T0244886

To:

....

From:

....

Date:

....

God Calls You
You
HIS,
Girl

BARBOUR
PUBLISHING

God Calls You
HIS,
Girl!

In a culture that fills your head and heart with lies about your value in the world, there is one who calls you HIS.

And He can be trusted. His Word is truth.

This delightful daily devotional will encourage and inspire your soul with deeply rooted truths from God's Word. Each devotional reading and heartfelt prayer will assure you that you are truly HIS—because God says so and His Word is unchanging!

Each of these 365 readings will help you grow in your faith and increase your self-confidence as you become the beautiful, courageous young woman the heavenly Creator intended you to be!

Be blessed!

You Are His

*Let them praise the LORD for his great love and for
the wonderful things he has done for them.*
PSALM 107:8 NLT

Identity is a big deal in our culture. You can see how warped the issue of "identity" can get when someone tries to figure out who they are outside the truth of God's Word. So when you consider identity, the best way to figure it all out is to think of how God views you.

This little devotional book you're holding right now is *all about* your identity in Christ. When you are trying to figure out the answer to your deepest question "Who am I?"...the answer lies in God's Word alone. You are loved. You are valued. God sent Jesus to show His love for you. No matter what anyone else says about you or does to you, these are the facts!

Isaiah 43:1 (ICB) says: "Now this is what the Lord says. He created you, people of Jacob. He formed you, people of Israel. He says, 'Don't be afraid, because I have saved you. I have called you by name, and you are mine.'"

. . . .

I believe these truths from Your Word, Lord God. I am Yours!

Poured into Your Heart

*And hope does not put us to shame, because God's love has been poured
into our hearts through the Holy Spirit who has been given to us.*
ROMANS 5:5 ESV

Have you asked Jesus to be your Lord and Savior? If you've committed your life to Jesus Christ, then God has poured His love into
your heart through the Holy Spirit, whom He has also given you!

Check this out: "I pray that the eyes of your heart may be enlightened in order that you may know the hope to which he has called
you, the riches of his glorious inheritance in his holy people, and
his incomparably great power for us who believe. That power is the
same as the mighty strength he exerted when he raised Christ from
the dead and seated him at his right hand in the heavenly realms,
far above all rule and authority, power and dominion" (Ephesians
1:18–21 NIV).

Now, read that again, asking the Holy Spirit to help you understand what that means for you as God's beloved child! What is God
saying to you in these verses? What kind of power is available to
you right now?

*Holy Spirit, please make these truths from God's
Word come alive in my heart. Help me know the
power of Your love that is alive inside me.*

The Throne Room

*So let us come boldly to the throne of our gracious
God. There we will receive his mercy, and we will
find grace to help us when we need it most.*
HEBREWS 4:16 NLT

When Jesus became the ultimate sacrifice for us, we were given direct access to God. Before Jesus came, sin prevented us from being close to the holy and one true God. In Bible times, God chose priests to come between sinful people and Himself, offering sacrifices so that their sins could be forgiven.

Can you imagine standing in the throne room of God? Picture it: You're a little bit frightened as you look around at the magnificent palace. And before you, the way is closed. A large wall of thick curtains prevents you from going to the throne of God.

When Jesus died on the cross, the Bible tells us that curtain was torn in two (Matthew 27:51)! Now you have direct access to God! Picture yourself walking boldly toward the throne of God just like Hebrews 4:16 says.

You are God's beloved daughter, a chosen princess!

. . . .

*Jesus, thank You for making a way for me to know
and love God. I ask You to come and fill me with Your
love and Your Spirit. I choose to follow You.*

Day 4

Press In to Know Him

*"Let us acknowledge the LORD; let us press on to acknowledge him.
As surely as the sun rises, he will appear; he will come to us like
the winter rains, like the spring rains that water the earth."*
HOSEA 6:3 NIV

God's faithfulness is as dependable as the sun rising or the rain pouring in spring. He always shows up when we need Him—He always comes through for us. Beautiful friend, acknowledge the Lord today. Press in for the revelation of Him in His Word. It takes time, it takes effort, and it requires you to cast off your earthly desires. But it is so worth it to find the Lord in His Word.

Learning more about who God is and growing deeper in your relationship with Him are beautiful treasures! The Father loves to be found by us! Press on in your journey to know Him more—you will not come up empty!

. . . .

*Lord, come meet me in my quiet time like a beautiful sunrise or
spring shower. Bring light and refreshment to my life. I enjoy
spending quiet moments with You in prayer and worship. Amen.*

Day 5
He Made It All!
(Including You!)

By him all things were created, in heaven and on earth,
visible and invisible, whether thrones or dominions or rulers or
authorities—all things were created through him and for him.
COLOSSIANS 1:16 ESV

Imagine you walk into a house. You see all the furniture, the rugs, the paintings on the walls. You see the people, the pets, the food on the table. You see the clocks, the microwave, and the refrigerator. And, in most cases, every single one of those "things" is made by a different manufacturer. How weird would it be to walk into a house and find out that (literally) every single thing was made by one company?

Now, think about God. He created everything that would ever be necessary to make that rug. And that clock. And those paintings. He created the humans and the pets, but He also created foods and trees and all the things that would one day become meals. And tables. And chairs. And refrigerators.

He made it all. No other "manufacturer" can boast that. But everything that is—is, because of God. And to think, He thought the world needed one of you too!

You're amazing, God! By You all things were created—
the things we see and the things we can't. Wow! Amen.

Quietness and Confidence Forever

The fruit of that righteousness will be peace;
its effect will be quietness and confidence forever.
Isaiah 32:17 niv

Isaiah prophesied of a time that was to come when God's Spirit would be poured out and His righteousness would be like a fertile field. He said His righteousness would bring forth peace, quietness, and confidence forever.

We live during an exciting time in history, friend! We have the full Bible, we know that the Messiah has come and will return, and we have the Holy Spirit, who has been poured out on the earth and empowers us in our Christian walk. As a result, we can experience the fruit of Jesus' righteousness in our lives: peace, a quiet life, and confidence in our God-given identity!

There is beauty in peace. God wants us to rest in Him, to be quiet and still so that we can hear His voice, and to walk in confidence that we are exactly who He created us to be!

. . . .

Father God, please give me Your perfect peace. I want to
walk in righteousness so that I can rest in the kind of quiet life,
free of striving and turmoil, that You designed for me. I want
to exude confidence that I know who I am in You! Amen.

Created through Him and for Him

All things were created through him and for him.
And he is before all things, and in him all things hold together.
COLOSSIANS 1:16–17 ESV

We know that all things were created *by* God, but sometimes I think we forget that we were also created *for* Him! We were made to know Him, to spend time with Him, and to give Him glory. He came before all things, and that is why we give Him all glory and honor—because He is the reason we exist!

Paul reminds us here that it is because of Jesus that all things hold together. When it feels like everything in your life is falling apart, you can trust that the same God who created the heavens created you and knows your life intimately. He will hold it all together even when you feel like it's about to collapse! Praise Him today for the beautiful ways that He sustains you and restores you so that your life brings Him glory!

. . . .

Jesus, I praise You for holding my life together. I know I could never make my life go the way I've planned for it to go. Only You have the perfect plan for my life, and You will bring everything together for my good and Your glory!

He Is the One You Need

For to us a child is born, to us a son is given; and the government
shall be upon his shoulder, and his name shall be called Wonderful
Counselor, Mighty God, Everlasting Father, Prince of Peace.

ISAIAH 9:6 ESV

Isaiah prophesied the coming Messiah long before Jesus was placed in a manger. He knew that Jesus would be many things to many people, including those of us born two thousand years later! He called Jesus the "Wonderful Counselor, Mighty God, Everlasting Father, [and] Prince of Peace."

How beautiful is it that Jesus is exactly who you need in any situation you might face? When you need guidance, He is your Counselor. When you're swamped by troubles that overwhelm you, He is the "Mighty God" who can tackle any problem. He is the "Everlasting Father" when you need a Father's love. When you're mired in chaos and confusion, He is the "Prince of Peace." No matter what you need today, Jesus has you covered!

. . . .

Jesus, thank You for always being exactly who I need, right when
I need You. Today, I need You to be my Everlasting Father, and
sometimes I need You to bring me Your perfect peace. You never fail
to show up for me in the exact way I need You. Thank You! Amen.

Day 9

He Knows You, Inside and Out

O Lord, You have looked through me and have known me. You know when I sit down and when I get up. You understand my thoughts from far away. You look over my path and my lying down. You know all my ways very well. Even before I speak a word, O Lord, You know it all.

PSALM 139:1–4 NLV

God knows you. He knows every little quirky thing about you. He knows when you're mad. He knows when you're sad. He's completely clued in when you're having a bad day, and He even knows what you're thinking. (Crazy, right?)

When you realize that your master artist, the one who designed you, knows every single thing about you, does it calm you down? He's got everything under control! Those issues you're facing at school, that relationship you're struggling with, that fight you had with your mom—He knows. He cares. And He's already working on it.

You can trust Him, girl. Even before you speak a word, He's taking care of the things that matter to you.

* *

Lord, I'm so glad You know me. (Hey, I do my best not to let others know the hidden details of my life, but I can't hide anything from You!) Thanks for caring. Amen.

While We Were Sinners

But God clearly shows and proves His own love for us,
by the fact that while we were still sinners, Christ died for us.
ROMANS 5:8 AMP

Beloved daughter of God, there's nothing you can do to earn God's love for you. Before the creation of the world, God had His heart set on you. He knows everything you've ever done and everything you ever will do. . .and He loves you completely anyway! You are loved, valued, and cherished by God, simply because you're His kid.

When you mess up, God loves you. When you succeed, God loves you. When you fail big-time, God loves you. You cannot disappoint God. Thinking that God is disappointed in you is a form of unbelief. Disappointment has to do with expectation. Would God ever be surprised by something you do? Nope. Because He already knows everything, from beginning to end.

God looks on you and smiles because He sees you through the love and sacrifice of Jesus Christ. Anytime you make a mistake, you can go boldly to the throne of grace and find mercy (Hebrews 4:16) and forgiveness from the one who loves you and has great plans for your life.

. . . .

I'm so amazed at Your amazing grace and love for me,
heavenly Father. Thank You for sending Jesus to make
a way for me to be in Your presence forever.

My God Hears Me

But as for me, I will look to the Lord; I will wait for
the God of my salvation; my God will hear me.
MICAH 7:7 ESV

In this chapter, Micah describes all the bad things going on in the world and the people who are against one another. Wow—sounds familiar! All it takes is one glance at the news to see that things aren't rainbows and sunshine all the time in our world either. But we can make a choice, friend. We can become bogged down in the despair of everything going wrong in the world, or we can look to the Lord!

We can have complete confidence that the God who sent His Son to save humanity is the same God who hears our prayers. He hears you when you call out to Him and will give you the guidance you need even when everything seems to be going sideways. That is the beautiful thing about looking to God, and not the world, for answers!

. . . .

Lord God, I look to You for the answers I need. When I see
everything that is going wrong in the world around me,
I can get overwhelmed. Give me Your peace that passes
all understanding as I wait for Your answer. Amen.

Day 12
Adopted and Chosen

*God sent him to buy freedom for us who were slaves to
the law, so that he could adopt us as his very own children.
And because we are his children, God has sent the Spirit of his
Son into our hearts, prompting us to call out, "Abba, Father."*
GALATIANS 4:5–6 NLT

Think about all the fairy-tale movies you've ever seen. The princess lives in a castle as an heir to everything her father owns. She has everything she could ever need. The same is true with us. Galatians 4:7 (NLT) says, "Now you are no longer a slave but God's own child. And since you are his child, God has made you his heir."

The Bible tells us that we are adopted into God's family. We get to call Him *Abba*, which is a warm and affectionate term for "Father." We are heirs to everything our Father owns. And He made it all!

No matter what your day holds, remember who you are and whose you are. Your Father is the King of the universe, and He can do anything! Worship Him today. Greet Him with a smile. Talk about your problems, big and small. He cares and He wants to bless you with His love.

. . . .

*Abba, You are my loving Father.
I'm so thankful to be Your child.*

Day 13

Future Plans

Within your heart you can make plans for your future,
but the Lord chooses the steps you take to get there.
PROVERBS 16:9 TPT

You're at a time in your life when the entire world is at your fingertips. There are so many amazing and beautiful things you can do with your life. You can go anywhere and choose any number of different paths for your life. You can make plans for your future. But just as the writer of this proverb acknowledges, you can make plans, but God will lead you down the path He has for you.

You have free will and the passions the Lord has given you that can lead you down many amazing paths. Don't forget to seek Him as you make plans, because His way is the best way, and He will never steer you wrong! Ask Him to open the doors to the places He wants you to go and to close the doors you shouldn't enter. You can trust His beautiful plan for your life. After all, He knows you even better than you know yourself!

. . . .

Lord, I surrender to Your will for me. I want to take only
the paths that You have for my life and not try to forge my
own way. I know that following my own way could lead
me away from You. I never want to be apart from You, so
please stay with me and guide me on my life path! Amen.

Pleasing God

God gives wisdom, knowledge, and joy to those who please him.
ECCLESIASTES 2:26 NLT

God is such a good Father that He showers His children with good gifts. As His children, we receive wisdom, knowledge, and joy. We receive these when we walk with Him in daily relationship. He is pleased when we seek Him. And we see the beautiful fruit of a relationship with Him: the good gifts He gives.

Wisdom is the very thing that Solomon asked God for when he became king. He knew how important it would be to have God's wisdom when leading others and making decisions. We need wisdom in our own lives. We need knowledge too. And joy! That's a big gift! The ability to find joy in all circumstances is something the world can never take away. Your joy and contentment are God-gifts! How beautiful it is to have a God who is pleased with you and gives you these good gifts!

. . . .

Father God, I pray that You are pleased with me and the way I seek You. I want to know You more every day. I don't just seek You to get Your good gifts, but I do want to receive Your gifts of wisdom, knowledge, and joy! Amen.

What Others Are Thinking

We serve God whether people honor us or despise us, whether they
slander us or praise us. We are honest, but they call us impostors.
2 Corinthians 6:8 nlt

Do you worry about what others are saying and thinking about you? It's hard not to sometimes, right? Especially with a room full of other girls your age! But when God's power is at work in you, you can be confident in who you are as His child, no matter what anyone else thinks.

Don't get me wrong: when other people say bad things about you, it can definitely hurt. But as you bring those hurts to Jesus, He reminds you of the truth. One youth pastor said: "The only way to get over what someone else says about you is to get under what God says about you!" Another person said: "What someone else thinks about you is none of your business." Meaning, you can't know or control other people's thoughts. Their thoughts are between them and God.

You are a dearly loved daughter of the King of kings! You have access to all of God's power. You can walk right up to God because of how loved you are.

. . . .

Lord, thank You that I never have to worry about what
other people think of me because I'm Your beloved child.

Family History

*This is the family history of Adam. When God created
human beings, he made them in his own likeness.*
GENESIS 5:1 NCV

Have you ever pulled out the family photo albums and looked at all
the pictures inside? No doubt you were stunned to see how much
you look like your grandmother. Or your great-aunt. Or even how
much you look like your mom when she was your age.

Family resemblances get carried down from generation to generation. But here's a cool thought: godly resemblances have been
carried down from the time of Adam until now.

Think about it this way: God created Adam and Eve in His
image. They messed up and were tossed out of the garden of Eden,
but that didn't stop their family from going on. . .and on. . .and on.
You're part of that original family, believe it or not. And, like Adam,
you were created in God's likeness. Isn't it cool to think that some
of Adam and Eve's DNA lives in you too? Even more exciting, if
you could see a photo of your heavenly Father, you might just think,
Wow, I can definitely see the family resemblance!

· ·

*I love being part of Your big family, Lord!
Thanks for including me. Amen.*

Joined to Christ

Since we are now joined to Christ, we have been given the
treasures of redemption by his blood—the total cancellation of
our sins—all because of the cascading riches of his grace.
EPHESIANS 1:7 TPT

The language in this verse is so beautiful! Because of the overflowing, cascading riches of Jesus' grace, we have received a total cancellation of our sins! They aren't merely forgiven; they are canceled! They no longer exist on our record because of the treasure of Jesus' redemptive blood!

If you are holding on to the shame and guilt of your past sins today, take this verse to heart. You have received full redemption! Jesus took all the sin of your past on Himself two thousand years ago, and now that you have joined your life to His, your sin is canceled! Soak in the beauty of this rich grace and walk like a daughter of the King, a coheir with Christ! You no longer bear your sin and guilt!

. . . .

Jesus, thank You for not only forgiving my sin but completely
canceling it off my record! You don't even remember the sins of my
past. Help me not to return to that guilt and shame. They are no longer
my portion—my portion is your rich and beautiful grace! Amen.

Everything You Need

"But I do not need the bulls from your barns or the goats from your pens. For all the animals of the forest are mine, and I own the cattle on a thousand hills."

Psalm 50:9–10 NLT

Being an heir of God isn't just about waiting for heaven. You have access to all of Your Father's wealth and wisdom and goodness at all times. You simply need to ask. When you have a need, go to your Father, the King, and talk to Him about it. He promises to meet your every need.

Philippians 4:19 (NIV) says, "My God will meet all your needs according to the riches of his glory in Christ Jesus." The Amplified Bible explains it like this: "My God will liberally supply (fill until full) your every need."

Does that mean you're getting everything you want? Not really. It means that God knows you better than you know yourself and knows your every need. Talk to Him about everything you think you might want or need. He'll fill you up with all the right stuff—wisdom, healing, resources—you name it, He has it! You can trust Him to take care of your every need.

. . . .

Lord, help me trust that You see me. You know everything I need. Help me sort it all out.

Resounding Yes!

Jesus Christ is the Son of God, and he is the one whom Timothy, Silas, and I have preached to you—and he has never been both a "yes" and a "no." He has always been and always will be for us a resounding "YES!"

2 CORINTHIANS 1:19 TPT

When you were younger, did you ever ask one of your parents for something and, when they said no, then go to the other parent to try to get a yes from them? With Jesus, we have the promise that He will always answer our needs and prayers with a resounding "Yes!" We can ask boldly for the things we need and the things we desire, so long as they align with His Word, and we will see Him come through for us with an answer that is for our good!

Pray big, bold prayers today and see the way Jesus answers the desires of your heart with the "yes" that is right for you in this season!

· ·

Jesus, thank You for being the perfect "Yes!" You know the desires of my heart and don't hold back anything from me that is for my good and Your glory. Thank You for giving me every reason to trust in Your perfect answer, because You are always faithful!

Day 20

Like Father, Like Son, Like Daughter

The Son radiates God's own glory and expresses the very character of God, and he sustains everything by the mighty power of his command. When he had cleansed us from our sins, he sat down in the place of honor at the right hand of the majestic God in heaven.

HEBREWS 1:3 NLT

Jesus is the Son of God. But check out what this verse says about the Son. If you read this verse carefully, you'll see one very important fact: Jesus is a lot like His Dad! Like Father, like Son. And now that you've accepted Jesus as your Savior (you have, haven't you?), you're a lot like Him too!

So what can a daughter or son of God expect to have? Look at the list: the character of God. Power. Cleansing (a clean heart), and a special place in heaven.

Like Father, like Son, like daughter. And one day you'll all be together for all eternity. God must really think you're something special to include you in all of that!

. . . .

Sounds like we've got a lot in common, Lord!
I can't wait to meet you face-to-face. Amen.

Day 21
Hearing from Our Loving God

Give thanks to the LORD, for he is good!
1 CHRONICLES 16:34 NLT

Starting a journal and writing out your thoughts and feelings to God can help you grow in your relationship with Him in powerful ways! God wants to hear all about you, even though He already knows everything about you. Why do you think that is?

Consider this: God wants to speak to you—today! Yes, the same God of the Bible, Creator of all things, wants to speak directly with you! That might sound impossible, but it's true.

Look up the following scriptures and take a few notes in your journal:

- John 10:27–28
- Romans 10:17
- Jeremiah 33:3
- John 16:13

Some of the ways that God speaks to His kids are through His Word, in creation, in music and worship songs, through other people, and the list goes on!

Matthew 11:15 (ESV) says: "He who has ears to hear, let him hear." Ask God to give you ears to hear His voice in your life.

* *

Lord, I want to know Your voice. Would you give me ears to hear?

Day 22
Worthy of Love

God so loved the world that he gave his one and only Son,
that whoever believes in him shall not perish but have eternal life.
JOHN 3:16 NIV

God gave His Son so that you could have eternal life.

Stop to think that through. God didn't have to send His Son. And Jesus didn't have to follow through and come to earth to die for you. But, out of a great love for you, that's exactly what God and Jesus did.

God decided you were worth it. His love was so strong that He gave. . .and gave. . .and then gave some more.

How do you feel when you think about how deep, how wide, how long, and how high the Lord's love is? Does it boggle your mind? Here's some great news: He loves the people you love—your parents, siblings, friends, and even your enemies. He loves humankind with a passion that drove Him all the way to the cross. And He did it all so that you could live with Him forever in heaven one day. (That's a lot of love!)

. . . .

Thank You for Your sacrifice on the cross, Jesus!
You thought I was worth dying for. Wow! Amen.

Day 23
Beautiful Brightness

*For your royal Bridegroom is ravished by your beautiful
brightness. Bow in reverence before him, for he is your Lord!*
PSALM 45:11 TPT

This psalm is both a song between Solomon and his bride, the princess of Egypt, and—metaphorically—a song between Jesus and His bride, the church. Jesus is the groom who is ravished by *your* beautiful brightness. You shine His light right back to Him as He gazes on you, beautiful friend!

Jesus is so easy to worship because He loves you so much. Bow before Him in prayer and adoration today, friend, because He is your Lord and God. He is all at once the Creator of the whole world and your closest and dearest friend. He concerns Himself with the affairs of every nation around the globe as well as with the most trivial issues you face. Remember this truth today as you go about your day: the groom is absolutely taken by you and your beauty! Show Him the same adoration and devotion through your worship and praise!

*Lord, show me how to love You in the best way I can!
I want to be as captivated by You, Jesus, as a new bride
is by her husband on her wedding day. Please give me
a passion for You and Your Word daily. Amen.*

Day 24
Fruit That Lasts

"You didn't choose me. I chose you. I appointed you to go and produce lasting fruit, so that the Father will give you whatever you ask for, using my name."
JOHN 15:16 NLT

Today's scripture is pretty clear, right? God chose you for a purpose. You were not an accident. He created you to know Him and to produce fruit. Galatians 5:22–23 tells us a little bit more about this fruit: "The Holy Spirit produces this kind of fruit in our lives: love, joy, peace, patience, kindness, goodness, faithfulness, gentleness, and self-control" (NLT).

If you look through the New Testament, Jesus has quite a bit to say about fruit. He talks about being connected to the vine. Have you ever picked a grape straight from the vine? Or picked blueberries from a bush? Or even picked some flowers from a garden? What happens after a few days? The fruit or flower starts to dry up or wilt. But if you stay connected to the vine (Jesus!), you won't wilt! You'll produce fruit that lasts and multiplies.

As the Holy Spirit fills you with fruit, those fruits overflow and bless everyone around you.

. . . .

Holy Spirit, I ask You to fill me to overflowing with Your fruit so that it lasts and blesses others.

He Sings Over You!

The Lord your God is with you, a Powerful One Who wins the battle. He will have much joy over you. With His love He will give you new life. He will have joy over you with loud singing.
ZEPHANIAH 3:17 NLV

God loves to throw a good party. No, really! He gets so giddy when He looks at you that He bursts into song. He's like that new mother who sings lullabies to her baby. He's also like the guy from that over-the-top musical you saw, the one who spontaneously burst into song for no obvious reason. That's how crazy He is about you, girl.

Maybe you didn't realize how strongly God feels about you. Maybe you look at your life—your looks, your actions, your lack of talent—and wonder how anyone could possibly celebrate you, of all people.

It's time to realize your worth! The Creator of the universe thinks you're so special that He's writing chart-topping songs just for you. Can you hear them? Lean in close! He might be singing one at this very moment.

. . . .

Lord, You really love me that much? You're seriously bursting into song? Over me? Wow! Thank You for finding value in me. I can't wait to hear what You're about to sing next. Amen.

Day 26
Jesus Understands How You Feel

*Jesus asked them, "Have you never read in the Scriptures:
'The [very] Stone which the builders rejected and threw
away, has become the chief Cornerstone; this is the Lord's
doing, and it is marvelous and wonderful in our eyes'?"*

MATTHEW 21:42 AMP

Have you ever felt forgotten, ignored, or left out? Jesus knows exactly what this feels like. God's Word tells us that Jesus was rejected. He had some friends and followers, but most people rejected Him and sent Him to die on a cross. They humiliated Him. Even His best friends didn't stick around when He needed it most (Matthew 26:36–46). How lonely that must have felt! It's hard to imagine how difficult this must have been for Jesus. He endured all of it out of His deep love for us.

Humankind rejected Jesus, but God chose Him. Remember this the next time you feel alone or forgotten. God chose you to be His much-loved daughter. Jesus sees everything that is happening to you, and He understands your heart. He is with you. You are never alone.

. . . .

*Jesus, help me remember that You know exactly how I
feel. Thanks for choosing me and understanding me.*

God Meant It for Good

*Even though you intended to harm me, God intended
it only for good, and through me, He preserved the lives
of countless people, as He is still doing today.*

GENESIS 50:20 VOICE

Friend, I hate to say it, but I'm sure you already know: there are people
who will intentionally hurt you. These are the people who will put
us down so that they appear better in the eyes of others. They aren't
thinking of your heart and your feelings; they are thinking only of
themselves. And it hurts! In this passage it was Joseph's own brothers
who sold him into slavery when he was just a young man. But while
his brothers meant to harm him, God used those circumstances to
build Joseph up and ultimately save thousands of lives.

That is the beauty of serving a good God who loves justice.
He will not let you break, no matter how much you might bend.
He loves you with an unfailing love, so when you go through those
trying times, ask Him to show you how He's forming your character
through the trials.

. . . .

*Father God, I'm struggling right now. There are people in my life
who seem to find happiness in belittling me. Their hateful words
and haughty attitudes are impacting the way I feel about myself.
I have a hard time remembering who I am in You when others
seek to put me down. Remind me of my identity in You, and
show me how You are growing me through these trials. Amen.*

Infinitely More Than
You Can Imagine

Now all glory to God, who is able, through his mighty power at work within us, to accomplish infinitely more than we might ask or think.
EPHESIANS 3:20 NLT

No matter what your plan is for your life, friend, God's plan is much greater than anything you could ever imagine. Paul reminds us in this verse to give all glory to God because He works powerfully in our hearts and in our lives! What He can do in your life goes far beyond what you could ask of Him or what your brain could even plan out!

The path will not always look the way you thought it might. Sometimes, it seems like you aren't headed the way you wanted to go: but when you look back weeks, months, or years later, you will see exactly why you walked the path you did. God had a plan all along! Following Him in faith will lead you down the best path, and He will prepare you for everything you'll encounter along the way. How beautiful it is to trust in His plan!

Father God, thank You for having a plan for my life that is better than I could ever ask or imagine! Help me to trust You with my steps each and every day. I know You won't let me down, because all that You do in me and for me and through me is for my good! Amen.

Give Up, Girl!

We have power over all these things through Jesus Who loves us so much. For I know that nothing can keep us from the love of God. Death cannot! Life cannot! Angels cannot! Leaders cannot! Any other power cannot! Hard things now or in the future cannot! The world above or the world below cannot! Any other living thing cannot keep us away from the love of God which is ours through Christ Jesus our Lord.
Romans 8:37–39 nlv

You can try all day, but nothing you ever do will drive God away. Even your worst behavior. (Think of that time you slammed your bedroom door in your mom's face.) Even when you say something truly hateful. (Think of that time you told your kid sister you wish she'd never been born.) Even then, Jesus still adores you. He still finds value in you and thinks you're worthy of love.

Nothing that happens in this lifetime can separate you from the love of Jesus. He's not going anywhere. Sure, you might feel like He's a million light-years away, but the one who's pulling back is you, not Him.

Give up, girl. You're His. He's yours. Ain't nothing gonna change that.

. . . .

I give up, Jesus! You've chased me down with Your love.
Thank You for thinking I was worth the chase. Amen.

God Delights in You

"The LORD your God is with you, the Mighty Warrior who saves. He will take great delight in you; in his love he will no longer rebuke you, but will rejoice over you with singing."

ZEPHANIAH 3:17 NIV

Today's verse is one to write down and post on your wall! God, the one who made every ocean and mountain and tree, who holds the solar system in place, and positions each star in the sky. . .delights in YOU! The Bible says He sings over you with joy. Imagine that: a heavenly Father who sings over His child with love and joy.

You, dear one, bring great joy and delight to God! And not because of anything you have done or could ever do or not do. . .simply because He created you. And God created you with the ability to choose. He gave you free will. He wants you to choose Him in return—choose to love Him and follow Him. Not because you have to, like a robot, but because you want to.

What will you choose?

. . . .

Lord God, You are amazing! It makes my heart so happy thinking about how You created all things and want a relationship with me. I choose to follow and love You, Lord.

Love, Love, and More Love!

*GOD told them, "I've never quit loving you and
never will. Expect love, love, and more love!"*
JEREMIAH 31:3 MSG

Love, love, and more love! God's love never fails. He never quits loving us, no matter our past or our present. And He cares about our future! His love and kindness are what lead us to reject our old, unfulfilling ways and draw closer to Him. There is no end to His love!

Friend, how beautiful is it that nothing you've ever done or ever could do would make God stop loving you? His one desire is that you would learn to love Him just as He loves you—without fail and without conditions! Keep expecting more and more love, and give Him all your love in return! Shower others with His love in you!

* * *

*Father God, I praise You for being so generous with Your
love. I find security in knowing that nothing I could ever
do would separate me from Your love, because You call me
worthy. Show me how to love like You do! Amen.*

Day 32

Thankful for Love

Give thanks to the God of heaven, for his steadfast love endures forever.
PSALM 136:26 ESV

God's love is steadfast. It's not fluctuating. (Hey, it's not like the weather—hot one day, cold the next. He's got boiling-hot love for you every day of the week!)

So how do you feel about that? When you ponder His steadfast love, is your heart overwhelmed? (Hint: It should be!) If so, take the time to thank Him. Spend a few minutes in prayer saying things like, "Jesus, I don't get it, but I'm so grateful!" When you come to Him with a heart filled with praise, guess what your supernatural Savior does? If you said, "Pours out even more love!" you would be right. He keeps that waterfall coming.

Now, here's the tricky part: He wants you to share steadfast love with others, not just with a few but with all the people in your circle of influence—at school, in your neighborhood, everywhere!

Before your heart hits the floor, remember: no pressure, girl! Ask for His help and He will love them through you. No, really!

. . . .

*I'm going to need Your help to love others as You love
me, Jesus, but I'm willing to give it a try! Amen.*

Day 33

United as One

*Arise, my darling! Come quickly, my beloved. Come and be the
graceful gazelle with me. Come be like a young stag with me.
We will dance in the high place of the sky, yes, on the mountains
of fragrant spice. Forever we shall be united as one!*

SONG OF SOLOMON 8:14 TPT

Sometimes, it seems as though we must meet a certain level of criteria
in our Christianity. We check our boxes of going to church, reading
the Bible, and saying prayers before meals, but is this really what
God wants from us? This passage shows that all He wants is for us
to simply be with Him.

Soak in the beautiful poetry describing how the Lord sees you.
He wants you to run with Him and dance with Him. Simply be
united with Him forever because you love to be in His presence.
Ask Him to deepen your longing for Him. Make your relationship
with Him the most important and meaningful thing in your life. He
is worthy of all your love and adoration, and He gives you all His
attention! Simply *be* with Him.

. . . .

*Lord God, deepen my desire for You. I pray that nothing else in
my life will seem more important to me than being with You.
All else is an unworthy substitute in light of who You are!*

Chosen and Equipped

*All Scripture is God-breathed and is useful for teaching,
rebuking, correcting and training in righteousness, so that the
servant of God may be thoroughly equipped for every good work.*
2 TIMOTHY 3:16–17 NIV

Imagine being chosen to be on a team to play a special game during gym class but then the teacher leaves the room without telling you how to play. Oh, and if you don't figure out the rules, you fail the class and have to take it again next semester. Talk about being set up to fail!

God didn't just choose you and leave you to figure things out on your own. He wouldn't set you up like that. He has given you His Word and His Spirit to teach you everything you need to know about winning in this life and the next. God doesn't play games with you. He wants you to know Him and how to follow Him. He wants you to hear His voice.

So get into God's Word and allow the Holy Spirit to bring His Words to life in you. You've been chosen and thoroughly equipped for everything God wants to do in your life.

. . . .

God, I'm so thankful that You didn't leave me to figure things out on my own. Thanks for being with me always and giving me Your Word.

Day 35
Chosen Treasure

*But you are God's chosen treasure—priests who are kings,
a spiritual "nation" set apart as God's devoted ones. He called
you out of darkness to experience his marvelous light, and now
he claims you as his very own. He did this so that you would
broadcast his glorious wonders throughout the world.*

1 PETER 2:9 TPT

You are a chosen treasure whom God has set apart for His glory!
When you realize that you have been brought out of darkness and
belong to God Himself, how can you do anything but broadcast His
glory throughout the world? It's like when you find the perfect pair
of jeans or a really good new moisturizer—you want to tell all your
friends so that they can experience those things too. Share about
God's goodness like you do a great fit!

Think of how others in your life could be affected by God's
mercy. Don't keep His glorious goodness to yourself, but spread it to
everyone you know! You have been drenched in the mercy of God,
so overflow to others!

*Father God, thank You for calling me out of darkness so that I could
experience Your light that is beyond all comparison! Show me how
to broadcast Your glorious wonders throughout my world! Amen.*

God's Amazing and Empowering Grace

But God's amazing grace has made me who I am!
And his grace to me was not fruitless. In fact, I worked
harder than all the rest, yet not in my own strength but
God's, for his empowering grace is poured out upon me.

1 Corinthians 15:10 TPT

Grace has made you who you are, friend! By grace you were saved! God's grace poured out on you is what gives you the power and strength to live out a life that honors Him! Your life is beautiful and fruitful because of the good work that He has been doing in you that will not be completed until He comes again!

Continue to walk in His strength and power and be amazed at all the ways He enables you to produce good fruit! It doesn't matter how many messed-up choices you've made in the past or how much longer it took you to come to Jesus than others you may know—the key is that you let His grace transform you and pour out through you!

. . . .

God, thank You for Your amazing grace. You are
producing Your fruit in me so that I represent You well.
I want to work hard at serving You and others, so please
empower me with Your strength and grace. Amen.

A Covenant of Love

*"The mountains may move and the hills disappear, but even then
my faithful love for you will remain. My covenant of blessing
will never be broken," says the LORD, who has mercy on you.*

ISAIAH 54:10 NLT

Have you ever made a covenant with someone? What's a covenant,
you ask? It's more than a promise. It's a pledge, a commitment.
Maybe you committed to do something for your teacher. Or maybe
you covenanted with a friend that you would stick with her, even if
everyone else walked away.

God takes covenants very seriously. In the Old Testament days,
He "sealed the deal" (made the promise public) with the shedding
of animal blood. Priests would offer sacrifices in the temple. In the
New Testament we see the ultimate bloodshed when Jesus went to
the cross as the final sacrifice for us all.

God could have chosen a different way, but He opted to covenant
with you, girl. And He wants you to know that He's covenanted His
love for you. You were worth it to Him. Worth the trip to the cross.
Worth the pain of the death of His Son. And worth the mercy He
continues to pour out, even now.

. . . .

*I'm so grateful for Your love covenant, Lord!
Thank You for thinking I was worth it. Amen.*

Day 38

Power through Passionate Prayer

Confess and acknowledge how you have offended one another and then pray for one another to be instantly healed, for tremendous power is released through the passionate, heartfelt prayer of a godly believer!
JAMES 5:16 TPT

Did you know that tremendous power can be released through your prayers, friend? Maybe you thought your prayers were just to bless your meals or to help you pass a test. Pray bigger! James reminds us that when we are sincere in our prayers and our lives are reflecting Jesus, we can see miracles happen!

Don't stop praying when you don't see an immediate answer. Press in! Persevere! Passionate, persistent prayer releases power. Spend time in prayer and go after God until you receive a clear answer. He doesn't hold back from His children. If you are earnestly seeking His will, His power, His healing, His salvation—you will see it! Make your heart clean before God by forgiving others or asking for forgiveness, and then pray for the areas where you need Him to move. You may be surprised how quickly He answers your prayer!

. . . .

Lord God, I want my prayers to move heaven and earth because You are in them. I don't want my prayers to be empty or just memorized words. I want to have such a close relationship with You that when I pray, I know You will hear and answer me. Amen.

Day 39
Come Away

My love responded and said to me, Arise,
my dearest, my beauty, and come away with me.
SONG OF SOLOMON 2:10 VOICE

Have you ever wanted to just get away to be alone with God? You figure it would be so much easier to read the Word or worship Him if you didn't have all the other distractions of the world around you. It's unlikely you'll ever have a significant amount of time in your life when you can just escape the world and spend time alone in God's presence.

However, He is calling you to come away with Him into His presence. How can you get away to be alone with Him? Be intentional about setting aside the time each day! Set an alarm to get up early, or just an alarm at a typically open time of the day. Turn off your notifications. Close your door. Let your family know you're having quiet time. Then spend that time praying, listening, and worshiping. Getting away with God doesn't have to be a production; it can be as simple as just doing it.

. . . .

Lord, show me how to come away with You into the secret place
where I can know You more and spend time alone with You,
sharing my heart's needs and desires and hearing from You.
Remind me to set aside intentional time to be with You. Amen.

Day 40

The Loving Kindness
of Our God

The LORD is righteous in all his ways and kind in all his works.
PSALM 145:17 ESV

God is loving and kind toward you because you are in Christ Jesus (Romans 8:1—You are in Christ Jesus and Christ Jesus lives in you!). Let's see what else the Bible says:

- "How precious is Your lovingkindness, O God! The children of men take refuge in the shadow of Your wings" Psalm 36:7 (AMP).

- "In order that in the coming ages he might show the incomparable riches of his grace, expressed in his kindness to us in Christ Jesus" Ephesians 2:7 (NIV).

- "But when the kindness and love of God our Savior appeared, he saved us, not because of righteous things we had done, but because of his mercy" Titus 3:4–5 (NIV).

- "For His lovingkindness prevails over us [and we triumph and overcome through Him], and the truth of the LORD endures forever. Praise the LORD! (Hallelujah!)" Psalm 117:2 (AMP).

· ·

Lord, fill my heart with Your joy as I share Your truths with anyone You put in my life who needs to hear them too.

Fragrance Fills the House

Mary picked up an alabaster jar filled with nearly a liter of
extremely rare and costly perfume—the purest extract of nard,
and she anointed Jesus' feet. Then she wiped them dry with her
long hair. And the fragrance of the costly oil filled the house.

JOHN 12:3 TPT

Mary loved to sit at the feet of Jesus and learn from Him. She didn't do the traditional things that her sister Martha did when Jesus was present—cooking and cleaning—she just soaked up Jesus' presence and His teaching. On this occasion, she brought out a huge jar of perfume, one that cost a year's salary, and poured it out on Jesus' feet and then dried His feet with her hair. That fragrant perfume, probably overpowering due to the sheer amount poured out, filled the whole house.

We don't have the pleasure of spending time with the man Jesus, but we do spend time in His presence, soaking up His Word and worshiping at His feet. We pour out our own costly perfume when we pray and worship with no time limits, distractions, or ulterior motives. This incense offering of our prayers fills the throne room of heaven with a sweet aroma. Today as you spend time with Jesus, imagine pouring out your prayers on His feet like a beautiful perfume. Imagine His eyes full of love smiling down at you. Enjoy being in His presence.

. . . .

Jesus, let me linger in Your presence today with
no hurriedness or distraction. Amen.

Like a Watered Garden

*The LORD will guide you continually and satisfy your desire in
scorched places and make your bones strong; and you shall be like a
watered garden, like a spring of water, whose waters do not fail.*
ISAIAH 58:11 ESV

Have you ever been to the desert and seen just how extremely dry
the ground is? The sun simply scorches most things that try to grow,
and they become hard and brittle. I spend time in the Middle East
doing mission work and I've never failed to be amazed at how much
can grow and be so beautiful when given just a bit of water. You will
see a vast expanse of sand and then a random patch of fertile beauty.

Our lives can be like that. Before we're in relationship with God,
our lives are scorched by sin and the desires of the world. Good
character has a hard time growing in those conditions. But then we
come to know Christ and He waters us. We turn into a garden, and
He tends us with care and becomes our living water. When we are
watered by Him, we find ourselves producing His beautiful fruit!

* *

*Father God, be my living water today and every day.
Tend me with Your wisdom—prune what needs pruning,
water what needs to be watered, and help me to produce
the fruit of the Spirit that draws others to You. Amen.*

Day 43
When Things Get Awkward

Your unfailing love is better than life itself; how I praise you!
PSALM 63:3 NLT

You tried to fix the broken friendship, but you failed. Nothing you did worked. Not that I'M SO SORRY! text. Not that LET'S JUST MEET AND TALK THIS OUT suggestion. Or that I TOTALLY MESSED THIS UP, PLEASE FORGIVE ME! note you sent. The relationship is now a thing of the past. You've parted ways. You don't speak. Things are. . .awkward. You keep thinking this is a hurdle your friend has to jump, that she will eventually come to her senses, but she doesn't.

Now think about your relationship with God. Can you ever picture a time when He will shun you like that friend did? It's impossible. It goes against the nature and character of God to shut you out, to walk away, to let things get awkward.

Girl, if things between you and God ever feel out of sorts, consider this hard truth: it's probably you, not Him. In fact, it's definitely you!

His love is unfailing. Even in the hardest of times, He will fight for a relationship with you. Why? Because He thinks you're totally worth it.

. . . .

Thank You for not giving up on me, Lord. I don't ever want things to get awkward between us. Amen.

Day 44

His Higher Ways

*For just as the heavens are higher than the earth, so my ways are
higher than your ways and my thoughts higher than your thoughts.*
ISAIAH 55:9 NLT

Have you ever climbed to the top of a mountain or looked out of a
window on the top floor of a tall building? Your perspective of the
scene is much different than the perspective of someone standing on
the ground looking in the same direction. You have a better view of
the big picture, but the person on the ground can see only the large
buildings or mountainside in front of them. In a similar way, God's
perspective is much broader than ours.

He is omniscient: He knows all and sees all. He knows the
direction your life will take. You, on the other hand, are looking at
each major decision, and each one seems so big at the time that it's
all you can see. This is where trust comes in! You have to trust that
God can see the big-picture view and will direct you as you navigate
those big life choices. Letting go and giving control to God is a
beautiful release!

- -

*Lord God, I trust that You can see my life from Your heavenly
vantage point. Even when I can only see the mountainside
in front of me, I know You can see the entire vista.
I'm depending on You to keep directing me and bringing me
closer to You until one day I see the whole beautiful view too.*

Day 45
Planted for His Glory

All your people will be righteous and they will possess the land forever. They are the shoot I have planted, the work of my hands, for the display of my splendor.

ISAIAH 60:21 NIV

Friend, you have been put into your family, your community, and your nation for such a time as this. The Lord planted you there like a small tree, watering and tending you with love, to display His glory. Though your family may change, or you may switch cities or even countries, God has given you the possession of the land where you live. No matter where you are throughout your life, you can claim that place for God's glory!

You are the beautiful work of God's hands, so use your influence in this moment to proclaim who He is. Share His wonders with those around you, go into the streets with your church and pray for the sick and the unsaved, worship the Lord with your life. He will continue to water you, to prune you, and to grow you into a beautiful, fruitful tree for His name's sake.

. . . .

Jesus, I want to live a righteous life that gives glory to You no matter where I'm planted. Please grow me and make me fruitful right where I am now. I want to find ways to glorify Your name here and now and in each place I end up throughout my life. Amen.

Day 46
Off-Roading

No temptation has overtaken you except what is common to mankind. And God is faithful; he will not let you be tempted beyond what you can bear. But when you are tempted, he will also provide a way out so that you can endure it.

1 CORINTHIANS 10:13 NIV

Imagine yourself driving down the road. Suddenly, you see signs that say CAUTION and BRIDGE OUT. You turn around and head in another direction, right?

That's kind of like this verse. Temptation comes in lots of forms: Excess dessert. Cheating. Looking at something you shouldn't. Bending the rules. Going somewhere online you're not allowed. When you're tempted and your heart starts pounding while the enemy entices you in a direction that you know is wrong, look for the signs. Pay attention. The Holy Spirit is speaking and nudging you to stay on the right road.

Girl, you've been chosen by God. He sees you. He is always with you. And He promises to give you a way out when you're tempted to do wrong. Look and listen for the warning signs when they come up.

. . . .

Lord, please soften my heart to hear Your voice when I'm tempted to go off-road. Give me wisdom and strength to make the right choice.

Day 47
God Is Love

*Those who are loved by God, let his love continually pour from
you to one another, because God is love. Everyone who loves is
fathered by God and experiences an intimate knowledge of him.
The one who doesn't love has yet to know God, for God is love.*

1 JOHN 4:7–8 TPT

It's easy to throw around the word *love* in our Western culture. We
love pizza. We love that new show. We love a good pair of shoes.
There's nothing wrong with enjoying the beautiful and enjoyable
things in the world. But love is so much greater than the simple
statements we toss around. Love comes from God, and God is love.
There is no real love apart from God.

When you understand the vastness of God's love for you, you
can't help but pour it out onto other people. The realization that we
are loved by God draws us into a deeper relationship with Him. And
when we show His love to others, we're drawn into deeper relationships with them too! Nothing is more beautiful than God's love!

*Father God, I want to show Your love to others. I know that
Your light and love shining through me are what make me
beautiful. Remind me that nothing is greater than being
loved by You and showing Your love to others! Amen.*

Your Master Gardener

*GOD's loyal love couldn't have run out, his merciful
love couldn't have dried up. They're created new every
morning. How great your faithfulness! I'm sticking with
GOD (I say it over and over). He's all I've got left.*
LAMENTATIONS 3:22–24 MSG

You glance out at the garden and notice the leaves on your mom's favorite plant are turning brown. Ugh. Is that beautiful flower doomed to death? Sure looks like it. Then you check again the next week and notice it's springing back to life. What happened? Did she water it? Add fertilizer?

God is the best gardener of all! He pours out love like early morning dew on the plants in your proverbial garden. Just when you think there's no chance, He waters again. And again. And again. He fertilizes with His mercy, His grace, His peace. And before long, you're springing to life just like that flower.

No wonder you're so in love with Him now! You've figured out that He finds you so lovable, so precious, that He won't quit, no matter what. He'll go to any lengths to prove His love for you.

. . . .

*Thank You for being a Master Gardener, Lord!
I won't wither as long as You take care of my heart. Amen.*

Day 49

Overwhelming Delight

Whenever my busy thoughts were out of control, the soothing comfort of your presence calmed me down and overwhelmed me with delight.

PSALM 94:19 TPT

Overwhelm—it has a negative connotation, right? When you think of overwhelm, you probably think of situations where you were overwhelmed with anxiety over unmet expectations or disappointment. Here the psalmist describes how God's presence would comfort him, calm him, and overwhelm him with delight when his busy thoughts were out of control. When my own thoughts are out of control, spiraling with worries and what-ifs, I don't experience a breakthrough until I lean into worship and prayer—into the soothing comfort of God's presence.

If you are burdened by anxiety today, trade it in for the overwhelming delight of being in God's presence. Lay down your worries at His feet and feel His comfort drape over your shoulders like a blanket, replacing the tension and anxiety you carried there.

· ·

Jesus, I lay down my busy thoughts. I give them over to You when I feel out of control. I know I'm not in control anyway, so I would rather give all of my anxiety over to You. Please replace my concerns with Your comfort. Amen.

Day 50
Truths about God

The Lord, Who makes you, bought you and saves you,
and the One Who put you together before you were born,
says, "I am the Lord, Who made all things. I alone spread
out the heavens, and I alone spread out the earth."

ISAIAH 44:24 NLV

We can learn a lot of truth about God from these verses in Isaiah 44, namely:

1. God made you.

2. He bought you with His blood on the cross and saved you, so you now belong to Him.

3. He knew you before you were even born.

4. God made all things, including heaven and earth.

The maker of the universe made you and knows everything about you. He loves you so much that He paid for your life and all your sins on the cross. Through Jesus, you belong to God and have His Spirit alive inside you.

. . . .

Lord, I believe the truth from Your Word that You made me and
saved me. Thank You for taking away all my sins and showing
me how much You love me. I choose to follow You. Thank You
that Your Holy Spirit is alive and at work in my heart.

The Holy Spirit, Your Friend

"And I will ask the Father and he will give you another Savior, the Holy Spirit of Truth, who will be to you a friend just like me—and he will never leave you. The world won't receive him because they can't see him or know him. But you know him intimately because he remains with you and will live inside you."

JOHN 14:16–17 TPT

When Jesus was leaving the earth to ascend into heaven, He promised that the Father would send the Holy Spirit of Truth. We have the Holy Spirit as our friend who will never leave us. We know Him even though we cannot see Him because He lives within us.

Have you ever had a friend who moved away? Maybe a childhood friend just slowly drifted out of your life. Though friends will come and go throughout the course of your life, you will always have the Holy Spirit with you. He will stay by your side no matter what you encounter. Through Him, there is no judgment or condemnation but rather forgiveness when you sin and guidance and correction to keep you on the right path.

· ·

Holy Spirit, thank You for being the best kind of friend. You won't lie to me to make me think I'm something I'm not, and You won't ignore or desert me if I slip up and make mistakes. You love me and guide me in my relationship with You, offering comfort and correction. Show me how to know You more intimately. Amen.

Day 52

Do Your Part

By putting our trust in God, He has given us His loving-favor and has received us. We are happy for the hope we have of sharing the shining-greatness of God. We are glad for our troubles also. We know that troubles help us learn not to give up. When we have learned not to give up, it shows we have stood the test. When we have stood the test, it gives us hope.

ROMANS 5:2–4 NLV

"Insert your debit card, please," the clerk says. So you do. You stick it in the slot and the transaction goes through. But what if you refused to put the card into the slot? Would you still receive the item? No way!

The same is true when you choose to put your trust in God. In some ways, it's like sticking that debit card into the slot. In goes your trust, out comes His loving favor and hope. In goes your obedience, out comes His shining greatness.

Doing what He asks you to do is the key that unlocks nearly every door. Life will give you a zillion tests. You'll want to do things your way. But every time, your heavenly Father will ask you to insert your trust in Him. When you do, He'll always come through for you. You mean that much to Him.

. . . .

I get it, Lord! I do my part, You do Yours.
Thanks for caring so much about me. Amen.

You Can Trust God's Word

*We also thank God constantly for this, that when you
received the word of God, which you heard from us,
you accepted it not as the word of men but as what it really
is, the word of God, which is at work in you believers.*

1 Thessalonians 2:13 esv

Do you ever stop and wonder, or do some of your friends ever ask you, "How do I know the Bible is true? Why should I trust it?" If you take time to look, you will find amazing research from experts throughout history who verify why the Bible can be trusted far more than any other book ever written. Check out great resources like Answers in Genesis and author Josh McDowell for some good information. More importantly, constantly remember that you have a relationship with God Himself through Jesus Christ, and you have the Holy Spirit within you. As you read the Bible consistently over time, ask God to show you more about Himself through His Word. Ask Him to grow your faith, and then trust Him to do it! You will be amazed at how He answers your prayers.

- -

*Heavenly Father, please keep growing my faith in
You as I read Your awesome Word! Show me how
and why it's true and can be trusted. Amen.*

Day 54

You Can Run Far Away from Sin

Happy is the man who does not walk in the way sinful men tell him to, or stand in the path of sinners, or sit with those who laugh at the truth. . . . For the Lord knows the way of those who are right with Him. But the way of the sinful will be lost from God forever.
PSALM 1:1, 6 NLV

Especially in your teenage and young adult years, the world will tell you how fun it is to play around with sin and risky behavior. But the world lies. God's Word tells you to run away from the evil desires of youth and pursue righteousness, faith, love, and peace instead (2 Timothy 2:22). Watch even a few minutes of the daily news. Do you want to trust this crazy, broken world and dabble in sin, or do you want to trust the never-changing God who gives you life and your every breath and who loves You so much He even let His only Son die for you?

. . . .

Dear Lord, please help me to stand strong in my love for You, my faith in You, and my obedience to You, no matter what crazy thing the world is telling me is harmless and just for fun. Remind me of Your deep love and great sacrifice to pay for my sin so that I will never want to play around with evil. Amen.

Day 55
An Open Declaration

For "everyone who calls on the name of the Lord will be saved."
ROMANS 10:13 ESV

Why do you suppose God is so keen on you making an open declaration of your faith in Him? Why not just keep it hidden in your heart?

Here's a cool nugget of truth: the Lord wants to use you. Yes, you. He didn't just choose you to be saved, to live forever with Him; He also wants you to realize that you have the potential to lead others to Him.

He thinks you're amazing! But He thinks the rest of humankind is pretty amazing too. And someone has to tell them about what Jesus did on the cross. If not you, then who?

It's simple math, really. Think of it this way: if every Christian led just one other person to the Lord, then the number of Christians on the planet would double. Whoa!

He picked you. So don't keep your faith to yourself, girl! Declare it—openly!

. . . .

I'll share the news of what You've done, Jesus! Thanks for saving me. And thanks for using me to reach others. Amen.

Day 56

In God's Presence

Because of Christ and our faith in him, we can now
come boldly and confidently into God's presence.
EPHESIANS 3:12 NLT

The New International Version says, "In him and through faith in him we may approach God with freedom and confidence."

Because of our trust in Jesus and all He's done for us, we get to come before God boldly, confidently, and freely. Even when you've messed up, you don't need to hang your head in shame before God. He already knows everything about you and loves you anyway. He has already paid for your sin, completely, forever.

So if you've messed up recently with temptation or screens or whatever your struggle may be, God sees you and loves you the same. Nothing you could do will ever change His mind about how much He loves you and values you.

Look to Him. Get close to Him. Share with Him what's on your heart and mind. Confess your sins and ask for help. He's the only one who knows you completely and knows exactly what you need. As you read His Word and allow the Holy Spirit to help you understand it, you'll be amazed at how much you begin to hear from God about your life.

. . . .

Lord, I'm so thankful I can come to You to be
restored and forgiven and fully loved.

You Can Trust in the Lord

*"Blessed are those who trust in the LORD and have made the
LORD their hope and confidence. They are like trees planted along
a riverbank, with roots that reach deep into the water. Such trees
are not bothered by the heat or worried by long months of drought.
Their leaves stay green, and they never stop producing fruit."*
JEREMIAH 17:7–8 NLT

Can you name a single person who has never let you down? Even
if you can, it just means you don't know the person well enough or
haven't known them long enough. No person on earth is perfect.
Yes, God mercifully blesses us with trustworthy people; it's just that
even the most reliable person on earth is never 100 percent reliable.
They're always capable of disappointing or hurting us, intentionally
or not, because they are human and have a sin nature. We need and
are grateful for good people relationships, but we are most blessed
when we look to God above all and put our full trust in Him, knowing
our most important relationship is with Him. He alone is perfect
and worthy of our praise.

* *

*Lord, my relationship with You is the most important
relationship in my life. You are love itself, and You are
my real hope. I trust in You more than anyone else.
You give me all the strength and confidence I need. Amen.*

Day 58
Work Won't Work

People are counted as righteous, not because of their work, but because of their faith in God who forgives sinners. David also spoke of this when he described the happiness of those who are declared righteous without working for it: "Oh, what joy for those whose disobedience is forgiven, whose sins are put out of sight. Yes, what joy for those whose record the LORD has cleared of sin."
ROMANS 4:5–8 NLT

We are so greatly blessed that work won't work to save us from our sin and get us to heaven. Imagine how exhausting working for our salvation would be, how much anxiety we'd feel as we wondered if we were doing a good enough job! Thankfully, our salvation is a gift from God that we receive from Him because of our faith. We believe that God provided Jesus to pay the price for our sin, and we believe that Jesus died on the cross and rose again. We believe that the only way to be made right with God is through Jesus Christ. We admit our sin and ask God to forgive us for it, and we let Jesus be Lord over our lives, doing our best to obey Him and follow His ways, which we learn from the Bible and guidance of the Holy Spirit.

Father God, thank You that I could never work my way to heaven. You never expected me to. I could never pay the price for my sin on my own, so You gave Jesus as my Savior. I am beyond grateful, and I want to live all my life to honor and praise You. Amen.

Day 59
It's Nothing You Did, Girl!

It is not given to you because you worked for it.
If you could work for it, you would be proud.
EPHESIANS 2:9 NLV

You love those pats on the back, don't you? They can make you feel so good. Some people work really hard but never get the encouragement they need from others. That's a tough way to live.

No matter how hard you work, no matter how many good deeds you do, you can't save yourself. You could give money to the poor, travel to developing countries, feed the homeless, and even take care of the sick, and it wouldn't earn you a ticket to heaven. There's only one way to get there, and that's through the sacrifice of Jesus on the cross.

Does this mean God doesn't want you to do good deeds? Oh, He definitely wants you to live this way. Good deeds are, well, good! Even though they don't save you, they shine a light on Him, which is a wonderful thing!

Jesus thought you were worthy enough to save. And He would do it again too!

. . . .

I get it, Lord. I didn't earn it. But that doesn't mean I
can live any way I like. So I'll live for You! Amen.

You Can Hold
Your Head High

The LORD will be your confidence.
PROVERBS 3:26 ESV

We've all done things that were embarrassing or awkward. You know, those things that made us want to melt into the floor or become invisible. And after these kinds of experiences, the weirdness can live on in our minds for a long time. But the awkward or embarrassing moment is usually much bigger in our own minds than in the minds of others. Yes, whoever was watching might remember for a while. You might even get teased a little. But that shows others' character, not yours. You can choose to show strong character and courage by remembering that everyone has embarrassing moments. So shake it off. Hold your head high, remembering you are a child of the one true God who loves you and is always looking out for you—no matter what embarrassing things you (and everyone else) might do.

. . . .

Heavenly Father, when I'm dealing with embarrassment, please comfort me and help me to shake it off. Help me remember that You are my confidence. Thank You for loving me no matter what. Amen.

Trust and Obey

If the LORD delights in us, then He will bring us into this land
and give it to us, a land which flows with milk and honey.
NUMBERS 14:8 AMP

After God led the Israelites out of slavery in Egypt and through the wilderness, they were almost ready to enter the Promised Land. God's people sent scouts into the land to see what was there and what kind of people lived there.

Caleb and Joshua were two of those scouts. These guys were faithful to God and trusted that He would be with them, even when the other scouts spread bad reports about the land and urged the people not to enter it. Caleb and Joshua reminded God's people that the people in the land, although much larger, did not have God's protection like they did.

Because Caleb and Joshua trusted God and obeyed Him, they were the only two of the scouts that survived and were able to enter the Promised Land.

God has a Promised Land for you too. He delights in You and is preparing a place for You to be with Him for all eternity.

• •

Lord, help me trust and obey You like Caleb and Joshua did!

Day 62
You Have Noah's Example

Noah. . .did all that God commanded him.
GENESIS 6:22 ESV

Most people know at least a little about the story of Noah in the Bible, and it's good to read and remember it. God was pleased with Noah, and then He gave Noah some instructions that must have seemed totally crazy! Build a giant ark? Collect two of each animal and load them up along with the family? Then wait while the rains fall and completely flood and destroy the whole earth? Even though Noah was an exceptionally good man, he probably shook his head sometimes, wondering what on earth was going on. Still, he continued to obey God. And in the end, God did exactly what He said He would do: He destroyed every living thing with a great flood. Only Noah and his family and the animals they had gathered survived, safe inside the ark. Noah and his family were greatly blessed because of Noah's obedience.

Have you ever sensed God leading you to do something that seemed to make zero sense, but you obeyed and then were blessed for it? Remember those times regularly, and thank and praise God for them!

. . . .

Heavenly Father, please help me to learn from Noah's example of obedience to You. Even when I don't understand, I want to follow Your commands and direction. Amen.

Day 63
Say the Name!

Because, if you confess with your mouth that Jesus is Lord
and believe in your heart that God raised him from the dead,
you will be saved. For with the heart one believes and is
justified, and with the mouth one confesses and is saved.

ROMANS 10:9–10 ESV

There's so much power in the name of Jesus. If only you realized!
You would be calling on Him first, in every situation.

Picture yourself in the middle of a crisis. Instead of calling a
friend or a family member, you cry out one name: Jesus! And in that
moment, peace floods your soul.

You were created by Him to want and need Him, not just in crises
but on good days too. He wants you to love Him and to recognize the
power in His name. He sees value in you, but He wants you to see
the full value in Him as well! (Hey, if you had a bodybuilder friend,
wouldn't you call on him to protect you if a dangerous situation arose?)

Call on Him. Don't wait. Don't pick up the phone and punch
in your friend's number. Call Jesus instead. He can do, in an instant,
what your friend couldn't do in years of trying. He saved you for
relationship, girl!

· ·

I call on You today, Jesus. You're the answer to every problem.
Your power can fix anything. I'm so blessed to call on You. Amen.

Day 64
You Are the Light of the World

"You are the light of the world—like a city on a hilltop that cannot be hidden. No one lights a lamp and then puts it under a basket. Instead, a lamp is placed on a stand, where it gives light to everyone in the house. In the same way, let your good deeds shine out for all to see, so that everyone will praise your heavenly Father."
MATTHEW 5:14–16 NLT

What a beautiful thing to get up in the morning and tell yourself as you look in the mirror: "You are the light of the world." That's what Jesus has said of you and me when we trust Him as Savior. With the Holy Spirit living inside us, our job is to shine our lights so that others will want to trust Jesus as Savior and praise God too! We should never want to cover up our light. The dark world around us needs the good news and love of Jesus desperately, so we need to shine as brightly as possible!

Dear Jesus, I am blessed to be the light of the world because of You! I want to shine Your love brightly to everyone around me and give God all the praise! Amen.

The Hands and Feet of Jesus

Now you [collectively] are Christ's body, and individually [you are]
members of it [each with his own special purpose and function].
1 CORINTHIANS 12:27 AMP

As God's children, we are part of His family together with all other Christ followers all over the world. If you were an only child before, now you have tons of brothers and sisters! We are also the body of Christ, the church.

After Jesus rose from the grave and went back to heaven, He sent His Spirit to live in our hearts. And we became the hands and feet of Jesus here on earth. Jesus gets His physical work done here on earth by using us. It matters what you do and how you feel and what you believe because you are God's representative here on earth. When people see you, they are experiencing God through you.

Ask Jesus to fill you up with His love and joy so that others can see His body at work in the world.

. . . .

Lord, thank You that Your Spirit is alive in me.
Please fill me up with love and joy so that I can be
Your hands and feet and love others like You do.

Day 66
Your God Is Holy

I saw the Lord sitting on a throne, high and honored. His long clothing spread out and filled the house of God. Seraphim stood above Him, each having six wings. With two he covered his face, and with two he covered his feet, and with two he flew. One called out to another and said, "Holy, holy, holy, is the Lord of All. The whole earth is full of His shining-greatness."

ISAIAH 6:1–3 NLV

In this scripture, the prophet Isaiah is describing a vision he had of God sitting on His throne with angels called seraphim surrounding Him and worshiping Him. To call God holy means to lift Him high above all others, esteeming Him as perfect and worthy of total devotion—meaning all your attention. No matter what is going on in your life, you'll be blessed if you take time each day to stop and think about God's holiness and praise Him for it. He is above all and absolutely perfect and awesome. And He loves you and cares about every detail of your life. That's an incredible blessing to be grateful for!

• •

Almighty God, You are holy, holy, holy!
I'm in awe of You and so blessed by You. Amen.

Day 67

More Than Enough Room

"Don't let your hearts be troubled. Trust in God, and trust also in me. There is more than enough room in my Father's home. If this were not so, would I have told you that I am going to prepare a place for you? When everything is ready, I will come and get you, so that you will always be with me where I am."

JOHN 14:1–3 NLT

Remember the story of Mary and Joseph? They got to Bethlehem and Mary went into labor. They started looking for a place to stay but the inn was full. "No vacancy." So they ended up in a stable, where baby Jesus was born.

Aren't you glad God never hangs out the No VACANCY sign? His door is open to you, His child. In fact, you're so valuable to Him that He gives you a key and says, "Come in anytime, girl!"

This is one of those free gifts that you received when you gave your heart to Him. Twenty-four seven access is yours. And when you come into His presence, you never have to be afraid. He's never going to greet you with a harsh word. No way! He'll spread His arms wide and say, "What took you so long, kiddo? I've been waiting on you!"

. . . .

Lord, I won't wait! I'll come to You with my problems, my joys, my sorrows. I'm so grateful Your doors are always open. Amen.

Day 68

Identified as His Own

*And now you Gentiles have also heard the truth,
the Good News that God saves you. And when you
believed in Christ, he identified you as his own by giving
you the Holy Spirit, whom he promised long ago.*

EPHESIANS 1:13 NLT

When you put your trust in Christ, God marked you as His very own. He sent His Holy Spirit to live inside you, identifying you as His. The very Spirit of God Himself is alive in you!

The Holy Spirit can comfort you, teach you, lead you, speak to you, give you good advice, help you think good thoughts, and remember God's words. Wow!

This is why Jesus said this: "But I tell you the truth, it is to your advantage that I go away; for if I do not go away, the Helper (Comforter, Advocate, Intercessor—Counselor, Strengthener, Standby) will not come to you; but if I go, I will send Him (the Holy Spirit) to you [to be in close fellowship with you]" (John 16:7 AMP).

. . . .

This is so amazing, Lord! Thank You for marking me as Your child by putting Your Spirit in my heart. My identity is secure in You alone.

You Are the Beautiful Work of God's Hand

But now, O LORD, you are our Father; we are the clay,
and you are our potter; we are all the work of your hand.
ISAIAH 64:8 ESV

Do you remember drawing or painting something or sculpting something out of clay when you were little, and you knew exactly what it was meant to be, but no one else seemed to? That's because you were the creator, so of course you knew, even if no one else could see it. Never forget that the one true God is your Creator. Sometimes, you might not be sure exactly who you are meant to be and what you're supposed to be doing as you're growing and still figuring life out, but God always knows. Keep following Him and asking Him to guide you into the extraordinary life He made you for, full of the good things He has planned for you.

. . . .

Dear God, You are the potter and I am the clay. Thank You for
making me and having good plans for me. Please show me day by
day what those plans are. I want to follow You forever! Amen.

Day 70

You Have Salvation and Purpose

God saved you by his grace when you believed. And you can't take credit for this; it is a gift from God. Salvation is not a reward for the good things we have done, so none of us can boast about it. For we are God's masterpiece. He has created us anew in Christ Jesus, so we can do the good things he planned for us long ago.
EPHESIANS 2:8–10 NLT

You can probably think of friends and classmates who seem hopeless and without purpose. They don't seem to care much about anything. They don't seem to have goals or plans. Or maybe they do have goals and plans, but they're on the wrong track or they're doing good things but for the wrong reasons. Any of those can lead to depression or anxiety. But focusing on Ephesians 2:8–10 is the best motivation. When you think about how God gave you the gift of salvation and created you on purpose with good plans for your life, you should feel full of gratitude and enthusiasm, eager to keep seeking God and asking Him to guide you in doing all those good things He has ready and scheduled for you in His perfect timing.

. . . .

Heavenly Father, thank You for salvation and new life in Jesus Christ. Thank You for creating me with purpose and plans. I'm excited for You to show me all the good things You want me to do with my life. Day by day, I'll trust You and follow Your lead. Amen.

Nothing to Be Ashamed Of

I'm not ashamed of the Good News. It is God's power to save
everyone who believes, Jews first and Greeks as well.
ROMANS 1:16 GW

There's an ongoing conversation about which "people group" God loves the most. He first revealed Himself to the Jewish people, and they're pretty high on the list! But then when Jesus came, the floodgates were open. For the first time, other people had access to the Savior too.

People of every skin color, every nation, every culture, every lifestyle. Jesus died for every single one. And He loves and values every human being exactly the same.

This is one reason we can't be ashamed of the gospel message. It truly is good news, not just for certain people groups but the whole world. And the whole world needs to hear. Will you tell them? Or will you hide your light under a bushel and pretend it's not important?

Look around you, girl! This world is in chaos. There are signs everywhere that the return of Christ is near. There's no time to waste. He adores you. He saved you. He's given you eternity. Will you share that message with others while you can?

. . . .

Lord, I won't hesitate! I sense that time is short.
I'll share the gospel with my friends and loved ones so that
we can all live in heaven together one day. Amen.

Day 72
You Can Be Totally Content

I have learned to be happy with whatever I have. I know how to get along with little and how to live when I have much. I have learned the secret of being happy at all times. If I am full of food and have all I need, I am happy. If I am hungry and need more, I am happy. I can do all things because Christ gives me the strength.
<small>PHILIPPIANS 4:11–13 NLV</small>

"Comparison is the thief of joy" is a well-known quote attributed to Theodore Roosevelt. And social media is often where the most comparison and joy-stealing goes on these days. The way to not let your joy be stolen is to be totally content the way God's Word says. Contentment means being happy and satisfied with what you have. It means you're not wanting something other than what you already have. God can give you total contentment when you focus on how you can do anything, get through any circumstance, with Jesus Christ giving you strength. Sometimes in life you might have more than enough, while other times you feel like you don't have nearly enough, especially when you look around too much in comparison. But when you focus on God and trust that He gives you exactly what you need when you need it, then you can be peaceful and thankful all the time.

. . . .

Dear Jesus, please help me remember how to be totally content—by trusting I can do all things because You make me strong to face anything! Amen.

Day 73
When You're Tested and Tempted

God blesses those who patiently endure testing and temptation.
Afterward they will receive the crown of life that God has promised to
those who love him. And remember, when you are being tempted, do
not say, "God is tempting me." God is never tempted to do wrong, and
he never tempts anyone else. Temptation comes from our own desires,
which entice us and drag us away. These desires give birth to sinful
actions. And when sin is allowed to grow, it gives birth to death.
JAMES 1:12–15 NLT

Anyone who thinks that becoming a Christian means enjoying an
easy life is clearly not actually reading the Bible or growing closer to
God. His Word plainly says that we will be tested and tempted to
do wrong. Even so, loving God and trusting in and following Jesus
as Lord and Savior make for the best kind of life. In every test and
temptation, every bit of suffering and heartache, God is working out
His good plans in our lives when we faithfully obey Him no matter
our circumstances. He blesses us with His supernatural comfort and
peace and joy even in the midst of the trials and pain, until one day
we will have total comfort, peace, and joy—and no tears or hardship
ever again—when we are at home forever in heaven.

Heavenly Father, please help me to patiently endure the tests
and temptations in my life. I want to prevail over them as I
follow You and keep my faith in Your eternal blessings.

Day 74
The Look of Love

To the church of God in Corinth, to those sanctified (set apart, made holy) in Christ Jesus, who are selected and called as saints (God's people), together with all those who in every place call on and honor the name of our Lord Jesus Christ, their Lord and ours: Grace to you and peace [inner calm and spiritual well-being] from God our Father and the Lord Jesus Christ.

1 CORINTHIANS 1:2–3 AMP

You are so special to God. God says you are set apart and made holy because of what Jesus did for you. He offers you grace and peace. And He is always looking on you with love.

Parents have a certain love look on their faces reserved just for their children. You have a special place in God's heart too. And He is the perfect parent. He is always looking at you with a special look of love. Even though there are billions of people in this world He made, You are still very special to Him.

. . . .

Heavenly Father, thanks for Your great love for me. I'm thankful for all that Jesus has done for me to make me holy in Your sight.

You Have Extras on Top

*God will supply every need of yours according to his riches in glory
in Christ Jesus. To our God and Father be glory forever and ever.*
PHILIPPIANS 4:19–20 ESV

Frozen yogurt is so good, especially piled high with amazing toppings.
Froyo is great on its own, but it's definitely even better with lots of
extra little treats on top!

When you eat froyo, you can think about how God gives us
good blessings and then often gives even more on top. When you're
needing a mental boost in a hard situation, sometimes you need to
take time to focus on the blessings you have and then the extra-
special blessings God has piled on top. Write them down and pray
over them with thanks. Showing gratitude for what God has done
and what He has given you in the past is a great way to build hope
and confidence for how He is going to supply your needs again right
now and in the future!

. . . .

*Heavenly Father, thank You for blessing me so
generously, even giving me extras on top of what I truly
need. Thank You for all the ways You've provided for me
and helped me in the past. I trust You for all the ways You
will keep on giving and blessing in the future. Amen.*

You Are Blessed with Forgiveness

The LORD is compassionate and merciful, slow to get angry and filled with unfailing love. He will not constantly accuse us, nor remain angry forever. He does not punish us for all our sins; he does not deal harshly with us, as we deserve. For his unfailing love toward those who fear him is as great as the height of the heavens above the earth. He has removed our sins as far from us as the east is from the west.

PSALM 103:8–12 NLT

If someone treats you badly again and again and again, it can be really hard to forgive them. So think about how awesome it is that God forgives us endlessly even though we all mess up a lot. We hurt our relationship with God when we don't acknowledge our sin and ask for His forgiveness. But as soon as we admit our sins and ask God to take them away, He does—as far as the east is from the west, actually! And then we can draw close to God and His goodness once again.

. . . .

Heavenly Father, no one forgives like You do! I'm so grateful for Your compassion, because I need Your mercy and forgiveness often. Remind me to admit my sins to You and let You take them far, far away. Thank You! Amen.

The Joy of My Salvation

Let the joy of Your saving power return to me.
And give me a willing spirit to obey you.
PSALM 51:12 NLV

Maybe you've heard the expression, "The excitement wore off." That's how it is with Christmas presents. Kids get the things they've begged for. Then time goes by and those gifts are shoved to the back of the closet, forgotten.

The same is true with great news. Maybe your parents have purchased a newer, bigger home. Everything is so exciting at first. You commit to keeping your new room in tip-top shape. But a few months in, it looks like a trash pile—just like the old place.

How easily we forget! We don't keep the celebration going.

When it comes to your salvation, Jesus wants you to keep the party going, girl! Every day can be just as fresh, just as new, just as powerful, as the day you gave your heart to Him. You don't have to lose your joy on the rough days. No way! You're still His child, filled with His Spirit.

Today, if you're struggling, pray the simple prayer below.

. . . .

Lord, restore the joy of my salvation. May I feel exactly as I felt in that moment when I first came to know You. Amen.

You Are Blessed by the Little Things

*"There is a boy here who has five barley loaves and two fish,
but what are they for so many?" Jesus said, "Have the people sit
down."... So the men sat down, about five thousand in number.
Jesus then took the loaves, and when he had given thanks, he
distributed them to those who were seated. So also the fish, as
much as they wanted. And when they had eaten their fill, he told
his disciples, "Gather up the leftover fragments, that nothing may
be lost." So they gathered them up and filled twelve baskets with
fragments from the five barley loaves left by those who had eaten.*

JOHN 6:9–13 ESV

Think about what a great thing Jesus did with a small act of generosity from a young boy who gave up his lunch. It might not seem like too big of a deal, but the boy probably was a little worried he might not get to eat that day! And then Jesus did an amazing miracle, taking that little lunch and feeding a huge crowd of people with many baskets left over. Think about how many of those people must have believed in Jesus that day after seeing such a stunning miracle. Be faithful even in the smallest things God calls you to do. Who knows how He will bless you and show you miracles because of your obedience and generosity?

*Heavenly Father, I want to be faithful to You even
in the little things You ask of me. Amen.*

Your Times Are in God's Hands

But as for me, I trust in You, O Lord. I say,
"You are my God." My times are in Your hands.
PSALM 31:14–15 NLV

You may feel stressed about the future and plans for after high school. Or maybe you're stressed because you can't seem to decide on any good plans. Or maybe you're just trying not to worry at all and taking things day by day. Whatever the case, never stop talking to God and asking for His leading and His help in setting goals in your life. You are so blessed that, like the psalmist says in Psalm 31, your times are in God's hands. Ask Him to give you wisdom in all things and to open the right doors of opportunity for you—the ones that He knows are best for you to walk through, that match up with His will for your life and the good things He has planned for you to do. Remember that He sees and knows everything that is going on with you. He is loving and taking care of you in every situation.

. . . .

Heavenly Father, thank You that I can trust that my times
are in Your hands. Nothing anyone says or does against
me can change the fact that You are my God who holds
me, protects me, and takes good care of me. Amen.

Day 80
Worthy of His Gifts and Abilities

Christian brothers, I want you to know about the gifts of the Holy Spirit. You need to understand the truth about this.
1 CORINTHIANS 12:1 NLV

Imagine you're a parent with a houseful of kids. (This might be a bit of a stretch, but use your imagination!) Now imagine you've got all the money in the world. (Woot!) You can give your kids anything you please. Money. Cars. Houses. Anything.

What would you give them? Would their attitudes help you determine which gifts would go to which child?

Now picture your heavenly Father. He's the owner of, well, everything. He could give you any gifts He likes. But He's choosing based on what's best for you. There are a host of spiritual gifts listed in 1 Corinthians 12: wisdom, teaching, faith, prophecy, miracles, and so on.

There are also artistic and academic gifts. Maybe you're a singer or a dancer or an artist. Maybe you excel at math or writing.

Here's the point: your Father has unlimited resources, and He values you so much that He wants to lavish His gifts on you. Today, open your hands and heart to receive!

. . . .

Lord, pour them out! I'll use those gifts for Your glory. Amen.

Even If You Suffer, You Are Blessed

Who is going to harm you if you are eager to do good? But even if you should suffer for what is right, you are blessed. "Do not fear their threats; do not be frightened." But in your hearts revere Christ as Lord. Always be prepared to give an answer to everyone who asks you to give the reason for the hope that you have. But do this with gentleness and respect, keeping a clear conscience, so that those who speak maliciously against your good behavior in Christ may be ashamed of their slander. For it is better, if it is God's will, to suffer for doing good than for doing evil.

1 PETER 3:13–17 NIV

Sometimes you do the right thing and suffer for it, while the one who did wrong seems to win. In those times, it's easy to feel bitter—but God wants you to feel blessed. He wants you to remember He's watching and He cares. He knows when you are suffering and whether or not you are faithful in the midst of it. He wants you to expect hard times and be prepared to honor and praise Him and point others to Him in the midst of them. What's more, He promises He will greatly reward you for your faithfulness.

* *

Father God, help me never to feel bitter but always to feel blessed. No hard time that I go through here on earth can ever keep me away from Your goodness and gifts, which You give me in Your perfect timing when I am faithful to You. Amen.

Day 82
Marked

*And you also were included in Christ when you
heard the message of truth, the gospel of your salvation.
When you believed, you were marked in him with a seal,
the promised Holy Spirit, who is a deposit guaranteeing
our inheritance until the redemption of those who
are God's possession—to the praise of his glory.*
EPHESIANS 1:13–14 NIV

When you put your trust in Christ, God marked you as His very own. You're His—forever! How did He do this? He sent His Holy Spirit to live inside you. Isn't that amazing? The very spirit of God Himself is alive in you!

The Holy Spirit is able to comfort you, teach you, lead you, speak to you, give you good advice, help you think good thoughts, and remember God's words. This is why Jesus said it was better for Him to leave the earth after He rose from the dead so that the Holy Spirit could come (John 16:7)! His Spirit can be in all of His children at the same time.

. . . .

*Jesus, thank You for sending Your Spirit to live inside me and mark
me as one of Your own. I'm so grateful for this miraculous gift!*

Day 83
Everything Will Be Perfect One Day

After you have suffered for awhile, God Himself will make you perfect. He will keep you in the right way. He will give you strength. He is the God of all loving-favor and has called you through Christ Jesus to share His shining-greatness forever. God has power over all things forever.

1 PETER 5:10–11 NLV

A perfect life here on earth would be so nice. But you know it's just not possible. You know there are all kinds of troubles and hurts in this world: little ones like a bad grade and big ones like the loss of a loved one. But God's Word promises that suffering and pain are just for a little while in this world as we wait for perfection forever in heaven. Meanwhile, God will keep you on the right path and give you strength to deal with the hard things of this life. None of them can ever overpower you because you trust that God has power over all of them.

. . . .

Heavenly Father, I hate the hurt in this world, but I love that You have complete power over all of it. I trust that You are working to make all things perfect and pain-free forever in heaven, for me and all who trust in Your Son, Jesus. Amen.

Day 84

He's Not Taking It Back!

God's gifts and his call can never be withdrawn.
ROMANS 11:29 NLT

Picture yourself at your best friend's birthday party. You've purchased the perfect-for-her gift, something you know she'll love. Sure enough, she opens it and is ecstatic. You hit the nail on the head.

Now picture yourself holding out your hands and saying, "Okay, now that you've seen it, you have to give it back. I never meant for you to keep it." Wait, what? Who does that? No one, and certainly not God!

And yet some people think He's ready to snatch back the gifts He's given them. They forget today's verse from Romans 11:29. God's gifts can never be withdrawn. If He created you with certain giftings, He means for you to develop and use them. But even if you don't (which is totally up to you) He's not asking for them back. He won't say, "I never meant for you to keep that, girl."

He *does* mean for you to keep that gift. And to grow it into something of beauty. Don't question Him. Don't get caught up in the "Does God really want me to use this gift?" dilemma. He does. So stir it up, girl!

. . . .

Lord, I guess I'd better keep going, even when I don't feel like it. You're not a quitter, and I won't be either! Amen.

Day 85
Loved and Free

"Do not be afraid. For I have bought you and made you free.
I have called you by name. You are Mine! You are of great
worth in My eyes. You are honored and I love you."
ISAIAH 43:1, 4 NLV

Read these verses from Isaiah again. Can you picture Jesus speaking these words to you? Close your eyes and talk to God about it. Do you really believe that God loves you this much? Stop and write down anything you hear Jesus saying to you during your time of prayer.

The first time Grace heard these words from Isaiah 43, she was overwhelmed with love for God. She'd never heard anything like that before. She let go of her shame, trusting in the love of Christ and truth of God's Word instead. She began to live her life in freedom.

When God Himself tells you who you are, it changes everything! Let Him speak to your heart every day. Let Him remind you of your worth and how much you matter to Him. You are His, held securely in the palm of His hand. You're His beloved daughter.

. . . .

Lord, change my heart so that I begin believing these truths in Your
Word. I want to walk in the freedom and love that You offer me.

Day 86
God Keeps You Steady

*If you had not helped me, LORD, I would soon have gone to
the land of silence. When I felt my feet slipping, you came
with your love and kept me steady. And when I was burdened
with worries, you comforted me and made me feel secure.*
PSALM 94:17–19 CEV

If you live in an area where winter is long and cold, you surely know
the feeling of your feet slipping. Ice and snow make everything slick,
and you have to be extra careful not to fall. Or if you do fall, you
want to make sure you have a big pile of soft snow to land in! When
you read Psalm 94, you can think of that slippery feeling but then
picture God's strong hand reaching out to steady you and keep you
safe. In any slippery situation, you can remember that God is always
ready to reach out His hand and help you.

*Heavenly Father, thank You for being the one who
steadies me and holds me up. Thank You for comforting
me and making me feel secure. Amen.*

Day 87

The Truth and Goodness of God's Word

Every word of God has been proven true.
He is a safe-covering to those who trust in Him.
PROVERBS 30:5 NLV

Memorizing scripture is a powerful way to stay encouraged. God loves to bring verses to your mind exactly when you need them. Sometimes repeating a calming scripture like Psalm 23 in your mind can help you to relax your breathing when you feel panicky. Sometimes singing praises like Psalm 136 is exactly what you need to have joy or combat the fear creeping up on you. Sometimes a powerful scripture that recounts the faith of others and the miracles of God, like Hebrews 11, is just what you need to grow your faith that God can do any kind of miracle in your situation too. Keep filling your mind with God's Word every chance you get, and see how He uses it to guide you and care for you and protect you.

* *

Heavenly Father, I'm so blessed by Your powerful Word.
Please bring specific verses and passages to my mind exactly when
I need them so that I can keep my focus fixed on You! Amen.

Day 88

Those Who Have Not Seen

But [Thomas] said to them, "Unless I see the nail marks in his hands and put my finger where the nails were, and put my hand into his side, I will not believe." A week later his disciples were in the house again, and Thomas was with them. Though the doors were locked, Jesus came and stood among them and said, "Peace be with you!" Then he said to Thomas, "Put your finger here; see my hands. Reach out your hand and put it into my side. Stop doubting and believe." Thomas said to him, "My Lord and my God!" Then Jesus told him, "Because you have seen me, you have believed; blessed are those who have not seen and yet have believed."

John 20:25–29 NIV

We can relate to Thomas sometimes. He just wanted to see in person, with his own eyes, that Jesus was alive. And Jesus blessed Thomas by coming to him. Yet Jesus also said, "Blessed are those who have not seen and yet have believed." That includes you and me, and it encourages us to keep the faith.

. . . .

Dear Jesus, I can't deny that it's hard sometimes to keep my faith since I didn't get to be there in Bible times and see You with my own eyes. Yet I do believe You are alive and You love me. You have shown me Your presence in my life through the Holy Spirit. You are the one and only Savior. No one else is like You, Lord, and I love You! Amen.

Every Gift Is from Him

*Every good gift and every perfect gift is from above,
coming down from the Father of lights, with whom
there is no variation or shadow due to change.*

JAMES 1:17 ESV

Some people might look at your musical abilities and say, "Girl, you get that from your mama! She's always been musical too." Or maybe they look at your book smarts and say, "Your grandfather was the same way. He loved math too."

It's true that family traits and propensities can be passed down, but guess who handed out those gifts in the first place? If you said, "God!" you're 100 percent right! Every good and perfect gift comes down from the Father of lights, passed out to those He loves. And isn't it interesting that today's verse uses the phrase "Father of lights" when talking about the gifts He gives His kids? They're meant to be used as a light, to illuminate the pathway for those you meet.

Walk in your gift and it will make a way for you. It will light your path. It will guide you to where you need to go. The Father of lights will make sure of it, girl!

. . . .

*My gifts are from You, Lord!
Thanks for letting them light my way. Amen.*

Day 90
God Can Make It Good

Joseph replied, "Don't be afraid of me. Am I God, that I can punish you? You intended to harm me, but God intended it all for good. He brought me to this position so I could save the lives of many people. No, don't be afraid. I will continue to take care of you and your children." So he reassured them by speaking kindly to them.

GENESIS 50:19–21 NLT

God can take the very worst of situations and turn it upside down. He can take anyone's evil plans toward you and work them out for your good. Consider the story of Joseph. It doesn't get much worse than being sold by your siblings into slavery in another country. Yet read the whole story of Joseph's life and look at the way God blessed Joseph through that awful experience. Whatever you're going through today, no matter how hard it is, choose to be loyal and obedient to God like Joseph was—and in His perfect timing, God will surely bless you for your faithfulness.

. . . .

Heavenly Father, thank You for Joseph's true story in the Bible to inspire and encourage me to keep being faithful to You even in the very worst of circumstances and injustices. You can take anything that's meant to be bad for me and turn it into good. I believe that, and I trust You! Amen.

Filled Up and Overflowing

I pray that God, the source of hope, will fill you completely with joy and peace because you trust in him. Then you will overflow with confident hope through the power of the Holy Spirit.

ROMANS 15:13 NLT

The Holy Spirit fills our hearts with the love of God. And that same power is what gives us hope. Colossians 1:27 (NLT) says, "For God wanted them to know that the riches and glory of Christ are for you Gentiles, too. And this is the secret: Christ lives in you. This gives you assurance of sharing his glory."

Christ lives in you! His Spirit is alive and at work in you at every moment! Think about this: When you fill a cup up with water to the very top, what happens if you jiggle the glass a little? It overflows and spills out! The Holy Spirit wants to fill you up just like that so that you overflow with love and hope—and then you can sprinkle a little of that on everyone around you.

. . . .

God, You are the source of my hope! Please fill me up to the top with love, joy, and peace so that I can sprinkle Your love all around me.

Day 92
You Can Honor God

Do you not know that your bodies are temples of the Holy Spirit,
who is in you, whom you have received from God? You are not your
own; you were bought at a price. Therefore honor God with your bodies.
1 CORINTHIANS 6:19–20 NIV

Always remember how blessed you are as a child of God, and take good care of yourself and the body God has given you! Ask Him every day to help you make healthy and wise choices. Because if you have asked Jesus to be your Savior, the Holy Spirit lives in you—and that makes your body a house for the Holy Spirit! The Bible says you are not your own but you belong to God. That's a good thing—the very best thing, actually!—because no one loves or cares for you like God does.

Father God, thank You that I belong to You!
Thank You for living in me! Please help me to take care
of my body the best I can so that as You live in me I can
do the good things You have planned for me. Amen.

His Spirit: A Lovely Gift

*The Helper, the Holy Spirit, whom the Father will send
in my name, he will teach you all things and bring to
your remembrance all that I have said to you.*

JOHN 14:26 ESV

God gives His kids many, many gifts. Some you can see with your eyes.
Some you can hear with your ears. But there's one gift that shows up
in a completely different way, and that's the gift of the Holy Spirit.

In the second chapter of Acts, you can read the remarkable story
of a remarkable day when the Spirit of God showed up. The disciples
were gathered together in an upstairs room, praying and waiting on
God. They were pressing in (praying with great anticipation). Then
from out of the blue, the Spirit swept in like flames! And everyone
began to speak in other tongues as the Spirit gave them the ability.
Wow! What a scene that must've been! They prayed, and God moved!

The Spirit is still moving today—healing hearts, bringing comfort, giving power to the powerless. Miracles are still taking place.
The Spirit of God lives inside of every believer, so He's right there,
ready to go to work on your behalf. Today, ask for a filling of the
Spirit so that you have all the power you could possibly need to do
the work God has given you.

* *

Holy Spirit, fill me today, I pray! Amen.

Day 94

Set Apart for a Purpose

He has saved us and called us to a holy life—
not because of anything we have done but because of
his own purpose and grace. This grace was given us
in Christ Jesus before the beginning of time.

2 TIMOTHY 1:9 NIV

Before time began, God had a plan for you. He called you to be His child and His friend. He set you apart because He has an amazing plan and purpose for your life.

God knew what He was doing when He created you. He has placed you right where you are for a season and a reason. Instead of wishing your life was a lot different, ask God to show you His plans and purposes for you in this season. Ask Him to give you eyes to see your circumstances from His perspective.

The path you're on is not random, dear one!

. . . .

Lord, I trust that You're doing something good in my life.
Please give me a vision for this season I'm in. Help me be
content and joyful on the path You've chosen for me.

Day 95

Glory to God Forever

Oh, the depth of the riches of the wisdom and knowledge of God! How unsearchable his judgments, and his paths beyond tracing out! "Who has known the mind of the Lord? Or who has been his counselor?" "Who has ever given to God, that God should repay them?" For from him and through him and for him are all things. To him be the glory forever! Amen.
ROMANS 11:33–36 NIV

This scripture reminds you how truly awesome God is! No one can ever fully understand Him. Does that mean you shouldn't even try? No way! He shows so much of Himself to you through His Word, through His creation, through His people, and on and on! Everything comes from Him and is made for Him and is held together by His great power. He wants you to keep getting to know Him better and better and to keep experiencing His amazing love for you.

. . . .

Almighty God, I worship You! You are truly extraordinary, awesome, and amazing! I want to take time every day to focus on how wonderful You are and how blessed I am to call You my heavenly Father! Amen.

You Belong to God

We know that we are children of God and that the world around us is under the control of the evil one. And we know that the Son of God has come, and he has given us understanding so that we can know the true God. And now we live in fellowship with the true God because we live in fellowship with his Son, Jesus Christ. He is the only true God, and he is eternal life.

1 JOHN 5:19–20 NLT

You might wonder sometimes why bad things happen in this world. It's because people sin, and the whole world is under the power of our enemy, the evil one, also called the devil or Satan. But those of us who believe in Jesus as Savior belong to God, so the evil one can never defeat us. Satan can attack us and hurt us, but God gives us life that lasts forever, no matter what! We should never want to follow any type of false god who will lead us into the ways of the evil one. Only the one true God leads us to life that lasts forever.

. . . .

Heavenly Father, I'm so blessed and grateful that I belong to You! Please show me and protect me from everything that is bad, and help me to keep away from false gods. I trust that because Jesus is my Savior, You give me life that lasts forever! Amen.

Fan into Flames

This is why I remind you to fan into flames the spiritual gift God gave you when I laid my hands on you. For God has not given us a spirit of fear and timidity, but of power, love, and self-discipline.
2 TIMOTHY 1:6–7 NLT

If you're trying to get a campfire going, you'll need to start with a few embers and then fan them into a flame big enough to use as a cook surface. All fires start small but grow, grow, grow!

Now think of the gifts and abilities your heavenly Father has poured into you. Right now, they're tiny embers—barely a spark. But if you "fan them into flames" (work hard to grow them) then before long those gifts (like that campfire) will grow!

It takes work. You have to keep that fire lit. Keep practicing. Keep working. Keep studying. Keep doing everything you need to do on your end to develop those gifts. But remember, the ember was placed there by God. You didn't start the fire. He did. So trust Him with it, girl. He's got this!

. . . .

I'll be disciplined, Lord! You are growing me into a spiritual powerhouse! I won't give up when the fire inside of me feels small. I'll make sure it keeps growing and growing. Amen.

Blessed to Be like Children

People were bringing little children to Jesus for him to place his hands on them, but the disciples rebuked them. When Jesus saw this, he was indignant. He said to them, "Let the little children come to me, and do not hinder them, for the kingdom of God belongs to such as these. Truly I tell you, anyone who will not receive the kingdom of God like a little child will never enter it." And he took the children in his arms, placed his hands on them and blessed them.

MARK 10:13–16 NIV

You're growing up and becoming an adult fast. As you look to the future, what are the things you're looking forward to about not being a kid anymore? What are the things you will miss? It's fun to hold on to childhood in some ways, even while it's good and necessary to grow and mature. We can be glad, then, that God's Word tells us a way we should always be childlike: in the way we receive His kingdom. As little kids, we don't usually worry and fret about too much. We're pretty carefree and eager and enthusiastic. We have great love for and faith in our parents or the ones who take care of us. And in that same kind of way, our heavenly Father wants us to remain like children forever—trusting in Him completely to provide for every single one of our needs and eagerly enjoying His great love for us.

Heavenly Father, even as I'm growing up, help me to always have childlike, enthusiastic love and joy and faith in You. Amen.

Talking with Jesus

*Jesus looked at them intently and said, "Humanly speaking,
it is impossible. But with God everything is possible."*
MATTHEW 19:26 NLT

Jesus wants to talk to you every single day. Can you hear Him?
Remember the scriptures we've read about Jesus wanting us to hear
His voice? Sometimes it helps to picture Jesus in your mind while you
pray. After all, God created your imagination for a reason! Christian
missionary reports out of the Middle East have stated that Jesus is
showing up in people's dreams who have never even heard of Him
before. That seems impossible, but nothing is impossible with God!

Jesus is a very personal God. He wants to be your friend and
your trusted counselor. He wants you to come to Him first for advice.

What do you need advice about today? Ask Jesus for help and
guidance. Talk to Him like you would your best friend. You can
talk to Him out loud, you can pray in your heart and mind, and it's
also very helpful to write down your prayers so that you can have a
reminder of how God answers you!

. . . .

*Jesus, thanks for creating my imagination so that I can see
and hear from You! I believe You can do the impossible!*

So Blessed to Be Saved

As he was approaching Damascus on this mission, a light from heaven suddenly shone down around him. He fell to the ground and heard a voice saying to him, "Saul! Saul! Why are you persecuting me?" "Who are you, lord?" Saul asked. And the voice replied, "I am Jesus, the one you are persecuting! Now get up and go into the city, and you will be told what you must do."
ACTS 9:3–6 NLT

The apostle Paul (previously called Saul) in the Bible was saved in an exceptionally dramatic way when God called him out of his life of darkness and destruction. You can read the whole account in Acts 9. Our stories of coming to faith in Jesus probably aren't quite as dramatic as Paul's, yet they are still just as important and meaningful. Faith in Jesus Christ as our Savior and Lord is the greatest gift we could ever receive. We are saved from the devastating effects of sin in our lives because Jesus took all the punishment upon Himself. His sacrificial love for us is so amazing, so awesome! We have every reason to give Him thanks and praise!

*Jesus, I praise You and thank You endlessly
for saving me from sin. Amen.*

More Grace to the Humble

*He gives more grace. Therefore it says, "God opposes
the proud but gives grace to the humble."*
JAMES 4:6 ESV

"She thinks she hung the moon." Maybe you've heard that expression. (Hopefully, no one has said it about you.) When someone thinks they're "all that," it means they've got a big head. They are arrogant, puffed up, hard to be around. To describe a girl like that, some would say, "She's full of herself."

God's not keen on His daughters being full of themselves. On the contrary, He wants you to be full of His Spirit, not yourself! All eyes on Him, not you. That's His way.

Sure, your heavenly Father adores you. He thinks you have incredible value. He feels so strongly about you that He went to the cross to cover your sin. But He doesn't want you to let things go to your head. He prefers you to humble yourself. In fact, today's verse says that he gives grace to the humble. So if you really want to walk in His favor, turn the spotlight on Him, not you! That's the best way to shine.

. . . .

*Forgive me for the times I've been prideful, Jesus.
I want to shine the light on You, not me. Amen.*

Life and Breath and Everything

"[God] himself gives everyone life and breath and everything else."
ACTS 17:25 NIV

It's not just material possessions that God blesses you with. It's every good thing—even the very next breath you take. Simply being alive and having opportunities to grow and learn and serve Jesus as You follow Him is the best blessing ever. Even if you feel like you are lacking in some way today—maybe there's something new you wish you had or an opportunity you wish would come your way—instead of focusing on what you don't have, how can you fix your thoughts on all the good things and opportunities you do have? What is God asking you to do with your gifts and your abilities and your life? How might He bring new blessings to you when you're obedient and faithful and grateful for what you already have?

. . . .

Dear Lord, please forgive me when I'm greedy and ungrateful. Help me to focus on all that You bless me with every single day. Just being alive is an incredible blessing. Thank You for my life and my possessions and my opportunities. I want to use them to serve You and show my love for You! Please guide and direct me. Amen.

Day 103

Blessed by the Promise Keeper

And the LORD gave them rest on every side just as he had sworn
to their fathers. Not one of all their enemies had withstood
them, for the LORD had given all their enemies into their
hands. Not one word of all the good promises that the LORD
had made to the house of Israel had failed; all came to pass.

JOSHUA 21:44–45 ESV

We are so blessed to love and worship the one God who is the true promise keeper. Time and again the Bible shows how God kept His promises to His people. The accounts of God's faithfulness in the Bible remind us that He keeps His promises to His people today as well. That includes you if you have accepted Jesus Christ as your Savior. The more you read God's Word, the more you learn about the many promises of God and how blessed you are because of them.

. . . .

Father God, thank You for making and keeping Your
promises to all of Your people, including me. Please help me
to learn more and more about Your promises and to grow
stronger and more confident in my faith as I do. Help me
to share about Your promises with others too. Amen.

Meet Him

Let us then with confidence draw near to the throne of grace,
that we may receive mercy and find grace to help in time of need.
HEBREWS 4:16 ESV

Imagine you've been invited to visit the queen of England. You're dressed in your finest, wearing everything you've been instructed. Now it's time to enter the throne room. Your knees are knocking. Your hands are trembling. You're terrified that she will turn you away.

When it comes to approaching Jesus, you can rest easy! Today's verse tells us that we can confidently approach His throne. And look at how the verse describes it: a "throne of grace." Wow! What an image! Instead of a throne of fear, it's a holy, welcoming place where you can expect to find forgiveness, mercy, and love.

God is good. And He adores His kids. He wants nothing but good things for us. So come boldly. No matter what you've done. No matter where you've been. No matter who you've been hanging out with. Just come. As you are. Meet Him at His throne of grace today.

. . . .

I'll come, Jesus. I'm a hot mess. I've done things I shouldn't have.
But here I am, ready for some face-to-face grace! Amen.

Day 105

God Promises That You Can Find Him

"You will seek me and find me when you seek me with all your heart."
JEREMIAH 29:13 NIV

True, we don't have God here in human form these days, and it sure must have been amazing to have learned from Jesus when He lived on earth. (Can you picture yourself as one of Jesus' followers back then? It's fun to imagine!) But today, we have the Holy Spirit present with us and we have God's Word to teach and guide us. We have God's promises that we can find Him (Deuteronomy 4:29) and that He is never far from us (Acts 17:27). If we ever feel that God is far away or we can't find Him, we need to consider what our attitudes and actions and habits have been like lately. Have we been holding on to any sin that we need to let go and seek forgiveness for? Have we been spending regular time with God through His Word and in prayer? James 4:8 (NLT) says, "Come close to God, and God will come close to you. Wash your hands, you sinners; purify your hearts, for your loyalty is divided between God and the world."

- -

Father God, thank You that You don't hide away from me. You want to be found and You want to be close to me. Help me to get rid of anything in my life that creates distance from You. Amen.

God Promises to Help and Protect You

I will lift up my eyes to the mountains. Where will my help come from? My help comes from the Lord, Who made heaven and earth. He will not let your feet go out from under you. He Who watches over you will not sleep. Listen, He Who watches over Israel will not close his eyes or sleep. The Lord watches over you. The Lord is your safe cover at your right hand. The sun will not hurt you during the day and the moon will not hurt you during the night. The Lord will keep you from all that is sinful. He will watch over your soul. The Lord will watch over your coming and going, now and forever.

PSALM 121 NLV

What are you needing God's help for today? It could be anything! Sometimes it's a smaller thing, like understanding your homework or finding your missing cell phone. Sometimes it's a big thing, like dealing with mean girls or grieving the death of a loved one. Or maybe you feel unsafe and desperately long for protection. Almighty God promises both to help you and to keep you safe, and you can trust Him to keep His promises.

. . . .

Heavenly Father, thank You for Your help and protection in every situation. Every person who helps me, everything that works out, every bit of safety I have ultimately comes from You as You watch over my life and care for me. I'm so grateful to be Your child, now and forever. Amen.

The Same God

*But the LORD made the earth by his power, and he preserves it
by his wisdom. With his own understanding he stretched out the
heavens. When he speaks in the thunder, the heavens roar with rain.
He causes the clouds to rise over the earth. He sends the lightning
with the rain and releases the wind from his storehouses.*

JEREMIAH 10:12–13 NLT

The God who loves and cares about you is the same God who
stretched out the heavens. The God who knows your name and the
number of hairs on your head is the same God who speaks in the
thunder and releases the wind from His storehouse.

God is always speaking love to you. Just look out at creation.
The grass is a beautiful green carpet designed by God. The birds and
the flowers all announce His existence. The person next to you is a
miracle, woven together by God.

When you think about God's unlimited power and His love for
you, what happens to your problems? Do you trust that God can
handle anything you have going on?

. . . .

*You are the same God who speaks water into existence, so I know
You can take care of anything that comes my way. Thank You, God!*

God's Love Is Unfailing

The steadfast love of the LORD never ceases;
his mercies never come to an end.
LAMENTATIONS 3:22 ESV

When was the last time you acted like a selfish brat? We all do at times, unfortunately! It's amazing that even on our worst days, when our worst attitudes and thoughts and actions are on display and we're feeling the most miserable and unlovable, God sees and knows them all yet still loves us endlessly. His love is steadfast and unfailing, and He promises it always will be. He proved His amazing love for us in this way: "While we were still sinners, Christ died for us" (Romans 5:8 NIV). He knew exactly how awful we can be in our sin, and still He loved and died for us. What an incredible blessing to have such a faithful Savior!

. . . .

Father God, even though You see the very worst of me,
You love me unconditionally, and I could never thank You
enough. I want Your steadfast, unfailing love to inspire
me to live my life the best way I can, avoiding sin as much
as I possibly can. You know I won't live life perfectly, but
as I try my best, You will continue to love me and help me
grow in goodness and grace. I am so grateful! Amen.

More Truth

*Both Jesus who sanctifies and those who are sanctified
[that is, spiritually transformed, made holy, and set apart
for God's purpose] are all from one Father; for this reason
He is not ashamed to call them brothers and sisters.*

Hebrews 2:11 amp

Today's verse is full of so much good stuff! Here's the breakdown:
Because of Jesus, you are...

- Spiritually transformed
- Made holy
- Set apart for God's purpose
- A child of the Father
- A sister to Christ

Wow! Whenever you're feeling low or worried, come back and read the truth of this scripture again. You are a precious part of God's family. He wants to talk with you and be with you. It's been said that if God had a refrigerator, your picture would be on it!

That might seem impossible with all the people in the world, but God is so big we can't possibly fathom His ways or have Him all figured out (Isaiah 55:8–9). Many of His creative and astonishing ways will remain a mystery until heaven. In the meantime, trust what God's Word says about you. He knows everything about you and loves you so, *so* much!

Lord God, Let Your love change me from the inside out.

God Lives in You

*God has given us his Spirit as proof that we live in him and
he in us. Furthermore, we have seen with our own eyes and
now testify that the Father sent his Son to be the Savior of the
world. All who declare that Jesus is the Son of God have God
living in them, and they live in God. We know how much God
loves us, and we have put our trust in his love. God is love,
and all who live in love live in God, and God lives in them.*

1 JOHN 4:13–16 NLT

What are you feeling anxious about today? So many sad and stressful
and scary things are happening in this world, but be assured that
you are never left to face any of them alone! When you believe that
Jesus is the one true Savior and the Son of God, then God is living
in you through His Holy Spirit and you are living with His constant
love and help. There's no better blessing than that!

*Heavenly Father, I believe in Jesus as my Savior, and so
I need to remember that You are with me always to help
with any hard thing. Sometimes I forget, and I'm sorry.
Please fill me up with awesome hope and peace and courage
as I trust that You live in me and never leave me. Amen.*

He Demonstrated It

The Word became a human and lived among us.
We saw his glory—the glory that belongs to the only Son
of the Father—and he was full of grace and truth.

JOHN 1:14 NCV

"We saw His glory" and "He was full of grace and truth."

Stop to think through those words about your Savior, Jesus Christ. Because He came to earth, because He was fully God and fully man, we were able to catch beautiful glimpses of what grace really looks like.

It looks like Jesus.

It looks like a Savior who stops on the side of the road and heals a lame man. It looks like a teacher who cared enough to provide lunch for five thousand people. It looks like an innocent man who hung on the cross, carrying the sins of people who didn't deserve His love.

That's what grace looks like. And it shines from the eyes of the only one who loved you enough to do all that because He thinks you're worth it.

The next time you're searching for glimpses of grace, look no further than Jesus.

. . . .

Oh, Jesus! Thank You for showing us what grace and
truth look like. We see it in Your eyes. We see it in Your
actions. We see it in Your Word. Your love for mankind is
immeasurable! What a glorious Savior You are. Amen.

Day 112

You Can Look Forward with Hope

*We should live in this evil world with wisdom,
righteousness, and devotion to God, while we look forward
with hope to that wonderful day when the glory of our
great God and Savior, Jesus Christ, will be revealed.*

TITUS 2:12–13 NLT

You should always be watching for Jesus to return. He promises He will, and His return will be incredible to see! It might sound rather scary because it will be unlike anything anyone has ever experienced, but it will be wonderful for everyone who loves and trusts Him. Mark 13:24–27 (NLV) says: "After those days of much trouble and pain and sorrow are over, the sun will get dark. The moon will not give light. The stars will fall from the sky. The powers in the heavens will be shaken. Then they will see the Son of Man coming in the clouds with great power and shining-greatness. He will send His angels. They will gather together God's people from the four winds. They will come from one end of the earth to the other end of heaven."

. . . .

*Dear Jesus, I'm watching and waiting for You to return
and gather Your people, including me! Your return is going
to be awesome! I love You and trust You. Amen.*

God Is Watching You

The eyes of the Lord are in every place, watching the bad and the good.
PROVERBS 15:3 NLV

No one watches out for you like God does. The Bible says He sees and knows everything that happens in every place, all the time. "No one can hide from God. His eyes see everything we do. We must give an answer to God for what we have done," says Hebrews 4:13 (NLV). And Job 28:24 (NLV) says, "He looks to the ends of the earth, and sees everything under the heavens." For people who make a lot of bad choices, these verses might seem scary, but for those who love God and want to follow and obey His Word, they are hopeful and encouraging. God only wants you to obey His good ways because He loves you and wants what's best for you. When you trust that He is always watching out for you, you can have peace and confidence, knowing He's able to help in every moment.

. . . .

Heavenly Father, please remind me that You are always watching me—in every place and every moment. Thank You for caring so much about me! Amen.

What Others Think

We serve God whether people honor us or despise us, whether they
slander us or praise us. We are honest, but they call us impostors.
2 Corinthians 6:8 nlt

Some people say they don't care what other people think of them,
but if you take a deep look at your heart, what people say can matter
a little too much. It's that whole "sticks and stones" thing. It's just
not true. Words can hurt.

Do you find yourself worrying about what others are saying and
thinking about you? Here's the thing: when God's power is at work
in you, you can be confident in who you are as His child no matter
what anyone else thinks.

When others say hurtful things about you, it can definitely sting.
But as you bring those hurts to Jesus, He reminds you of the truth.
You are a dearly loved daughter of the King of kings! You have access
to all of God's power. You can walk right up to God because of how
loved you are.

. . . .

Lord, thank You for reminding me of who I am. I never have to worry
about what other people think of me because I'm Your beloved child.

Your God Is Always Everywhere

Where can I go from your Spirit? Where can I flee from your presence? If I go up to the heavens, you are there; if I make my bed in the depths, you are there. If I rise on the wings of the dawn, if I settle on the far side of the sea, even there your hand will guide me, your right hand will hold me fast. If I say, "Surely the darkness will hide me and the light become night around me," even the darkness will not be dark to you; the night will shine like the day, for darkness is as light to you.

PSALM 139:7–12 NIV

God is omnipresent, meaning He is in all places all the time. Everywhere you go, He is with you. In good times and bad, He is right there, and you can call out to Him for help or in worship or just to talk to Him about anything. No person can ever promise you what God promises you. He says, "I will never leave you or let you be alone" (Hebrews 13:5 NLV).

. . . .

Heavenly Father, thank You for being in all places all the time. I need You with me every moment, and I'm so grateful You never leave me. Amen.

A Grace-Filled Calling

*Who saved us and called us to a holy calling, not because
of our works but because of his own purpose and grace,
which he gave us in Christ Jesus before the ages began.*

2 TIMOTHY 1:9 ESV

You have a holy calling on your life. Because of your faith in Jesus, He has placed His hand on you and His calling in your heart. You will follow hard after Him, not just now but forever. But what does it mean to "follow Jesus," exactly?

Imagine you got a phone call from a total stranger who said, "Hey, I have plans for you. Drop everything and come with me." Would you go? No way!

But Jesus won you over with His grace! He said, "Girl, I see the pain you've struggled with. I see the empty feelings in your heart. I see the insecurities. And I adore you anyway." Then He saved you and called you to give every part of your life to Him.

His actions are not the result of anything you've done. They are the result of everything He's done. He saved you. Gave you a new life. Set you free from the past. And, out of love and gratitude, you decided to take Him up on His offer to turn your life around. How could you resist so great a sacrifice?

. . . .

*You've offered me grace, forgiveness, and a sense of
purpose. I'll gladly follow after You, Jesus! Amen.*

What Are You Building On?

"Anyone who listens to my teaching and follows it is wise, like a
person who builds a house on solid rock. Though the rain comes in
torrents and the floodwaters rise and the winds beat against that
house, it won't collapse because it is built on bedrock. But anyone
who hears my teaching and doesn't obey it is foolish, like a person
who builds a house on sand. When the rains and floods come and the
winds beat against that house, it will collapse with a mighty crash."

MATTHEW 7:24–27 NLT

If you've ever gone to the beach, maybe you've seen some amazing sandcastles or even built some yourself. But we all know that a sandcastle never lasts for too long in the waves and weather. Jesus taught that it matters what you build on. Anything built on a strong foundation like rock is able to stand firm through all kinds of weather. If you build your life on the strong rock of Jesus and His Word, you will stand firm and brave through all kinds of situations.

Jesus went on to say that anything built on sand is not strong enough to last. He was contrasting people who hear His teaching and listen and obey it with people who only hear it but do nothing with it. Those who obey Jesus are built up strong for whatever life brings their way, while those who ignore Jesus are easily washed away.

* *

Dear Jesus, I don't want to ignore You and be easily washed
away. Please build me up with great faith as I depend on
You to be my rock in every kind of weather! Amen.

Day 118
You Know the One
True Religion

We need such a Religious Leader Who made the way for
man to go to God. Jesus is holy and has no guilt. He has
never sinned and is different from sinful men. He has the place
of honor above the heavens. Christ is not like other religious
leaders. They had to give gifts every day on the altar in worship
for their own sins first and then for the sins of the people.
Christ did not have to do that. He gave one gift on the altar and
that gift was Himself. It was done once and it was for all time.
HEBREWS 7:26–27 NLV

Many people say that all religions are the same and all roads lead to heaven, but that's just not true. Belief in Jesus as God and as our one and only Savior is what's true. Jesus alone was (and is) perfect and holy and without sin. He gave His own life once for all, for people of all time, and no other religion offers that kind of gift and love and miracle! To know Jesus as Savior is to believe in Him and accept His awesome gift of grace and the eternal life He provided when He took away our sins by dying on the cross for them and then rising to life again.

. . . .

Dear Jesus, no one else is like You! You are the one true God and
Savior, and I'm so blessed that You've revealed Yourself to me! Amen.

The Garden of Your Heart

Do not be deceived: God cannot be mocked. A man reaps what he sows.
GALATIANS 6:7 NIV

Have you ever grown a garden? Some people have a knack for it and really enjoy planting things and watching them grow. Jesus liked to use gardening illustrations in the Bible to help people understand what He was teaching. Many people in the crowds following Him were farmers and gardeners.

This verse in Galatians is a truth to remember for a lifetime. It's the law of sowing and reaping. The law of sowing and reaping means that what you plant is what you harvest. It's true in the natural world and it's true in the spiritual world. If you plant pumpkins, you'll harvest pumpkins. If you plant doubt and worry in your heart, that's exactly what will grow.

Your heart matters to God, and He wants to plant really good things there. If you have weeds growing in your heart, go to the master gardener, Jesus, and ask for His help.

. . . .

Jesus, I ask You to prepare the soil of my heart for the good things You want to plant there. Pluck out the weeds and help me sow good plants instead.

While You Wait

*Wait for the LORD; be strong, and let your heart
take courage; wait for the LORD!*
PSALM 27:14 ESV

It's hard to be patient. We want that new thing or opportunity or relationship or result or answer to prayer right *now*, please and thank you! But goodness and blessing result from patience. Consider the following scriptures on this topic and look for more in His Word. Draw close to God and let Him teach you to wait well.

- "But they who wait for the LORD shall renew their strength; they shall mount up with wings like eagles; they shall run and not be weary; they shall walk and not faint" (Isaiah 40:31 ESV).

- "The LORD is good to those who wait for him, to the soul who seeks him" (Lamentations 3:25 ESV).

- "But as for me, I will look to the LORD; I will wait for the God of my salvation; my God will hear me" (Micah 7:7 ESV).

- "Wait for the LORD and keep his way, and he will exalt you to inherit the land" (Psalm 37:34 ESV).

Heavenly Father, help me to be a patient person who trusts in Your perfect timing. Teach me the things I need to learn while I wait.

Abounding Grace!

*God is able to make all grace abound to you,
so that having all sufficiency in all things at all
times, you may abound in every good work.*

2 CORINTHIANS 9:8 ESV

Have you ever watched a group of kids at a trampoline park? It's overwhelming and a little terrifying watching them leap and twirl in the air, one on top of the other. The opportunity for disaster is everywhere, especially with the heavy bouncers. You know the ones. They go down hard: they come up high. Over and over, they jump. They "abound."

In some ways, God's grace is like that high jump. It's a little dangerous. It has reached into the low lows of your sin and propelled you to a higher place, one you've never been before. It's showing you a new perspective, girl. It's abounding!

God loves and values you so much that He's willing to go deep in order for you to go high. So jump! Leap! Twirl! Allow the freedom of His Spirit to propel you to new heights as you place your trust in Him.

• •

I get it, Lord! You found me worthy of grace, and You reached down to rescue me. How blessed I am! Amen.

You Might Get More Than You Dreamed

[Jesus] said to Simon, "Now go out where it is deeper, and let down your nets to catch some fish." "Master," Simon replied, "we worked hard all last night and didn't catch a thing. But if you say so, I'll let the nets down again." And this time their nets were so full of fish they began to tear! A shout for help brought their partners in the other boat, and soon both boats were filled with fish and on the verge of sinking.

LUKE 5:4–7 NLT

Jesus helped the fishermen catch far more than they could have imagined. They had just spent the whole night fishing and had caught nothing, but Jesus only had to say the words, and suddenly the fish were everywhere—enough to tear their nets and sink their boat! Never forget that God is able to bless you with so much more than you expect. Keep trusting Him, keep praising Him, keep waiting on His perfect timing, and keep asking Him for everything you need— and He just might provide so much more than you ever dreamed!

. . . .

Heavenly Father, so often You go above and beyond to show how You love to bless and care for Your people. Thank You for blessing me in above-and-beyond ways too! Amen.

None like the Lord

Among the gods there is none like you, Lord; no deeds can compare with yours. All the nations you have made will come and worship before you, Lord; they will bring glory to your name. For you are great and do marvelous deeds; you alone are God. Teach me your way, LORD, that I may rely on your faithfulness; give me an undivided heart, that I may fear your name. I will praise you, Lord my God, with all my heart; I will glorify your name forever.

PSALM 86:8–12 NIV

Do you ever stop to think about how awesome it is to know the one true God and to have a personal relationship with Him because of Jesus Christ (1 Timothy 2:4–6)? There is no one like Him in all the world. He alone is worthy of all your praise, so go ahead and praise Him for the privilege of being His child!

Heavenly Father, You are so awesome and so good to me. Only You are the one true God, and I am so thankful to know You and be loved by You! I love You too, and I want to follow You and worship You forever. Amen.

Family Life

Most important of all, continue to show deep love for each other, for love covers a multitude of sins. Cheerfully share your home with those who need a meal or a place to stay. God has given each of you a gift from his great variety of spiritual gifts. Use them well to serve one another.

1 Peter 4:8–10 nlt

God has good plans and purposes for His family. He wants us to love each other deeply. And like a good parent, He wants us to share. He's given each of us special gifts to serve others and honor Him.

Think of a mom with her toddler children. She teaches them to share and treat each other with kindness and love. But sometimes those little ones go rogue. Mom has to intervene before mutiny ensues. She lovingly gets them back in order.

Sometimes this happens in the body of believers too. We don't always agree. We get selfish. We don't want to serve others. When that happens, we are reminded to love one another deeply. That love helps us give each other grace so that we can get back to the family life God has intended for us.

· ·

Lord, help me learn to love others well. More like You do. Show me how to use my gifts to serve and love.

You Have God's Protection

The first time I was brought before the judge, no one came with me. Everyone abandoned me. May it not be counted against them. But the Lord stood with me and gave me strength so that I might preach the Good News in its entirety for all the Gentiles to hear. And he rescued me from certain death. Yes, and the Lord will deliver me from every evil attack and will bring me safely into his heavenly Kingdom. All glory to God forever and ever! Amen.

2 Timothy 4:16–18 NLT

Even when Paul had no one else to help, God Himself was with Paul and gave him strength. Paul trusted that God would protect him from every sinful plan or evil attack. And he knew someday God would bring him into heaven forever. Paul wrote these things in his letter to Timothy, but they are for you to remember today too. You are blessed to have God's mighty protection and the promise of safety in His heavenly kingdom!

. . . .

Heavenly Father, thank You for Your mighty protection. I trust that no matter what happens here in this world, You will ultimately always keep me safe because someday You are going to bring me into perfect paradise in heaven to live with You forever! Amen.

Day 126

God's Measuring Stick

*Grace was given to each one of us according
to the measure of Christ's gift.*
EPHESIANS 4:7 ESV

When you were a kid, your parents probably kept track of your height by using a measuring tape or measuring stick. Maybe there's a doorway in your house with markings on it from all of your different measurements. It's fun to watch kids grow!

Think about today's verse in light of those markings. God measures out how much grace He's going to give you. Now, you might read that and think, "Well, great. With my luck, He won't give me much!" Oh, but here's the truth: He doesn't base the measurement on anything you have or haven't done. (Whew!) Nope. He pours out grace according to the "measure of Christ's gift."

Whoa. The death of Jesus on the cross is the measuring stick! And, when you realize it goes to the heights, the depths, and the widths to cover your sin, you suddenly get it: His grace is immeasurable! It has no bounds. You will experience it every day in every way. What a remarkable God we serve.

. . . .

*Jesus, thank You for pouring out Your grace.
I love the way You measure! Amen.*

A High Calling

Therefore, holy brothers and sisters, who share in the
heavenly calling, fix your thoughts on Jesus, whom we
acknowledge as our apostle and high priest.
HEBREWS 3:1 NIV

Life is a series of choices. As God's dearly loved daughter, you share in a high and heavenly calling. You always have one choice or another to make. Surely, as soon as you make one, another presents itself. Mom might have a list of chores for you to get done. You can choose to obey or not. . . .

If you follow God's Word, the very best choice is to obey Mom and do what she's asked you to do. And if you need help making the right choice, talk to God about it. He will offer guidance and show you the right way. Stick with Him, and you'll always be prepared to make good choices.

It may seem like these mundane choices you are making today to obey and do the chores aren't very important, but they really are! God is training you and guiding you in every choice you make. Fix your eyes on Jesus, friend. Those chores and daily choices are an important part of who you are becoming!

. . . .

Lord, I pray You would give me a desire to obey you and
to do my daily tasks out of love for You and my family.
Help me to hear Your guidance and make good choices.

Day 128

You Have Forever Blessings

"Do not lay up for yourselves treasures on earth, where moth and rust destroy and where thieves break in and steal, but lay up for yourselves treasures in heaven. . . . For where your treasure is, there your heart will be also."
MATTHEW 6:19–21 ESV

The things you have in this world are nice, for sure. It's fun to collect things and get new clothes and jewelry and technology and stuff for your room and entertainment and vacations and all kinds of gifts and blessings, right? And it's okay to enjoy those things—as long as we don't fixate on them and worship them, making getting all that stuff our main motivation and goal. Nothing here on this earth lasts forever. Things break or wear out or get lost. Entertainment and vacations come to an end. You can't take one bit of your stuff on to heaven with you when your life on earth is over. So God tells us to store up treasures in heaven. That's where our blessings last forever. How do we do that? We ask God to show us the good works He has planned for us to do, and we love and follow and obey Him. We constantly make it our goal to live out what Jesus said are the two greatest commandments—to love God with all our heart, soul, mind, and strength, and to love others like we love ourselves (Matthew 22:36–40).

Heavenly Father, help me to focus on the forever treasures that await me in heaven because I love and live for You. Amen.

You Have a Safe Place Forever

*My soul is quiet and waits for God alone. My hope comes
from Him. He alone is my rock and the One Who saves me.
He is my strong place. I will not be shaken. My being safe
and my honor rest with God. My safe place is in God, the
rock of my strength. Trust in Him at all times, O people.
Pour out your heart before Him. God is a safe place for us.*
PSALM 62:5–8 NLV

When you think of your safe place, do you think of the place you
feel most comfortable and relaxed and understood? Maybe you think
of being at home with your family, cozy and well taken care of. Or
maybe you think of your safe place as with your best friend, the one
you can talk to about anything. Those are good safe places, but they're
not eternal like God is. He wants to be your best, rock-solid, forever
safe place! He is with you anytime and anywhere. Talk to Him, cry
out to Him, depend on Him, and trust Him for everything you need.

* *

*Heavenly Father, I'm so blessed that You are my unchanging, eternal
safe place. Thank You that I can pour out my heart to You and be
loved and understood—anytime, anywhere, forever. Amen.*

Rich in Everything

You are rich in everything. You have faith. You can preach.
You have much learning. You have a strong desire to help. And you
have love for us. Now do what you should about giving also.
2 CORINTHIANS 8:7 NLV

Today's verse says that you are rich in everything. Wait. . .everything, you ask? Like. . .everything?

God thinks you're worthy of the best, girl! So He lavishes His gifts on you. He's given you faith. He's given you the ability to share your story. He's placed a strong desire inside you to help others. (And you thought that was just your idea!) He also placed love in your heart.

All these things are holy gifts from a God who thinks you're awesome! He's made you rich—not so that you can hoard it and keep it all to yourself but so that you can share with those you come in contact with. That faith? Your BFF needs some of it right now. That love? Your mom is going through a hard time and could use a dose of it. That desire to help? Your grandmother sure could use some help cleaning out her garage.

Spread grace around. God lavished it on you; now lavish it on others!

. . . .

I want to be a grace spreader, Jesus! May I do my part to bring
joy to everyone I meet. I want them to see You in me. Amen.

You Can Pray All the Time, about Everything

Don't worry about anything; instead, pray about everything.
Tell God what you need, and thank him for all he has
done. Then you will experience God's peace, which exceeds
anything we can understand. His peace will guard
your hearts and minds as you live in Christ Jesus.
PHILIPPIANS 4:6–7 NLT

What a crazy cool blessing that the almighty, one true God of the universe wants you to talk to Him all the time. His Word tells us again and again to keep on praying to Him for everything, at all times. It literally says, "Never stop praying" (1 Thessalonians 5:17 NLT). Prayer is never just talking to yourself or to some fake god who doesn't care. Prayer is a direct line of communication with the King of all kings and Lord of all lords! Wow! He loves you enough that He sent His only Son, Jesus, to die to save you. He wants to empower you with courage and faith and joy in Him for whatever you're facing!

. . . .

Almighty God, my heavenly Father, I'm so grateful You want me to
pray to You and never stop for any reason. Thank You that You are
always with me, always listening to me. I love You, Lord! Amen.

Day 132
Let God Love You

We know and rely on the love God has for us. God is love.
Whoever lives in love lives in God, and God in them.

1 JOHN 4:16 NIV

Do you find it hard to simply be still? Some people are born with the "fidget gene." They always have to be moving something, jiggling their legs, fidgeting with something in their hands. People like that actually tend to think better while they're moving.

But even if you find that you must fidget, you can still learn to be still before God. This is simply sitting in God's presence and opening your heart up to God as He fills you and reminds you of His love (it's okay if you need to wiggle your legs or tap your fingers while you try this!).

In Psalm 46:10 (NIV), God said, "Be still, and know that I am God; I will be exalted among the nations, I will be exalted in the earth."

God wants you to know that you are deeply loved just because you're you. He made you. He loves you. Nothing you can do will ever change that. Think about that for a while before you do anything else today. Let God love you.

. . . .

Wow, God! You really love me just for being me. I
don't have to earn Your love. Thank You!

Your Paths Will Be Straight

*Do not forget my teaching, but keep my commands in your
heart, for they will prolong your life many years and bring
you peace and prosperity. . . . Trust in the LORD with all your
heart and lean not on your own understanding; in all your
ways submit to him, and he will make your paths straight.*

PROVERBS 3:1–2, 5–6 NIV

Even though so many movies and messages and people today will
tell you to "follow your heart," that's not actually great advice. Before
any of us really do follow our heart, we need to make sure our heart
matches up with God's. Too often, our own hearts and desires are
tempted by sin and everything that's bad for us. So God's Word
tells us to trust Him with all our hearts and to *not* lean on our own
understanding. We need to stay close to Him by reading His Word,
praying, worshiping Him, and serving Him. And we need to ask
Him every day to help us submit to Him and His will for us—that's
the only way we stay on a good, straight path.

. . . .

*Father God, I want to trust in You more than
myself. Please help me to follow my own heart
only when it's matching up with Yours because
I'm submitted to You and Your will. Amen.*

You Have Someone to Lift Your Head

*You, O Lord, are a covering around me, my shining-greatness,
and the One Who lifts my head. I was crying to the Lord with my
voice. And He answered me from His holy mountain. I lay down
and slept, and I woke up again, for the Lord keeps me safe.*
PSALM 3:3–5 NLV

Sometimes you just need to go to your bed and cry your eyes out.
And that's okay! Life can be crazy, and sometimes everything feels
way too hard. As you cry and release all that emotion, think of God as
being like your favorite blanket comforting you, just as this scripture
says He is the covering around you. He is the one who helps you and
gives you "shining-greatness" again. He lifts your head and wants to
help you get out of bed and face all the hard things head-on with His
power. It's good to cry to God and tell Him all your feelings, but then
be sure to let Him lift your head and empower you to keep on going.

. . . .

*Heavenly Father, I'm so grateful You comfort and cover me when I'm
crying to You. And then You lift my head again. I can face anything
with You as my constant encouragement and strength. Amen.*

Your Sadness Can Turn to Joy

*"Hear me, LORD, and have mercy on me. Help me,
O LORD." You have turned my mourning into joyful dancing.
You have taken away my clothes of mourning and clothed
me with joy, that I might sing praises to you and not be
silent. O LORD my God, I will give you thanks forever!*
PSALM 30:10–12 NLT

Only the one true God can take the worst kind of sadness or anger or pain in our lives and turn it into such joy that we feel like dancing. He might do that for us here on earth in certain ways, or we might have to wait until heaven, but He promises that He will. With every hard and sad thing you go through, you have a choice either to let your circumstances make you angry with God and pull you apart from Him or to trust His promises and grow closer to Him. The first choice will only make you sadder and sadder, but the second choice will make you do some happy dancing!

. . . .

*Heavenly Father, please keep me close to You and strong in my faith
in the midst of every kind of pain. I trust that in Your perfect timing,
You will turn all heartache and struggle into total joy. Amen.*

Worthy of a Good Life!

*I know the plans I have for you, declares the LORD, plans for
welfare and not for evil, to give you a future and a hope.*
JEREMIAH 29:11 ESV

God believes you're worthy of a good life. But what does that look
like? Is He planning to lavish expensive cars and jewels on you?
Does He have plans for you to live in a megamansion or hang out
with movie stars?

Nope. Not that those things are necessarily bad, but God's idea
of a good life definitely looks different from Hollywood's! His good
life includes great plans for a wonderful future. A future where you're
blessed. A future where you're spiritually and emotionally whole. A
future where your family sticks together, rooted and grounded in Him.

God knows the plans. You don't. (That's the hard part: you have to
trust Him.) But you do know this much: He has never let you down.
He's never given you bad gifts. So you can trust that His vision of
a "great future" is going to be pretty magnificent. That's how much
He adores you, girl!

. . . .

*Lord, I trust You with my future. I know You've
got awesome things planned for me. (Thanks!)
I can't wait to see them come to pass. Amen.*

God Helps You from the Highest Heavens

Our holy God lives forever in the highest heavens, and this is what he says: Though I live high above in the holy place, I am here to help those who are humble and depend only on me.

ISAIAH 57:15 CEV

Imagine if you could pick up the phone and call the president of the United States and ask him for help with anything at any time. The role of president is a powerful one, so you would feel confident knowing that the president could come to your rescue for anything you asked. Even though not many of us are going to have close connections with important world leaders, the fact is we do have a close connection to the highest King and ultimate world ruler: our one true God who lives in the highest heavens! We have instant communication with Him through the Holy Spirit living within us, and He promises to help everyone who is humble and depends on Him above all. What an amazing blessing!

. . . .

Almighty God, You are the highest and best and most powerful of all, and yet You love me and want to help me. I am amazed and thankful, and I love You too! Amen.

Day 138
God Can Speak to You in Amazing Ways

There the angel of the LORD appeared to him in a blazing fire from the middle of a bush. Moses stared in amazement. Though the bush was engulfed in flames, it didn't burn up. "This is amazing," Moses said to himself. "Why isn't that bush burning up? I must go see it." When the LORD saw Moses coming to take a closer look, God called to him from the middle of the bush, "Moses! Moses!"

EXODUS 3:2–4 NLT

God can speak to you through anything, in any kind of situation—like the amazing way He spoke to Moses through a burning bush. No one can know exactly why God chooses certain incredible ways to speak to His people, but it's just amazing to know He can! Listen to Him first and regularly through reading all of His Word, and also ask Him to speak to you in any kind of way He chooses. Let your heart and mind be open to hearing His voice!

. . . .

Dear Lord, thank You for Your Word and the amazing ways You speak to Your people. Please speak to me and help me always to listen well. Amen.

Day 139

He Will Complete It

So now finish doing it as well, so that your readiness in desiring it may be matched by your completing it out of what you have.
2 CORINTHIANS 8:11 ESV

Do you finish what you start? If you're like most girls, the answer might be, "Meh. Sometimes yes, sometimes no." It's so easy to start a project with zeal and gusto, but seeing it through to the end? Not so much.

Think of that big project you had to turn in last semester. You were excited. . .at first. Then your excitement fizzled out as the weeks went by and you realized how much work it was going to be. You found yourself throwing it together the night before it was due. Ugh! (Don't you hate it when that happens?)

God's not a fan of procrastination either. But here's some amazing news: When it comes to His plans for you and for your future, He's going to finish what He started. You can count on it. And He'll do it on His perfect timetable. That's how much He adores you, girl! He thinks you're worthy of an amazing life.

. . . .

I'm so excited about Your plans for my life, Jesus.
I can't wait to see what You've got up Your sleeve! Amen.

You Are Gifted

*Each of you has been blessed with one of God's many wonderful
gifts to be used in the service of others. So use your gift well. If you
have the gift of speaking, preach God's message. If you have the
gift of helping others, do it with the strength that God supplies.
Everything should be done in a way that will bring honor to God
because of Jesus Christ, who is glorious and powerful forever. Amen.*

1 PETER 4:10–11 CEV

The talents and things you're naturally good at and that come easy
to you are the gifts God has given you. He has given them to you
so that you can help others with them. If you're good at certain school
subjects, see what you can do to help your friends who struggle with
them. If you're especially friendly and outgoing, reach out to people
to make them feel included. If you have talents in music, see how
you can use them to help worship God at church. Most of all, continually thank God and give Him credit for every good thing you
can do. Each one is a gift from Him!

. . . .

*Heavenly Father, thank You for the unique talents and
abilities You've given me. I want to use all of them to
worship You and point others to You. Amen.*

What God's Word Says about You

But you are a chosen people, a royal priesthood, a holy nation, God's special possession, that you may declare the praises of him who called you out of darkness into his wonderful light. Once you were not a people, but now you are the people of God; once you had not received mercy, but now you have received mercy.

1 PETER 2:9–10 NIV

Have you ever felt left out? Lonely? Purposeless? God has some very important things to say to you that He wants you to take to heart:

- You are chosen.
- You are royalty.
- You are holy.
- You are God's special possession.
- You can praise Him.
- He called you out of darkness into His wonderful light.
- You are part of God's people.
- You have received mercy.

When you are feeling down, 1 Peter 2:9–10 is a great scripture to read out loud and declare over yourself. Insert your name in there and declare it again and again until you really start to believe it!

· ·

Lord, please plant Your truths in my heart so that their roots will grow deep and change the way I live my life!

Truly No Worries

*"Do not worry about your life, what you will eat or drink; or about
your body, what you will wear. Is not life more than food, and the
body more than clothes? Look at the birds of the air; they do not
sow or reap or store away in barns, and yet your heavenly Father
feeds them. Are you not much more valuable than they? Can any
one of you by worrying add a single hour to your life? And why
do you worry about clothes? See how the flowers of the field grow.
They do not labor or spin. Yet I tell you that not even Solomon in
all his splendor was dressed like one of these. . . . But seek first his
kingdom and his righteousness, and all these things will be given to
you as well. Therefore do not worry about tomorrow, for tomorrow
will worry about itself. Each day has enough trouble of its own."*

MATTHEW 6:25–29, 33–34 NIV

"No worries" is a nice thing to say, but the only one who can truly bless
us with no worries is our good heavenly Father, who cares the very
most about us—even more than our closest friends and loved ones.
If He knows and takes good care of even the birds and the flowers
that He created, surely He takes even better care of the people He
made in His own image.

. . . .

*Father God, thank You for the blessing of truly no worries when I
focus on Your great big love and Your all-knowing care for me. Amen.*

A Straight Path

Trust in the LORD with all your heart, and do not lean on your own understanding. In all your ways acknowledge him, and he will make straight your paths.
PROVERBS 3:5–6 ESV

God can make your path straight. That's an amazing promise. If you've ever been on a crooked road, you know how vulnerable you feel! It twists and turns, goes up and down, and leaves you feeling discombobulated. But when you give God the reins, He straightens out the road in front of you and makes it clear which way to go. (And He provides safety as you travel.)

Why would He go to all of this trouble for you? After all, there are billions of people in the world. God is pretty busy, right?

Sure, He's busy. But He's never too busy for you! He adores you. And He's going to keep guiding you no matter how busy He is with other things (like, say, world peace).

Giving *you* peace is just as important to Him. That's how much your heavenly Father values you!

. . . .

I get it, Lord. I matter to You. I matter so much that You take the time to carve out a straight path and watch over me as I travel along it. Thank You! Amen.

Day 144

In the Midst of Suffering and Misunderstanding

*What we are suffering now cannot compare
with the glory that will be shown to us.*
ROMANS 8:18 CEV

Sometimes when we're struggling with a problem or need or heart-ache, God doesn't just suddenly fix things like we hope. We sure wish He would, and we pray and cry out to Him, asking Him to see our needs and make everything okay again right away. And when He doesn't, our trust in Him can really be shaken as we wonder why. We question God. Maybe we even feel anger and blame toward Him at times—but anger and blame are not good to hold on to. Even when we're confused and hurting and frustrated over a prayer that seems to go unanswered, we need to look for the ways God is answering other prayers and showing His love in many other ways at the same time. We can continue to trust and know that we're blessed even through the hardest times. We can't possibly see all the good things God is doing in the midst of suffering, but one day in heaven we will understand. Then God will make all things perfect and new.

· ·

*Dear Lord, please help me to keep trusting You even when I'm
confused about what You're doing. When I don't see You answering my
prayers as I want them to be answered, please show me and remind
me of how You are caring for me and blessing me in other ways. Amen.*

Human Being or Human Doing?

This is love: not that we loved God, but that he loved us and sent his Son as an atoning sacrifice for our sins.
1 JOHN 4:10 NIV

It's easy for Christians to get into the bad habit of feeling like we're not doing enough. That we have to be better Christians so that God will love us and approve of us. That we have to get it right all the time or we must stink at following Jesus. That we have to say yes to everything at church and sign up for every good deed so that God and everyone around us will know that we are Christians.

But that's not the Jesus way. God wants to fill us up with His love first and foremost, and then He pours out that love to others as the Holy Spirit leads us day by day. God made you a human *being*, not a human *doing*. Be listening for His leading in your life before you say yes to anything. You have nothing to prove. You are chosen and dearly loved just for *being*.

· ·

Lord, I'm guilty of trying to earn love and acceptance from You and others. I'm sorry for that. Please fill me up with Your love and give me ears to hear Your leading in my life.

Day 146
You Have Real Joy

"As the Father has loved me, so have I loved you. Now remain in my love. If you keep my commands, you will remain in my love, just as I have kept my Father's commands and remain in his love. I have told you this so that my joy may be in you and that your joy may be complete. My command is this: Love each other as I have loved you. Greater love has no one than this: to lay down one's life for one's friends."

JOHN 15:9–13 NIV

The world around us tries to sell us all kinds of ideas about what love and joy are, and often they're really bad ideas. But Jesus tells us here in John 15 how to have *real* love and joy. When we obey Jesus the way Jesus obeyed God the Father, we stay close to God. And because God is love (1 John 4:8), our whole lives are lived in love. When we live in love, we can't help but be full of joy because we are living exactly the way God intended when He created us!

. . . .

Dear Jesus, I'm sorry for the times I don't obey You. Every time I disobey, I want to realize my mistake and come back to You to get on the right track again. I want to live in Your love and be full of real joy! Amen.

You Have God Guiding You

*By day the LORD went ahead of them in a pillar of cloud to guide
them on their way and by night in a pillar of fire to give them light,
so that they could travel by day or night. Neither the pillar of cloud by
day nor the pillar of fire by night left its place in front of the people.*
EXODUS 13:21–22 NIV

God is the very best guide. When He led His people, the Israelites,
out of slavery in Egypt, He did so with a pillar of cloud during the
day and a pillar of fire at night to give them light. That must have
been unbelievably cool to see! When you read this story in the Bible,
remember that God wants to be your guide. No, He may not lead you
in such dramatic ways as pillars of cloud and fire, but you can ask Him
to show you clearly, step-by-step and day by day, the places He wants
you to go and the good things He wants you to do. And make sure
you're spending time learning from His Word, especially because it's
a lamp to your feet and a light for your path (Psalm 119:105).

. . . .

*Heavenly Father, I want You to be my guide. I trust that
You can use anything to lead me in my life. Please help me
to keep my attention focused on You. Show me all the good
places and plans You have for me. Thank You! Amen.*

Day 148

The One Who Lives in You

The One Who lives in you is stronger than the one who is in the world.
1 JOHN 4:4 NLV

This is such a simple and powerful Bible verse to memorize and keep on repeat in your mind. Our enemy Satan is constantly stirring up all kinds of evil in this world. And you will sometimes be under attack from him in all sorts of different ways: through someone else's nasty words or actions, through stressful times for your family, through painful times of loss, through sickness, and on and on. But no matter how strong the enemy and his evil may seem against you and your loved ones, they are never stronger than the power of God in you through the Holy Spirit. Don't ever forget that! Call on God to help you be strong and calm and patient—and to help you see how He is working and taking care of you through it all.

. . . .

Father God, deep down I know You are always stronger than any attack on me, any hard thing I'm going through. But I do forget that truth sometimes, and I'm sorry. Please remind me and fill me with Your power and peace—and do the fighting for me. Amen.

His Timetable, Not Yours

*Do not overlook this one fact, beloved, that with the Lord
one day is as a thousand years, and a thousand years as one
day. The Lord is not slow to fulfill his promise as some count
slowness, but is patient toward you, not wishing that any
should perish, but that all should reach repentance.*

2 PETER 3:8–9 ESV

God has a completely different timetable than you, girl. It's true! You're
human. When you want something, you want it now. And hey, the
world has conditioned you to that idea. You can drive through and
pick up fast food. You sign on to the Internet and have immediate
access to information. You even put food in the microwave and it
cooks up lickety-split.

When it comes to the things you're waiting on, however, results
don't always come about so quickly. But before you give up and stop
praying, remember: God knows the perfect timing to bring you the
things you need. If He loves and values you as much as you know
He does, don't you think you can trust Him with His timetable?

You can. You should.

Deep breath. He's buzzing along behind the scenes, working all
things together for good.

- -

*I'll be patient, Lord! It's not easy, I confess,
but I'll keep waiting on You. Amen.*

You Are Accepted

"All those the Father gives me will come to me,
and whoever comes to me I will never drive away."
JOHN 6:37 NIV

The Amplified Bible says it this way: "The one who comes to Me I will most certainly not cast out [I will never, never reject anyone who follows Me]."

This is one of those verses to write down in your journal or on a sticky note. You're going to need it throughout your life. Rejection stings. We all face it from time to time. Whether it's not getting an invitation you are hoping for, finding no seat at the table you want to sit at, watching the boy you like choose another girl, or receiving a rejection letter from your college of choice, rejection hurts.

But something to remember in the midst of that is that you are always accepted in Christ. "Rejected" is not who you are. When rejection comes, acknowledge the hurt. Take it to Jesus. Let Him love you through it. And then start rejecting any lies the enemy flings at you. Stand on the truth that you are accepted forever.

You are loved.

Chosen.

His.

. . . .

Lord, You know I've felt rejected at different times.
I bring that to You now. Please heal up those places as
I reject any lies the enemy has labeled me with.

Your God Never Changes

Long ago you laid the foundation of the earth and made the
heavens with your hands. They will perish, but you remain
forever; they will wear out like old clothing. You will change
them like a garment and discard them. But you are always the
same; you will live forever. The children of your people will live in
security. Their children's children will thrive in your presence.
PSALM 102:25–28 NLT

Life is always changing, and sometimes we appreciate that fact and
sometimes we don't. What is something you wish could always stay
the same? What is something that you're glad always changes? No
matter what changes around us, though, it's so good to know that God
is constantly the same. We sure need His stability in this turbulent
world. We depend on Him to be steady and strong and true, and when
we look to Him to guide us, we can be steady and strong and true too!

Heavenly Father, I'm glad You never change, and I'm
especially glad that Your love and care for me never
change. Please keep helping and guiding me. Amen.

Day 152

You Can Be a Mighty Warrior

When the angel of the LORD appeared to Gideon,
he said, "The LORD is with you, mighty warrior."
JUDGES 6:12 NIV

Think of a person you really look up to. How does it make you feel when they give you a wonderful compliment? Pretty nice, right? So imagine how Gideon must have felt when God spoke to him through an angel's appearance and called him a "mighty warrior." Wow!

You can think of God telling you the same thing He told Gideon. You are totally capable of being a mighty warrior for God because He is with you always, constantly giving you courage and power. Those qualities don't come from yourself but from God's Holy Spirit within you.

. . . .

Dear Lord, I trust that You are with me in everything
I do. I want to be a mighty warrior who points other
people to You and Your love and truth! Amen.

Day 153

A Stranger to This World

*Beloved, I urge you as aliens and strangers [in this world]
to abstain from the sensual urges [those dishonorable
desires] that wage war against the soul.*

1 PETER 2:11 AMP

Fitting in can be tough stuff. Everyone wants to have friends and to feel like they belong somewhere. But fitting in to the patterns of this world is not a healthy or godly pursuit.

Fitting in to today's culture is something that believers can't do. God set you apart for a reason: to show a different way. . .to offer truth and hope to a dark and hurting world.

Hebrews 13:14 (NLT) says: "For this world is not our permanent home; we are looking forward to a home yet to come." Our citizenship is in heaven.

You *do* belong to the body of Christ. And when you ask God to give you healthy and godly friendships to come alongside you and uplift you, He will give you exactly what you need.

- -

*Lord, please give me purpose and contentment when I consider my
relationships and my place in this temporary world. Help me to shine
a bright light, pointing others away from darkness and toward You.*

Day 154

You're an Overcomer

Children, you belong to God, and you have defeated these enemies. God's Spirit is in you and is more powerful than the one who is in the world. These enemies belong to this world, and the world listens to them, because they speak its language. We belong to God.
1 JOHN 4:4–6 CEV

Have you ever heard someone brag that they're never afraid of anything? There is no way that's true. Everyone gets scared or anxious or worried about something sometimes. True bravery and courage come from admitting fears and worries and facing them anyway. You can't be brave unless you first know that you were scared of something but chose to deal with it. And sometimes you deal with things so well that you totally overcome them—and then they're never a fear or worry again! With God's Holy Spirit working in you to help, you can face anything and overcome it. Jesus said, "I have told you these things, so that in me you may have peace. In this world you will have trouble. But take heart! I have overcome the world" (John 16:33 NIV).

. . . .

Heavenly Father, I admit my fears and worries and how much I need Your help with them. I believe with all my heart that You can help me overcome them. Amen.

Peace Will Keep Your Heart and Mind

*The peace of God is much greater than the human mind can understand.
This peace will keep your hearts and minds through Christ Jesus.*

PHILIPPIANS 4:7 NLV

Maybe schoolwork is extra hard these days, or maybe you just started a new semester or even a new school and everything feels different. Maybe you or a loved one is sick and needing a lot of medical care. Maybe there's a lot of conflict in your home or with your friend group. But no matter what is going on, God can give you extraordinary peace. If you focus on all the stress, of course you will be stressed. So focus instead on what Philippians 4 goes on to say: "Keep your minds thinking about whatever is true, whatever is respected, whatever is right, whatever is pure, whatever can be loved, and whatever is well thought of. If there is anything good and worth giving thanks for, think about these things. Keep on doing all the things you learned and received and heard from me. Do the things you saw me do. Then the God Who gives peace will be with you" (Philippians 4:8–9 NLV).

. . . .

*Father God, help me to trust You in the middle of stress
and stay focused on what is good and right and true.
Please bless me with Your extraordinary peace. Amen.*

You Are Approved Of

For the Lord delights in his people; he crowns the humble with victory.
PSALM 149:4 NLT

Yes, God approves of you. Now let's clarify that: we're not talking about the things you do but about who you are. Make sense?

We all mess up. We choose selfishness sometimes. We choose sin. And like a good parent, God doesn't always approve of your choices. But He always approves of who you are.

Would a good and loving parent approve of their usually delightful toddler's behavior when she hits her sibling over the head with something hard? No. That toddler is getting appropriate consequences for what she's done so that she learns that it's wrong to hit and not to do it again. But those consequences also show how much that child is loved and valued. That child's parents still love that child unconditionally no matter what she's done. They still approve of who she is, just not her behavior at the moment.

God's Word tells you that He delights in you no matter what you do or don't do. You're His precious child, and He loves you for who you are.

. . . .

Lord, I think I'm starting to get it: Your love has nothing to do with my behavior. That's amazing love!

Day 157
Full Access

This is a faithful and trustworthy saying:
If we died with Him, we will also live with Him;
if we endure, we will also reign with Him.
2 TIMOTHY 2:11–12 AMP

Have you ever toured a castle or the White House? If you search online for Buckingham Palace, you can take multiple virtual tours online. Many guides have videoed their special tours of the palace. In every tour, you will see many halls and rooms that are roped off and locked. The public is not allowed to enter the royal family's private and personal areas. And that tends to be what most people are curious about!

As a beloved princess of God, you have access to all the private and personal areas in God's palace. Ephesians 2:6 (NLT) says, "For he raised us from the dead along with Christ and seated us with him in the heavenly realms because we are united with Christ Jesus."

You are welcomed into the royal family. You have a special seat at the dining table with your name on it. You are seated with Christ in the heavenly realms, reigning with Him.

• •

Wow, Lord! Your Word is coming to life before my eyes. Thank You for showing me who I really am and giving me a seat at Your table.

He's Whispering Directions (Even Now!)

Your own ears will hear him. Right behind you a voice will say,
"This is the way you should go," whether to the right or to the left.
ISAIAH 30:21 NLT

God has amazing plans for your life, but you feel lost. Stuck. Confused. (Remember, confusion is from the enemy, not from your heavenly Father, so don't hang out there long!)

God wants to give you clear directions. How, you ask? He's whispering in your ear, even now. It's true! You might say, "Whoa. I don't hear a thing." But think about this: He spoke to men and women in the olden days, right? And the Bible says He's the same yesterday, today, and forever. So if He did it then, what makes you think He wouldn't still speak now?

He's whispering through the voice of your parents. He's speaking through a close friend. He's giving directions through your circumstances. And His Spirit is actually speaking in that still, small voice of His to your heart. (This is how you "know" what to do, even when no one tells you—you discern it by His Spirit.)

He's given you everything you need to take steps in the right direction. Trust His plan. Follow His voice.

. . . .

Lord, I trust You. I'm listening close.
I want to hear You loud and clear! Amen.

A Royal Priest

You are a chosen people. You are royal priests,
a holy nation, God's very own possession. As a result,
you can show others the goodness of God, for he called
you out of the darkness into his wonderful light.

1 Peter 2:9 NLT

You may read this verse and be tempted to skip right past the part about you being chosen and God's very own, then think, *Wait, I'm a royal priest? What? Is this scripture really about me?*

The truth is you are chosen. You are God's very own possession. *And* you are a royal priest! Wow! What does that even mean? Let's take a look:

First Peter 2:5 (NLT) says, "You are living stones that God is building into his spiritual temple. What's more, you are his holy priests. Through the mediation of Jesus Christ, you offer spiritual sacrifices that please God."

Many other scriptures tell us that God chose us as His priests. Priests in the Old Testament were ministers of God who offered sacrifices for sin. But Jesus became the ultimate sacrifice, changing everything! And this is really good news for you and me!

· ·

Jesus, thank You for coming for us and changing everything!
Because of all You've done for me, I can belong to God.

Anointed by God

But you have an anointing from the Holy One [you have been set apart, specially gifted and prepared by the Holy Spirit], and all of you know [the truth because He teaches us, illuminates our minds, and guards us from error].

1 JOHN 2:20 AMP

Did you know that you were anointed by God? Check it out:

- "As for you, the anointing [the special gift, the preparation] which you received from Him remains [permanently] in you" (1 John 2:27 AMP).

- "Now it is God who establishes and confirms us [in joint fellowship] with you in Christ, and who has anointed us [empowering us with the gifts of the Spirit]" (2 Corinthians 1:21 AMP).

What does *anointed* even mean? Well, you might remember hearing this before: set apart for a reason. But it also means that you have been "specially gifted and prepared by the Holy Spirit." That's awesome news, right?

God knows exactly what you need to live the life He has for you, and He's anointed you and given you everything you need to live it out! So stand firm in the love and the anointing that God has for you, dear one. He has amazing adventures coming your way!

. . . .

Wow, Lord! I had heard that I was set apart, but anointed? . . . That's awesome! Thank You!

A Holy Sacrifice

*And so, dear brothers and sisters, I plead with you to
give your bodies to God because of all he has done for you.
Let them be a living and holy sacrifice—the kind he will
find acceptable. This is truly the way to worship him.*
ROMANS 12:1 NLT

Have you heard about the curtain that was torn in two when Jesus died on the cross? Go look it up sometime in Matthew 27:50–55. It's a crazy true story! This wasn't a curtain like you have in your house today. This thing was massive and thick. It closed off the holy of holies where only the high priest was allowed to go once a year to make a sacrifice for the sins of all people.

As Jesus gave up His last breath, the curtain was torn from top to bottom. God wanted everyone to know that Jesus had now made a way for all believers to enter the holy place to come to God themselves. Jesus is the only sacrifice ever needed. Because of His death for us, all believers have access to God all the time. Now, all He wants is your heart.

. . . .

*Lord Jesus, I give You my heart.
Thank You for Your amazing sacrifice for me!*

Day 162

Every Spiritual Blessing

Blessed be the God and Father of our Lord Jesus Christ,
who has blessed us in Christ with every spiritual blessing
in the heavenly places, even as he chose us in him before the
foundation of the world, that we should be holy and blameless
before him. In love he predestined us for adoption to himself as
sons through Jesus Christ, according to the purpose of his will.

EPHESIANS 1:3–5 ESV

Life is a blessing. Your breath is a blessing! Health is a blessing. Those relationships you share—they're a blessing.

Every minute of every day is filled with blessings from God. And when you remember to view them that way, then your heart will be full. Grateful. Overflowing with confidence in the one who values you enough to make sure you're blessed. . .coming and going.

Today, if you're not feeling blessed, take the time to write down the many, many blessings you might be overlooking. For instance, here's what you might write down: *Food in the pantry. Healthy family. My dad's job. Great Christian friends.*

There are many, many blessings if only you will see them for what they are. God has mapped out a great plan for your life, and He desires to bless you at every turn.

. . . .

Thank You for loving me so much that You pour out blessings,
Lord! I'm so grateful for Your tender, loving care. Amen.

Your Inheritance

For his Spirit joins with our spirit to affirm that we are
God's children. And since we are his children, we are his heirs.
In fact, together with Christ we are heirs of God's glory.
ROMANS 8:16–17 NLT

You, beloved daughter of God, have a bright future in this life and a beautiful inheritance waiting for you in heaven. First Peter 1:4 (NIV) tells us this inheritance "can never perish, spoil or fade. This inheritance is kept in heaven for you."

Remember, when parents decide to adopt a child, they are *choosing* to become parents to a child who doesn't biologically belong to them. It is a legal process as well. When a child becomes adopted, that child has the same legal rights as biological children and becomes a legal heir.

Being adopted into God's family means that you are God's heir. Everything He has belongs to you. It's not like a fancy car that can rust or money that can be taken away. Your inheritance is safe in heaven for all eternity.

The Bible tells us that heaven is a perfect place with no more tears, no more sin, and no more pain. And God is preparing a place there for you right now (John 14:2–6).

. . . .

Heavenly Father, I'm so thankful that You made me Your child!

You Are Affirmed

"No longer do I call you servants. . .but I have called you friends,
for all that I have heard from my Father I have made known to you."
JOHN 15:15 ESV

So what is affirmation, anyway? Dictionary.com says *affirm* can mean "to support (someone) by giving approval, recognition, or encouragement." Who isn't going around looking for encouraging support? That's how we find our friends, right?

But Jesus took care of this for us too. Sometimes we lose our support system—like when we move or have a serious disagreement with a friend. If we were to lose our affirmation when we lose our friends, that would be devastating! But Jesus wants us to find our affirmation in Him first.

- He is our support: "They attacked me at a moment when I was in distress, but the LORD supported me" (Psalm 18:18 NLT).

- He gives us recognition: "The sheep hear his voice, and he calls his own sheep by name and leads them out" (John 10:3 ESV).

- He gives us encouragement: "You, LORD, hear the desire of the afflicted; you encourage them, and you listen to their cry" (Psalm 10:17 NIV).

Jesus calls us friend.

. . . .

Jesus, thanks for affirming me and calling me Your friend. I love You.

Privilege and Responsibility

*But to as many as did receive and welcome Him, He gave the
right [the authority, the privilege] to become children of God, that is,
to those who believe in (adhere to, trust in, and rely on) His name.*

JOHN 1:12 AMP

The Bible is full of scriptures that tell about your authority in
Christ and the privileges you've been given as God's child. If you've
received and welcomed Jesus into your life, then you've been given
the right and the authority to become God's child. That comes with
certain privileges and responsibilities. Think about it: the light of
the whole world is alive inside you! So you have a responsibility
to shine that light in a dark world. Matthew 5:15 (NLT) says, "No
one lights a lamp and then puts it under a basket. Instead, a lamp
is placed on a stand, where it gives light to everyone in the house."

You also have the amazing privilege of calling the Creator of the
world your dad! At the beginning and end of every day (and 24-7
actually), you have the right and privilege to crawl up into the lap of
your heavenly Father and bask in His great love for you.

. . . .

*I'm so glad to be Your child, Lord! Shine Your light in and through
me so that others can see Your love at work in this dark world.*

How to Make the Devil Flee

Submit yourselves, then, to God.
Resist the devil, and he will flee from you.
JAMES 4:7 NIV

Did you know that you can make the devil flee? But first, the Bible says you have to submit yourself to God. Only then can you resist the devil.

Submitting to God is about obeying Him and getting in the habit of surrendering your will to God's will. For you, that might look like starting the day in prayer. You open your heart and your hands to God, and you hold everything loosely. You're willing to change your plans if you feel God leading you in a different direction. You've dressed yourself in God's armor, and you're ready for the day. You go online to do your homework, and you see an inappropriate ad on the side of the page. At first, you're tempted to click on it. But then you pay attention to that Holy Spirit nudge inside of you that says, "Don't do it!" You submit yourself to God by obeying Him, and you say no to temptation. You've resisted the devil, and now he's gone. (He'll be back to try again, so don't get too comfy. But you can get your homework done in peace for now.)

. . . .

Lord, I submit myself to Your will and Your plans for my life.
Help me resist the devil so that he will leave me alone.

The Spirit of God Alive in You!

"In the last days, God says, I will pour out my Spirit on all people. Your sons and daughters will prophesy, your young men will see visions, your old men will dream dreams."

ACTS 2:17 NIV

God knew we couldn't figure out life alone. He knew we would need a helper to teach us and lead us. So He sent His very own Spirit to live and grow inside of us. This is so very important to remember!

Listen to what God's Word says: "Spiritually alive, we have access to everything God's Spirit is doing. . . . Isaiah's question, 'Is there anyone around who knows God's Spirit, anyone who knows what he is doing?' has been answered: Christ knows, and we have Christ's Spirit" (1 Corinthians 2:15–16 MSG).

When we have the Spirit of Jesus alive in us, we are being transformed, God's Word is brought to life in us, and we are taught right and wrong. Because God loves you so much, He sent His Spirit to come alive in you. His Spirit is alive and at work in you this very moment!

. . . .

Lord God, I'm so thankful for Your Spirit alive and at work in me!

Flourish in God's Love

*And I pray that you, being rooted and established in love,
may have power, together with all the Lord's holy people, to grasp
how wide and long and high and deep is the love of Christ.*
EPHESIANS 3:17–18 NIV

We do a lot of gardening around here. Last year we dug up a bunch of yucca plants. These plants have huge roots. We had to chop up some of them and experiment with transplanting them to other sections of our yard. What we found was that the giant roots of this plant sustained the shock of being transplanted. The plant flourished even when we chopped some of it off.

God wants you to be rooted like that too—not rooted in the ground like plants but rooted in His love. Then when life feels like it's chopping you to bits, you can still flourish in the love of Christ.

Imagine yourself with roots growing deep into the love of God. That's where your strength and joy come from no matter what life brings your way.

. . . .

*Lord, I want to be rooted in Your love. Lead me close to
Your heart every day. I want to experience Your love in new
and refreshing ways. Help me flourish in Your love.*

Transformed to Live an Amazing Life

*Don't copy the behavior and customs of this world,
but let God transform you into a new person by changing
the way you think. Then you will learn to know God's
will for you, which is good and pleasing and perfect.*

Romans 12:2 NLT

Have you ever wondered why God wants to see your heart and mind transformed? Why is He so keen on you not looking like—or acting like—the people in this world? Is He out to ruin your fun? Does He want to force you to live a strict, rules-first life?

Nope. None of that! He knows a secret that you likely haven't figured out yet: life is easier when you think and act like Him. When your mind is transformed and becomes more like His and less like the world's, you'll live a safer, more controlled life. God's will is not about rules; it's about relationship with the one who knows you best and loves you most!

If He cared enough about you to transform your thinking, then no doubt He has amazing plans for your future. Trust Him, girl. But start by giving Him your thoughts, your heart, and your attitude!

. . . .

Lord, I give myself to You. Transform me! Make me into Your image so that things will go well in my life. I trust You! Amen.

Just Imagine

Now to him who is able to do immeasurably more than all we ask or imagine, according to his power that is at work within us, to him be glory in the church and in Christ Jesus throughout all generations, for ever and ever! Amen.
EPHESIANS 3:20–21 NIV

How's your imagination? Do you feel like you have a good one? God created us with the amazing ability to imagine and create. As we get older, many people tend to shut that down. But God created your imagination on purpose! He wants you to use it for His glory.

Take a look at today's scripture. It says that God is able to do immeasurably more than all we ask or imagine. Think about that for a minute. If you could imagine answering all of your prayers and deepest desires with the most perfect outcome—God can do it even better than that! Do you trust God with your prayers and deepest needs? He is good, and He loves to bless you. He may not answer everything the way you want, but that's because He has the best view of your life (from beginning to eternity!). He can do way more than you could ever think or imagine. Trust Him.

Lord, help me trust You with all my prayers and desires.

Deborah, the Prophet and Judge

Deborah, the wife of Lappidoth, was a prophet who was judging Israel at that time. She would sit under the Palm of Deborah, between Ramah and Bethel in the hill country of Ephraim, and the Israelites would go to her for judgment.

JUDGES 4:4–5 NLT

Deborah was a prophet! She was a wise, God-fearing woman. You can check out her story in Judges 4. Deborah was also a great leader. Her people respected her. Even the military general followed her leadership.

People flocked to Deborah to hear her advice, and God set her up as a judge over all the Jewish people, not just other women. She urged them to repent and turn back to God. She also commanded an army to go into battle, and God gave them victory.

God has great plans for you as a woman. As you grow up, seek out God's will for you as a woman. Don't let people put you in a box if God has given you a specific vision and mission for Your life. You just might be another leader like Deborah!

. . . .

Lord, I submit my heart, my will, and my life to You. Make me into all that You designed me to be.

Queen Esther

*"If you keep quiet at a time like this, deliverance
and relief for the Jews will arise from some other place,
but you and your relatives will die. Who knows if perhaps
you were made queen for just such a time as this?"*
ESTHER 4:14 NLT

Esther is the story of an orphaned Jewish girl who became queen. Sounds like a fairy tale, right? The awesome thing is that it's a true story! God used Esther to change the heart of a king and save an entire nation of people.

The king's evil adviser Haman was determined to kill all the Jews in the kingdom. God gave Esther extraordinary courage to stand up to evil, even if it might cost her her life. She was chosen for a special time in history—"for such a time as this"—and so are you!

God made you on purpose to be alive at this period in time for a reason. As you seek Him every day, He will be with you on your own courageous journey through life. Who knows what you'll accomplish in your lifetime! God does. And He is always with you and for you!

- -

*Lord, I believe You made me for more than I can
ever imagine. Please give me the courage and
strength to follow Your plan for my life.*

When You're Feeling Down

The righteous cry out, and the LORD hears them;
he delivers them from all their troubles.
PSALM 34:17 NIV

Anne of Green Gables used to talk about "Jonah days." When the bad things just keep piling up. Those days happen in this broken world, and when they do, these truths from God's Word can help:

- "The LORD is close to the brokenhearted and saves those who are crushed in spirit" (Psalm 34:18 NIV).

- "But God gives comfort to those whose hearts are heavy" (2 Corinthians 7:6 NLV).

- "Cast all your anxiety on him because he cares for you" (1 Peter 5:7 NIV).

- "Come to me, all you who are weary and burdened, and I will give you rest" (Matthew 11:28 NIV).

- "Trust in the LORD with all your heart and lean not on your own understanding; in all your ways submit to him, and he will make your paths straight" (Proverbs 3:5–6 NIV).

Chosen one, God sees you. He's close. Take these truths to heart as you let God love and comfort you.

. . . .

Lord, I believe the truths I read in Your Word. I believe
You are close. Please comfort me. Please hide these
words in my heart as I bring my feelings to You.

Mary of Nazareth

"I am the Lord's servant," Mary answered.
"May your word to me be fulfilled." Then the angel left her.
LUKE 1:38 NIV

You know the story of Christmas. An angel came to Mary and told her she would become the mother of our Lord and Savior, Jesus Christ. She was young. Most historians believe that Mary was a very young teenager although the Bible doesn't say how old she was. It was customary at the time to get engaged during the early teen years, sometimes earlier.

But even at that young age, we know this about Mary: God chose her. Luke 1:30 (NIV) says, "The angel said to her, 'Do not be afraid, Mary; you have found favor with God.'"

She went through some very difficult times in her life. She was pregnant without a husband, and her fiancé planned to leave her. She probably wasn't believed when she told others the story. But God was with her. He planned for Mary's relative Elizabeth to be an encouragement to her during that hard time.

Trusting God during difficult times is necessary to carry out His plans for your life. Be on the lookout for "Elizabeths" to encourage you along the way.

. . . .

Lord, help me trust that You're always with me.
Thanks for sending people to encourage me.

Day 175

An Inheritance
for Your Reward

*Work willingly at whatever you do, as though you were
working for the Lord rather than for people. Remember
that the Lord will give you an inheritance as your reward,
and that the Master you are serving is Christ.*
COLOSSIANS 3:23–24 NLT

Have you ever received an inheritance? Maybe one of your grand-parents passed away and you received a token, something that once belonged to them. A quilt. A piece of jewelry. Money.

People leave behind all sorts of things as an inheritance, but Jesus left the very best thing of all—worth far more than a diamond ring or a car. He left the promise of eternity, a "forever" experience with Him. (Hey, no one else left you that, did they?)

So work hard in this wonderful life He's given you, but remember: there's an even better life coming. Christians don't have to fear death. We have heaven to look forward to! Heaven is our reward for falling in love with Jesus and giving our hearts to Him.

Work for Him, not people. He's leaving you a crown that will sparkle longer than any earthly jewelry you might receive.

· ·

*Thank You for the reward of heaven, Jesus!
Nothing even comes close. Amen.*

Struggling with Anger

*We know that our old sinful selves were crucified with Christ so that
sin might lose its power in our lives. We are no longer slaves to sin.*
ROMANS 6:6 NLT

Have you ever struggled with your anger? Gotten really mad at
someone? Maybe a brother or sister, a friend, or even your parents?
Anger often happens when you feel slighted or you didn't get your
way in a situation. Then your whole body gets on board with your
anger. You feel it in your stomach. You feel it in your clenched jaw.
You might even get a headache!

The great news is, because of Jesus, those angry feelings don't
have to control your life anymore! Our old sinful self was crucified
with Christ so that sin has lost its power over us.

In those situations when you're tempted to get mad, remember
what Jesus did for you on the cross. Ask Him for help to calm down
and fill your heart with His love instead. Allow Him to help you
sort out your feelings before acting on them. You're not a slave to
your feelings anymore.

* * * * *

*God, thank You for forgiving me for the times when I've let
anger take control of me. Fill me with Your love instead.*

The Mouth Reflects the Heart

*Don't use foul or abusive language. Let everything
you say be good and helpful, so that your words will
be an encouragement to those who hear them.*
Ephesians 4:29 nlt

Whew! You can hardly go to the grocery store these days without getting an earful of foul language. It's everywhere. But the Bible says don't do it. Want to know why? Check out this verse: "A good man brings good things out of the good stored up in his heart, and an evil man brings evil things out of the evil stored up in his heart. For the mouth speaks what the heart is full of" (Luke 6:45 niv).

Do you see what God's Word is saying here? What's inside the heart of someone who uses bad language? "The mouth speaks what the heart is full of."

So what's your heart full of? If you find yourself wanting to say something bad the next time you stub your toe or have a bad day, ask Jesus to reveal what's in your heart. Let Him pull out any bad weeds that might be growing there and fill you with His love and grace instead.

. . . .

*Lord, please pull out any nasty weeds in my heart.
I want my mouth to reflect love and grace.*

The Life You've Been Given

*Only, let each one live the life which the Lord has assigned him,
and to which God has called him [for each person is unique and is
accountable for his choices and conduct, let him walk in this way].*

1 CORINTHIANS 7:17 AMP

Some of the Corinthians were becoming followers of Jesus and then making huge changes without being led to make those changes by God. For example, some spouses were ready to leave their unbelieving spouse. But that's not what God says to do. Paul tells the people to stay in their marriages and continue as before. You can share the message of Jesus right where you are, in the family you're in, in the job you have. That doesn't mean you can't hope for or make changes in the future. Just make sure to seek God's will before doing so.

God made you exactly the way He wanted you to be for a reason, and He put you where you are right now for a purpose. God wants you to be content with the life He has given you and not wish for someone else's.

. . . .

*Lord, help me to embrace the life that You gave
me and share Your love right where I am.*

Reigning in Life

For if, because of one man's trespass, death reigned through that one man, much more will those who receive the abundance of grace and the free gift of righteousness reign in life through the one man Jesus Christ.
ROMANS 5:17 ESV

You are a beloved daughter of God, covered in the righteousness of Christ. And, if you could see yourself the way God sees you, you would live differently. You would love differently. You would respond differently to difficult situations.

Everyone likes a good fairy tale, right? The lovely princess gets rescued and takes her rightful place in the kingdom. But the story of God's kingdom is true—and *you* are the lovely princess He's rescued. He showers you with an abundance of grace. He loves you, and you have much authority in the kingdom because of the Spirit of God alive in you!

You get to reign in life—now and for eternity—through Jesus Christ and all that He's done for you.

. . . .

Lord God, help me to see myself the way You do. Help me to begin to understand the authority You've given me because of Jesus Christ. Help me to reign well and to love others well.

Day 180
Seeking Soul

The LORD is good to those who wait for him, to the soul who seeks him.
LAMENTATIONS 3:25 ESV

Waiting for anything is difficult. Whether you're waiting for food to be cooked, waiting for the results of an exam, or waiting to open a gift on your birthday—waiting is not easy! God promises that He is good to those who wait on Him! When we wait patiently on the good things He has for us, we demonstrate our trust in Him. As we seek Him out, we wait on His good plan.

Let us remember the beauty in the mystery of God. The God who created everything, who must stoop down just to look upon the created world because He is so high above it, cares for us! We are on this earth for such a fleeting time in the expanse of eternity, yet He is good to us, and He cares for those who seek Him! What a marvelous God!

. . . .

Father God, I don't want to take for granted the magnificence of who You are. Waiting is hard, but when I remember that I'm waiting on a God who only has plans for my good, I relax and seek You and wait patiently to hear Your voice. Amen.

In His Image

*So God created man in His own image, in the image and likeness
of God He created him; male and female He created them.*
GENESIS 1:27 AMP

The book of Genesis tells us that we are created in the image of God. Human life is special and honored above every other living thing because each of us bears the mark of our Creator God. Just like a valuable piece of artwork, every human being is special because of who made us. We are God's creation. It's so important to remember as you grow up that every human life has value because every human is made in the image of God.

When you meet new people, don't judge them by their outward appearance. Their hair, shoes, and clothes don't make them who they are inside. They are God's precious creation no matter what they look like on the outside. Get in the habit of seeing other people as God's precious works of art. Even if they don't see it or believe it, you know it's true. This will begin to change how you treat everyone around you!

. . . .

*Lord, help me to treat other people like the valuable treasures
they really are. We are all Your precious masterpieces.*

His Prized Possession

He chose to give birth to us by giving us his true word.
And we, out of all creation, became his prized possession.
JAMES 1:18 NLT

Looking up Bible verses in several different translations and paraphrases can be fun, and it can help us get a better understanding
of what verses mean. If you have a Bible app, looking up verses in
multiple translations is easy.

Check out today's verse in a few different variations:

Amplified Bible: "It was of His own will that He gave us
birth [as His children] by the word of truth, so that we would
be a kind of first fruits of His creatures [a prime example
of what He created to be set apart to Himself—sanctified,
made holy for His divine purposes]."

The Message: "He brought us to life using the true Word,
showing us off as the crown of all his creatures."

International Children's Bible: "God decided to give us life
through the word of truth. He wanted us to be the most
important of all the things he made."

What does all this tell us? God gave us life through His true
Word, and we are the crown of His creation. His most prized possession. Set apart and made holy for His divine purpose!

. . . .

God, thank You for giving me worth and value!

We Need Each Other

*And let us consider how we may spur one another on toward
love and good deeds, not giving up meeting together, as some
are in the habit of doing, but encouraging one another—
and all the more as you see the Day approaching.*

HEBREWS 10:24–25 NIV

Bad days happen. And on those bad days, it can sometimes be easy
to forget who (and whose) you are! That's why we need each other.

You need friends and mentors who will always remind you that
you are loved and chosen by God for such a time as this. If you
don't have someone in your life like that, pray that God will provide
someone! I believe this is a prayer that God loves to answer. Ask
Him to send you someone who can encourage you in your faith and
who you can encourage too.

Be on the lookout for how God wants to answer this prayer.
Friends might show up in unusual places! And remember, if you want
good and loving friends, *be* a good and loving friend.

. . . .

*Lord, I'm praying now that you would bring someone into my
life who will encourage me in my relationship with You. Let us
pray for each other and help one another grow closer to You.*

Trust Him with Your Days

*There is a time for everything, and a season for
every activity under the heavens.*
ECCLESIASTES 3:1 NIV

This familiar verse from Ecclesiastes tells us that there's a time for everything. The scripture goes on to say there's a time to be born, a time to die, a time to plant, a time to harvest. God has (literally) ordained times for everything you could think of. He's on the job, girl!

Why, then, would you doubt Him when it comes to your days? He's got it all mapped out. There's a time for all the things you're going to accomplish. There's a season for every relationship. Your activities are in His hands.

You can trust Him with your days, girl. His heavenly clock has it all worked out, even if you can't see what's going on behind the scenes.

What season are you in? Trust Him in it, good or bad. He's got this. He's got you.

. . . .

*You're always on the clock, Lord! You have a time and a season
for everything I will ever go through. I know I can trust You
with my days, and today, I choose to do just that. Amen.*

Have No Fear–He Is Near!

*Even when your path takes me through the valley of deepest
darkness, fear will never conquer me, for you already have!
Your authority is my strength and my peace. The comfort of your
love takes away my fear. I'll never be lonely, for you are near.*

PSALM 23:4 TPT

At certain times in your life, you will walk through valleys of deepest
darkness. These valleys are the unfortunate side effect of living in a
fallen world. At some points, you'll feel as if all hope is lost. Loved
ones pass away, a dire diagnosis is received, jobs are lost, friendships
and relationships end. Through it all, however, fear cannot conquer
you, because God has already conquered fear!

Knowing that God is sovereign and that He works all things for
our good gives us strength and peace. We can find comfort in His
perfect authority. It's true, He may not change the circumstances for
you in the moment, but He will change you through the circumstances. He will grow you and draw you closer to Himself. You are
never alone, even in the darkest times.

. . . .

*Thank You for walking beside me on the darkest of days, Lord.
You are so faithful to be by my side through it all. I will not give
in to fear because I know that You have already conquered its
power over me. I rest in Your comforting embrace and peace.*

Day 186
Trouble

*Now if we are children, then we are heirs—heirs of
God and co-heirs with Christ, if indeed we share in his
sufferings in order that we may also share in his glory.*
ROMANS 8:17 NIV

This world can be rather troubling at times. It's not our true home.
Philippians 3:20 (NLT) reminds us, "We are citizens of heaven, where
the Lord Jesus Christ lives. And we are eagerly waiting for him to
return as our Savior."

Jesus Himself told us we're going to have trouble here, so we
should expect some days to be hard. But He also said, "Take heart!
I have overcome the world" (John 16:33 NIV).

So how can we live with joy in our hearts while we're expecting
trouble? Well, we wake up each morning expecting some challenges,
and we ask God to help us through each and every one. That doesn't
mean we're grumpy or negative, though. Always look at trouble as a
challenge that can be overcome with the power of Christ.

Life is an adventure full of good times and bad. We can find
Christ in each moment, and He will give us joy in His presence!

*Jesus, I'm expecting some adventures and challenges today,
and I know You will be with me through them all.*

Day 187
A Worthy Walk

Walk in a manner worthy of the Lord,
fully pleasing to him: bearing fruit in every good
work and increasing in the knowledge of God.
COLOSSIANS 1:10 ESV

God sees you as worthy—of love, care, gifts, joy, and so on. He adores you! You might read this and think, *Wow, it's all on Him! I can live the way I want, and He'll go right on finding me worthy now that I'm a believer.*

Well, that's true, but...don't you want to make His heart happy? Aren't you interested in drawing others to Him?

Today's verse sheds some light on how God feels His worthy ones should live. He wants you to "walk in a manner worthy of the Lord." But what does that mean, exactly?

It means you bear some responsibility to do the right thing, girl! Your life needs to line up with the Bible. You need to have the attributes of Christ. Does this mean you're expected to be perfect? Not even close! Does it mean you should be making an effort to be godlier? Absolutely.

Walk in a manner worthy of your calling. You can do it. You really can.

. . . .

I'll do my best, Lord! I want to be more like You. Amen.

Day 188

He Wants Us to Know Him

*For I want not animal sacrifices, but mercy. I don't want
burnt offerings; I want people to know Me as God!*
Hosea 6:6 voice

Even during Old Testament times, when burnt offerings were common and required by the Law, God wanted the people to know that burnt offerings weren't what He truly desired. God has always desired a relationship with His people.

Ever since Adam and Eve sinned and were banished from the Garden of Eden, God had a plan to restore humanity back to a relationship with Him. He desires nearness. He wants us to know Him just as deeply and intimately as He knows us!

These days we don't offer animal sacrifices, but we do think of sacrificing our time and serving others as ways to please God. While serving your church, your community, and others is important, what God primarily desires of you is your presence. Know Him! Spend time in His Word—that's the most beautiful way to spend your day!

*Father God, I want to know You more! I want to stay in Your
presence. Let me serve out of a heart devoted to knowing
You and being Your hands and feet, not merely because I
think it's what I ought to do or what You require of me.*

Carry the Light

You are the light of the world. A city set on a hill cannot be
hidden. Nor do people light a lamp and put it under a basket,
but on a stand, and it gives light to all in the house. In the same
way, let your light shine before others, so that they may see your
good works and give glory to your Father who is in heaven.
MATTHEW 5:14–16 ESV

Jesus calls you "the light of the world." And light is a pretty big deal.

Have you ever lost power in your house? Suddenly, nothing seems right at home. You've got to keep the refrigerator and freezer closed to keep things cool for as long as possible. There's no air conditioning. You can't use your washer and dryer. But the worst part is—there isn't any light!

You carry the light of Jesus with you everywhere you go. Without the light of Christ, the darkness in our world would be overwhelming. So let your light shine bright, pointing others to God.

. . . .

Lord, please help me shine brightly for You. I want others to come
to know You and give You glory because of the light they see in me.

Never Fails to Shine

*A fountain of life was in him, for his life is light for all
humanity. And this Light never fails to shine through
darkness—Light that darkness could not overcome!*
JOHN 1:4–5 TPT

It all points to Jesus, right? The Law that God gave Moses was to
show the people that they could never follow every rule well enough
to be in right standing with God. The kings proved that no ruler
could ever lead Israel better than the Lord. Then Jesus came to fulfill the Law and the Prophets. He came with all the light and life
within Him that humanity needed for thousands of years. And He
still never fails to shine in the darkness.

If you have felt let down by others, or even by yourself, remember that darkness could not overcome Jesus. Your failures and the
failings of others could never overshadow His great light. Run to
His beautiful light today and watch the darkness fade away!

. . . .

*Jesus, Your light sustains me and brings clarity. I'm not fearful
of what lies ahead or shamed by what came before because
Your light has erased the darkness. Remind me of this truth
whenever I begin to lose sight of Your light. Amen.*

Your Safe Place

God is our safe place and our strength. He is always our help
when we are in trouble. So we will not be afraid, even if the earth
is shaken and the mountains fall into the center of the sea.
PSALM 46:1–2 NLV

Trauma counselors will often counsel their clients to think of a safe space in their mind. This can be a happy memory, a vacation spot, a favorite place to go every day—anywhere that feels completely safe in your mind. Christian counselors have their clients invite Jesus into that space to help process difficult memories.

The Bible tells us that God is our safe place. As you grow up, your safe places may change as you move and grow. But your safe place in God will never change. You can always count on Him to be the same.

God wants to protect you, to comfort you, and to tell you how loved you are. Sometimes sitting in the quiet with God is the best way to pray. Ask Him to fill you with His love as you sit in His presence. Picture yourself close to Jesus and let Him love you.

* *

Lord, You are always my safe place. Thanks for giving me strength.

Day 192

He's There in Hard Times

*When you pass through the waters, I will be with you; and through
the rivers, they shall not overwhelm you; when you walk through
fire you shall not be burned, and the flame shall not consume you.*

ISAIAH 43:2 ESV

You've been through a lot. You've seen something you wish you hadn't.
Been through some challenges you'd rather forget. And yet you're
still here. You're still going. And God wants you to know that He
was right there with you, even in the hardest of times.

Did you realize that God actually carries you during the hardest
of times? He lifts you out of flood waters. He carries you through
the fire. And, if you take a close look at today's verse, you'll see that
you can come through those things unscathed (basically, without
the smell of smoke in your hair).

How is such a thing possible? When God takes control, He
can pull you through a dark situation and heal you from the inside
out. He can take the nastiness you experienced and wash it away,
removing the pain and lingering effects.

He was with you every step of the way, girl. That's how much He
loves you. And He doesn't plan to leave you hanging now!

* *

*Thanks for carrying me through the flood and the fire,
Jesus. Whew! I've been through some stuff. If not for
You, there's no telling where I'd be. Amen.*

Allow God to Love You

The LORD appeared to me (Israel) from ages past, saying, "I have loved you with an everlasting love; therefore with lovingkindness I have drawn you and continued My faithfulness to you."

JEREMIAH 31:3 AMP

In church, we are taught to share the gospel from a young age. And rightly so. But if you've been a Christian for a long time, you can forget that the gospel still applies to you too. "For God so loved the world" is meant for you. And sometimes you need a good reminder and a long refill of His love for you.

First John 4:19 (ESV) says, "We love because he first loved us." Today, take some time to crawl up into God's lap, lean your head on His shoulder, and let Him love you. Can you imagine that as you pray? Talk to Him about what's on your heart. But make sure to allow time to sit and be loved in His presence. Nothing else in life can fill you up the way God's love does. His love is kind, faithful, and everlasting.

. . . .

I love You, Lord, because You loved me first. I'm so thankful for Your everlasting and overwhelming love!

Wrapped around You

*His massive arms are wrapped around you, protecting
you. You can run under his covering of majesty and hide.
His arms of faithfulness are a shield keeping you from harm.*
PSALM 91:4 TPT

God finds your trust so beautiful. When you run to Him for protection, you are not left exposed. He covers you! Relax into His
protective hug today, whether things are going great or some things
are going poorly. His faithful arms welcome you gladly.

Notice the hugs from God as you go through this week: did
you receive an unexpected text from a friend, hear a favorite song
pop up on your playlist, or just have a really good day? Thank God
for the ways He has His arms wrapped around you, even when you
don't notice!

. . . .

*Thank You, Father, for the way You love and protect me. Thank You
for the unexpected moments in my day that are hugs from You. I know
You care about all things, big and small, in my life. Make me aware of
more of these small moments so that I am filled with gratitude. Amen.*

The Three As

But God demonstrates his own love for us in this:
While we were still sinners, Christ died for us.
ROMANS 5:8 NIV

Let's talk about the three As: acceptance, approval, and affirmation.
Most humans tend to walk around hunting for these three As.
They want to be accepted. They want to be approved of. They want
others to affirm them. Many will go to extreme lengths to have these
needs met. But did you know that Jesus has already taken care of
these? Take a look at this: "Christ arrives right on time to make this
happen. He didn't, and doesn't, wait for us to get ready. He presented
himself for this sacrificial death when we were far too weak and
rebellious to do anything to get ourselves ready. . . . But God put his
love on the line for us by offering his Son in sacrificial death while
we were of no use whatever to him" (Romans 5:6–8 MSG).

. . . .

Heavenly Father, open my heart and mind to understand
Your amazing love for me. While I was still a mess, while I
was still making bad choices, You loved me even then.

Lifter of My Head

But you, O LORD, are a shield about me,
my glory, and the lifter of my head.
PSALM 3:3 ESV

Have you ever walked around with your head hanging low, shoulders hunched, trying to make yourself as small and unnoticed as possible? When we're insecure, ashamed, or scared, we tend to look at the ground instead of walking with boldness and confidence. But God calls you beautiful, girl! He wants to see your beautiful face as you step forward in confidence and give Him glory!

He is the lifter of your head in those moments when you're struggling. Imagine Him reaching out His kind, strong hand to lift your chin so that all you see are His beautiful eyes! Are you filled with love and courage? This is what David describes in Psalm 3! When God is your shield and lifts your head, there is no battle you cannot face! Read all of Psalm 3 today (it's only eight verses) and think of how mighty our God is, and yet He still cares personally for each of His children!

. . . .

Lord God, sometimes the stress of what is going on in
my life weighs so heavily on my head and shoulders. I feel
like an unwatered plant that begins to droop and shrink.
You are calling me to walk in the glory of Your beauty,
so please lift my head so that I can be strengthened by Your love!

Count Your Blessings

*Let all that I am praise the LORD; may I never
forget the good things he does for me.*
PSALM 103:2 NLT

Check out these lines from the old hymn "Count Your Blessings":

> *When you are discouraged, thinking all is lost. . .*
> *Count your many blessings, name them one by one,*
> *And it will surprise you what the Lord hath done.*

Do you have a journal? If not, grab a blank notebook and start to record what you're thankful for every day. If you don't have a notebook, you could even find some blank space at the bottom of each of these devotionals. The point is to get in the habit of thanking God for all the good things He's done for you.

You may be thinking, *How could I ever forget what God's done?* But when times are hard or you're in pain, it can be easy to focus on the problems instead of God's blessings. And if you have lots of blessings written down, you can go back to them and see the days when God was working. The days when He answered your prayers. The days when He blessed you.

Give it a try, and You might be surprised at all the Lord has done!

. . . .

Lord, I'm so thankful for all You've done in my life.

Day 198
Protected

Now I am departing from the world; they are staying in this world, but I am coming to you. Holy Father, you have given me your name; now protect them by the power of your name so that they will be united just as we are.

JOHN 17:11 NLT

Did you know that Jesus was praying for you? In John 17, the Bible records several long prayers that Jesus prayed for Himself, for His disciples, and for future believers—that means *you*!

Among other things, Jesus prayed that you would be protected by the power of God's name. Psalm 3:5 (NLT) says: "I lay down and slept, yet I woke up in safety, for the LORD was watching over me."

God is watching over you and protecting you. You don't have to fear. You are dearly loved and never alone!

. . . .

Jesus, thank You for thinking of me and praying for me! That's amazing to think about. Help me not to fear, knowing that God is protecting me.

A Loving Daddy

*You see, you have not received a spirit that returns you to slavery,
so you have nothing to fear. The Spirit you have received adopts you
and welcomes you into God's own family. That's why we call out
to Him, "Abba! Father!" as we would address a loving daddy.*

ROMANS 8:15 VOICE

What a comfort to know that God isn't some fickle god in the sky
judging us on a whim and directing us to do things just to entertain
Himself? He is our loving Dad! He isn't looking to strike us down
with a trident for displeasing Him! Yes, He wants us to pursue holiness and follow His Word, but the reason is so that He can have a
relationship with us and bless us—not just boss us around!

The Holy Spirit adopted us and welcomed us into God's family
when we said yes to Jesus! We can approach our loving heavenly
Father with anything that concerns us, big or small. He is delighted
when we come to Him with our needs! He sees the beauty in our
childlike faith and rewards us for it.

. . . .

*Father God, I want to reach out to You with open arms like a child
running to her daddy. I'm so thankful You're a Father who loves me
unconditionally and doesn't judge or discipline out of anger. Show me
how to love You with complete abandon and childlike faith! Amen.*

When You Turn Back

"Simon, Simon, Satan has asked to sift all of you as wheat.
But I have prayed for you, Simon, that your faith may not fail.
And when you have turned back, strengthen your brothers."
LUKE 22:31–32 NIV

Before Jesus was betrayed by Judas and arrested, He was eating the Passover meal with His disciples. Jesus had something important to tell Simon here in Luke 22. Basically, Satan asked permission to smash the disciples. And troubles would come, for sure. But Jesus prepared and encouraged Simon Peter with these words. Jesus was praying for him, and He gave Peter direction for after he was tested.

A little later, Simon Peter denied Jesus three times because he was afraid. When Simon Peter realized what he had done, he wept. But God wasn't done with Simon Peter yet, even after he denied Jesus.

Jesus had instructed Peter to strengthen his brothers after he turned back. And that's exactly what Peter did. He was even a major part of establishing the early church.

God can use you even after you've messed up too. We all make mistakes. And when you turn back to Jesus, you can share your story with others to encourage them in their faith.

. . . .

Lord, please use my mistakes to help others in their faith.

Out of Darkness

You are a chosen people, a royal priesthood, a holy nation,
God's special possession, that you may declare the praises of him
who called you out of darkness into his wonderful light.

1 PETER 2:9 NIV

Have you ever been in a really dark room? Maybe you woke up in the middle of the night because you heard a younger sibling crying from down the hallway. You stumbled out of bed, flipped on the light, and the sudden shock of the overhead glow nearly blinded you.

That's kind of how it is for people who've been walking in spiritual darkness when they come to Jesus. It can be kind of shocking. Jarring! They aren't used to it. That's why you have to be patient—with yourself and with others. They won't always get it right the first time. Their eyes are just getting adjusted to walking with Jesus.

God has brought you out of the darkness, girl. You have seen some icky stuff. Some of your friends and loved ones are still involved in icky stuff. But Jesus has set you on a bright path. Don't get overwhelmed by the light. Just rest in the confidence that He loves you so much that He chose you to be His.

. . . .

Thanks for putting me on a bright path, Jesus! My eyes are
getting used to the light now. I like it here! Amen.

A Special Part

*Just as our bodies have many parts and each part has a
special function, so it is with Christ's body. We are many
parts of one body, and we all belong to each other.*
ROMANS 12:4–5 NLT

Jessa walked into youth group for the very first time. Thankfully,
she saw a friend she knew from drama group, and she instantly felt
better. But those first few minutes of looking around at a new group
of people can be a bit intimidating, right?

Here's the good news: Jesus says you belong! Especially at church.
He made you a special part of His body, a.k.a. the church. The Bible
says that Christ's body is made up of many parts and each of them
is important.

The next time you walk into a room not knowing anyone, remember that Jesus is with you. Ask Him for courage to go and talk with
someone new. Ask Him to show you where you belong, and try not
to worry about what others think of you. Jesus knew exactly what He
was doing when He made you part of His body. And you belong there!

. . . .

Lord, thank You for making me a special part of Your body.

Day 203

His Delight

He led me to a place of safety; he rescued me because he delights in me.
PSALM 18:19 NLT

Remember, before you took your first breath—before the creation of the world (remember Ephesians 1:4 tells us this!)—your worth was established. Your worth has nothing to do with your behavior. It has nothing to do with your choices. It has nothing to do with what you think or don't think. God loves you and delights in you simply because you are His creation. You're His precious child. He doesn't just tolerate you; He delights in you!

Think about how amazing that is! When God looks around at all of His creation, you are the best part! He chose you to be in relationship with Him. He leads you to places of safety. He rescues you from dangers—all because you are worth it to Him! He gave His very own life so that you could be with Him forever.

Doesn't that make you want to worship and praise God? Crank up your favorite worship song and sing your heart out in praise to the God who adores you!

. . . .

Your love is amazing, God! You are so good and kind. Thanks for loving me so deeply!

Day 204

Hearing God's Voice

Whether you turn to the right or to the left, your ears will hear
a voice behind you, saying, "This is the way; walk in it."
Isaiah 30:21 niv

Many people think that God stopped speaking long ago. Don't believe it! Check out what the Bible says,

- "My sheep hear my voice, and I know them, and they follow me. I give them eternal life, and they will never perish, and no one will snatch them out of my hand" (John 10:27–28 esv).

- "You shall walk after the Lord your God and fear him and keep his commandments and obey his voice, and you shall serve him and hold fast to him" (Deuteronomy 13:4 esv).

- "Does he who supplies the Spirit to you and works miracles among you do so by works of the law, or by hearing with faith?" (Galatians 3:5 esv).

- "As it is said, 'Today, if you hear his voice, do not harden your hearts as in the rebellion'" (Hebrews 3:15 esv).

Lord Jesus, I want to hear Your voice in my life.
Show me what that looks like. Please open my ears,
my heart, and my mind to hear from You!

Christ Will Be Revealed

For, at just the right time Christ will be revealed from heaven by the blessed and only almighty God, the King of all kings and Lord of all lords. He alone can never die, and he lives in light so brilliant that no human can approach him. No human eye has ever seen him, nor ever will. All honor and power to him forever! Amen.

1 TIMOTHY 6:15–16 NLT

Jesus—the Most Beautiful One. He shines with a light so brilliant that if we saw Him in the fullness of His glory, we would be struck dead. It's so easy to forget about the magnitude of His brilliance because He is our friend and Comforter. Yet He is also a fierce and mighty warrior, sitting on the throne of heaven. He is immortal. He is light and power. He is revealed by God.

If you seek beauty, seek Jesus. He is more radiant than the sun, and He is the Source of all. Thank Him today for the magnificence of who He is in your life. Get lost in His presence!

. . . .

Jesus, You are the Most Beautiful One. I want to know You more and be drawn into Your beauty. I want to get lost in Your presence!

Held Close to His Heart

He tends his flock like a shepherd: he gathers the lambs in his arms and carries them close to his heart; he gently leads those that have young.
ISAIAH 40:11 NIV

The Bible talks a lot about God being our shepherd. Since most of us don't live on farms or have sheep these days, that might not mean much to you. But in Bible times, everyone knew about the life of a shepherd. A good shepherd protects the sheep from wild animals and cares for them when they get hurt or wander off. Shepherds make sure their sheep always have food and fresh water.

Jesus is our good shepherd. He carries us close to His heart. Check out what Jesus said about Himself in John 10:11 (NIV): "I am the good shepherd. The good shepherd lays down his life for the sheep." And in verse 14 (NIV) He says, "I am the good shepherd; I know my sheep and my sheep know me."

Can you picture yourself being held in the arms of Jesus as you pray? He wants to speak to you and for you to know Him personally. He wants you to know that you are loved.

. . . .

Lord, be my good shepherd. Help me hear Your voice telling me how much You love me.

A Holy Walk

God has not called us to live in sin. He has called us to live a holy life.
1 Thessalonians 4:7 NLV

Holiness. It's an amazing word, isn't it? Maybe you look at that word and think, *Yeah, that's beyond me. I could never live a holy life!* Maybe you've tried and (according to your own estimation) failed.

Here's the truth: we all fail at holiness. We're human. We mess up. "All have sinned and fall short of the glory of God" (Romans 3:23 ESV). That's why we need Jesus so much! And here's some good news: He never fails the holiness test. Never. Ever. So when you give your heart to Him, when His Spirit comes to live inside of you, His holiness takes over.

It's not on you, girl, but you do have to walk it out. You have to try to live a holy life. You have to walk according to the purposes He's established. Stay away from sin. Don't engage in wicked behavior. And hang tight to Jesus in good times and bad.

The road ahead of you is a holy walkway, but you can travel it if you trust Him to live through you.

. . . .

I get it, Jesus. I'll stay away from sin and stick close to You.
You give me the power to live in holiness. I love it! Amen.

Day 208
Listening for God

*I hear the tumult of the raging seas as your waves and
surging tides sweep over me. But each day the LORD pours
his unfailing love upon me, and through each night I
sing his songs, praying to God who gives me life.*
PSALM 42:7–8 NLT

God is always speaking to you. Are you listening? Girl, you are so
loved by God. He cares about every need and every thought that
weighs heavy or light on your heart. He wants to speak to you about
every thought and circumstance.

The psalm writer sings of raging seas and discouragement. But
he remembers that God pours out His unfailing love on His children every day and that he can worship and talk to God throughout
every moment.

God is present in your circumstances. He is up to something
good, no matter what things look and feel like. You have a special
place in God's heart, and He wants you to bring every thought to
Him. He is speaking in the wind and rain, in His Word, through
songs, through people, and so much more.

What is God saying to you today?

*Lord God, please continue opening my ears to hear
from You. Sometimes busyness and fear get in the way.
Please remove those barriers so that I can hear from You.*

Lies about God and Faith

"Make them holy by your truth; teach them your word, which is truth."
JOHN 17:17 NLT

The enemy will try to lie to you about everything. After you've started counteracting Satan's lies with God's Word, he'll start trying to get you to doubt that the Bible is even true at all. Don't fall for it.

Lie: God is mad at you.
Truth: There is no condemnation for those who are in Christ Jesus (Romans 8:1).

Lie: The Christian life is too hard.
Truth: Jesus will give you rest. His yoke is easy and His burden is light (Matthew 11:28–30).

Lie: God doesn't talk to people anymore.
Truth: Jesus said that His sheep hear His voice and follow Him (John 10:27).

Lie: The Bible isn't true.
Truth: God's Word is living and active and God-breathed (2 Timothy 3:16; Hebrews 4:12; 1 John 1:1).

As for the Bible being true, countless eyewitnesses saw all that happened with Jesus and His death and resurrection. From archaeologists finding locations in the Bible that were exactly as described to scientific evidence for the flood in Genesis, you can trust that God's Word is true.

· ·

Thank You, Lord, that Your Word is truth!

Prosper in All You Do

*"And keep the charge of the LORD your God, walking in his
ways and keeping his statutes, his commandments, his rules,
and his testimonies, as it is written in the Law of Moses, that
you may prosper in all that you do and wherever you turn."*

1 KINGS 2:3 ESV

These are King David's last words to his son Solomon. God promised
David that if his descendants followed the Lord with their whole
hearts, one of them would always be on the throne in Israel. David
knew that being king brought not only many opportunities to do
good but also opportunities to turn from the Lord out of selfishness
and pride. He encouraged Solomon to pursue the Lord so that he
would prosper.

While we know that Solomon ultimately followed his own path,
we can learn from his mistakes. We can take the wise words of his
father, David, and live them out in our own lives. When we follow
God and walk in His ways, pursuing holiness, we will prosper in
all we do!

. . . .

*Father God, I want to prosper in the ways that matter.
I want to honor You in all that I do. Remind me of Your Word
when I begin to stray. Convict me and draw me into repentance
so that I can stay in right relationship with You. Amen.*

No One Like Our God

*Who has directed the Spirit of the LORD, or has taught Him as
His counselor? With whom did He consult and who enlightened
Him? Who taught Him the path of justice and taught Him
knowledge and informed Him of the way of understanding?*

Isaiah 40:13–14 amp

When you're worried, when you're in trouble, when you're over-whelmed, when life seems too hard, remember this: your God is greater than any power on earth and in the heavens. And He knows you by name. He chose you as His own. He loves you dearly. You can go to Him with every problem and every need. He welcomes you in. He has a solution.

No legal system, no surgeon, no government, no authority in all the world can tell Him what to do! He is the ultimate authority over everyone and everything. As verse 9 says, "Here is your God!" This is the God who rolls out the night sky every evening, knows all the stars by name, and is holding you (verse 26)!

*There is no one like You, God! I'm so grateful that I can
come to You with everything and know that You care.*

Bought with a Price

Do you not know that your body is a temple of the Holy Spirit within you, whom you have from God? You are not your own, for you were bought with a price. So glorify God in your body.
1 CORINTHIANS 6:19–20 ESV

If you've ever been to an auction, you know the excitement that can build as bidding wars get underway. People fight one another to take the prize.

Now picture yourself on the auction block. You're up for sale. And the devil is fighting it out with God. The devil wants you. God wants you. And, in the end, God places the highest bid anyone has ever seen—He offers His Son as a sacrifice for your sin. He buys you, once and for all.

Wow! When you think of it like that, does it make you want to honor Him more with the way you live? You were bought with a price, girl! And you are a temple of the Holy Spirit, which means that He's living inside of you even now.

So how you live matters. How you love matters. What you say and do matter. Every single moment matters because you were purchased at such a high price.

. . . .

I get it, Jesus. I was on the auction block, and You bought me with Your very life. I'll do my best to honor You with mine. Amen.

A Safe Shelter

The Eternal One is good, a safe shelter in times of trouble.
He cares for those who search for protection in Him.
NAHUM 1:7 VOICE

Have you ever needed protection? A safe place to run when you were scared? There have been many times in my life when the only place I could turn when I was scared was to the Lord in prayer. He is my shelter and my strength. He is yours too! Nothing in this life is too big or too small for the Eternal One.

When you find yourself fearing a time of trouble, turn to Him and rest in the perfect peace He gives. Many scary things are happening around the world each day. We see them on the news, on social media, and in our own neighborhoods. God knows the world can be a scary place, but He is good. He cares for us when we seek protection in Him. There is beauty in running to the arms of our Father when we are scared.

. . . .

Father, thank You for being my safe place. I'm so grateful You know the end from the beginning. Nothing is a surprise to You, and You will sustain me no matter what comes my way.

Day 214

A Holy Purpose

*"But you will receive power when the Holy Spirit
comes upon you. And you will be my witnesses, telling
people about me everywhere—in Jerusalem, throughout
Judea, in Samaria, and to the ends of the earth."*

ACTS 1:8 NLT

Is Jesus real or not? Can He help you? Does God still speak to His people today? The struggles, the blessings, the problems, and the adventures in your life all happen for a reason. God is using every single thing to tell you—and the world—that He is real. That He is close.

These lessons you're learning right now are not just for you. When you face something hard and have evidence that God is with you, write it down so that you don't forget. Every time you hear from God, write it down in a journal. When God answers your prayers, make a note.

These life lessons have great purpose. They are to share with your friends, your parents, your future spouse, your future children. God uses everything to bring hope, light, and love to a dark world.

· ·

Lord, I commit my life to You. Please use me for Your holy purposes in this world. I want to share the reality of who You are with the world!

Day 215
Looking for Miracles

O LORD, You are my God; I will exalt You, I will praise and give thanks to Your name; for You have done miraculous things, plans formed long, long ago, [fulfilled] with perfect faithfulness.
ISAIAH 25:1 AMP

Have you experienced any miracles? Maybe you or someone you know was healed of an illness. Maybe you received an answer to something right in the nick of time. Maybe you saw something that doesn't make any physical sense.

God is in the miracle business. He always has been and always will be. He can do all the miracles from long ago that you've heard of (the parting of the Red Sea, raising Jesus from the dead, healing multitudes), and He still does all kinds of miracles today. Just start looking around. Spend a few dollars at the store for a new note-book. Start writing down your prayer requests, and keep a record of all the answers and miraculous ways you start seeing God at work all around you. Some are little. Some are huge. God is still at work today—speaking, changing things, working on His kids' behalf.

. . . .

*I believe You are the God of miracles, Lord.
Help me to see You at work in my life.*

Peace of Mind and Heart

*"I am leaving you with a gift—peace of mind and heart. And the peace
I give is a gift the world cannot give. So don't be troubled or afraid."*
JOHN 14:27 NLT

Jesus really wanted us to understand that His peace is a gift and that
it is meant to free us from our fear and anxiety. Why do you think
this was such a major point for Him to drive home for His disciples
and for us? I think it's because fear is the biggest reason we don't trust
God in certain areas of our lives. Our fear tells us there is something
we can do to make things better if only we try harder or know what
to do. Faith in God, on the other hand, is an acknowledgment that
He is sovereign over everything and that there is nothing we can do
to add even one more day to our lives.

Internalize this gift of peace in your heart and mind today. It's a
gift you won't find anywhere else in the world—it comes only from
God. You don't need to be afraid.

. . . .

*Thank You for Your gift of peace, Jesus. I know I can cling to
it when I begin to worry about what tomorrow will bring.
Help me to understand this gift of peace better so that You
are the first face I seek when I start to be afraid. Amen.*

Coming and Going

The LORD will guard your going out and your coming in
[everything that you do] from this time forth and forever.
PSALM 121:8 AMP

You are important to God. He sees you. The Bible says that He guards your coming and going—forever! That doesn't mean that you'll never get hurt or that bad things won't happen. (Life won't be perfect until heaven). It does mean that God has a plan and purpose for your life and that He will finish what He started in you. Philippians 1:6 (NLT) says, "And I am certain that God, who began the good work within you, will continue his work until it is finally finished on the day when Christ Jesus returns."

That means as you head out the door to church or school or camp, God sees you. As you make new friends and work your first job, God is with you. He is always available to talk with, get wisdom from, and remind you of your value and identity in Him. How can you reach out to God today during your coming and going?

. . . .

Lord, thank You for keeping constant watch over me.
Remind me throughout this day that You are close.

Worthy of a Second Chance

Some of you were once like that. But you were cleansed; you were made holy; you were made right with God by calling on the name of the Lord Jesus Christ and by the Spirit of our God.
1 CORINTHIANS 6:11 NLT

God thinks you're worthy of a do-over. That's right, girl! He's going to give you second chances. And third. And fourth. That's how merciful and gracious He is.

Does this mean you should deliberately disobey or mess up since you know He's going to forgive you anyway? Of course not! Flat-out disobedience would be wrong. But if you do slip up and do something wrong, He's right there, ready to forgive and give you another opportunity to get it right.

Why do you suppose God is in the "second chances" business? Why not just punish you when you mess up? Wouldn't you learn from your mistakes? Maybe, but at what cost? He would be pushing you away if He always came down hard on you. You would stop trusting Him if He never showed mercy and grace. He wants you to know that you are valuable to Him. You are His child, after all!

· ·

Thanks for offering second chances, Lord! Amen.

For His Glory

*"I will say to the north and south, 'Bring my sons and
daughters back to Israel from the distant corners of the
earth. Bring all who claim me as their God, for I have
made them for my glory. It was I who created them.'"*

ISAIAH 43:6–7 NLT

You've been chosen to be God's child. He made you for His glory.
Second Corinthians 3:18 (NLT) says, "So all of us who have had
that veil removed can see and reflect the glory of the Lord. And the
Lord—who is the Spirit—makes us more and more like him as we
are changed into his glorious image."

As you grow as a follower of Jesus, He changes your heart more
and more to look like His. He's not taking away your personality. He
made you that way on purpose. He is in the process of making you
holy, more like Him in your thoughts and actions. You were made
to know and love God and to reflect the glory of God to the world.

. . . .

*Lord, I invite You to keep changing my heart to look more and more
like Yours. Help me think Your thoughts and walk in Your ways.*

Walking Closely with God

*God the Father knew you and chose you long ago, and his Spirit has
made you holy. . . . May God give you more and more grace and peace.*
1 Peter 1:2 nlt

See? Here's another great reminder that God knew you and chose
you long ago! Peter is praying that God would give His children more
grace and peace. The Amplified Bible says, "May grace and peace [that
special sense of spiritual well-being] be yours in increasing abundance
[as you walk closely with God]."

Have you ever felt closer to God at certain times than at others?
Like maybe at church or when you're singing worship music? But
what is the truth? The truth is that no matter what it feels like, Jesus
has promised never to leave you (Hebrews 13:5; Matthew 28:20).
Get in the habit of picturing yourself walking closely with Jesus, arm
in arm or hand in hand.

Hebrews 11:1 (niv) says, "Now faith is confidence in what we
hope for and assurance about what we do not see." When feelings
get in the way of the facts, remind yourself of the truth. You can walk
closely with God, and He is always with you!

*Lord God, remind me of the truth that You are
close and that You'll never leave me.*

Day 221

Come to Me

*Then Jesus said, "Come to me, all of you who are weary
and carry heavy burdens, and I will give you rest."*
MATTHEW 11:28 NLT

What a comfort that Jesus promises that when we bring our heavy
burdens and weariness to Him, He will give us rest. What a beautiful
trade! What a relief to know I don't have to carry around my anxiety,
fear, heartache, and grief—I can turn it all over to Jesus and He will
give me peace and rest.

Think of a way to turn over your weariness and heavy burdens
to Jesus today. You could write them on a slip of paper and then
shred it. You could write them on rocks and throw them into a lake.
Anything you come up with is a good symbol of releasing those cares
and taking on His perfect peace instead!

. . . .

*Dear Jesus, I turn my burdens over to You, exchanging
them for Your peace and rest. I trust You. Amen.*

Joy!

Satisfy us in the morning with your unfailing love,
that we may sing for joy and be glad all our days.
PSALM 90:14 NIV

Your feelings and your attitude are important to God. And guess what? Jesus promises to fill you with His joy just by spending time with Him.

Take a look at these verses from the Bible about joy:

- "You make known to me the path of life; you will fill me with joy in your presence" (Psalm 16:11 NIV).

- "I am coming to you now, but I say these things while I am still in the world, so that they may have the full measure of my joy within them" (John 17:13 NIV).

Spend time with Jesus, and He'll fill you with joy. Jesus is with you in this very moment. If you're having trouble feeling joy in your life, get alone somewhere and just talk to God. Tell Him exactly how you feel—either out loud, in your mind, or jot it down in a journal. Jesus wants you to have joy in your heart. And if you're not feeling particularly joyful, He will help!

. . . .

Jesus, I'm thankful for Your promise of joy as I spend time
with You. Help me know and experience Your true joy.

Healed and Saved

*O LORD, if you heal me, I will be truly healed; if you save
me, I will be truly saved. My praises are for you alone!*
JEREMIAH 17:14 NLT

Jeremiah was a prophet in the Old Testament. His job was to share
messages with God's people so that they would turn their hearts back
to God. But God's people had forgotten Him. They were choosing
sin and idols instead of following God's ways. In Jeremiah 2:13
(NLT), God said, "For my people have done two evil things: they
have abandoned me—the fountain of living water. And they have
dug for themselves cracked cisterns that can hold no water at all!"

But God offered a way out. If they would repent and turn back
to Him, He would heal and save them. He offers us the same thing
today. When God heals us, we are truly healed. When He saves, He
saves completely.

Turning to people or things to heal and save us will never work.
Only God can heal and save completely.

. . . .

*Lord, I choose You. You are the fountain of living water,
the only one able to heal and save the way I need.*

Day 224

In Heavenly Peace

*"But the one who always listens to me will live undisturbed
in a heavenly peace. Free from fear, confident and courageous,
that one will rest unafraid and sheltered from the storms of life."*

PROVERBS 1:33 TPT

This proverb is given as a promise from Wisdom. Wisdom, personified as a woman, says that when we listen to her, we will live in peace, confident and courageous. This is not to say we won't have trouble. We know that just because we are Christians doesn't mean we are exempt from difficulty. Yet as we trust in the Lord and lean on His wisdom, we discover a supernatural peace that transcends our circumstances.

We won't be taken down by the storms of life because we are sheltered under His wings; we have nothing to fear because He is with us. Listen to Wisdom today and rest in God's heavenly peace.

. . . .

*Lord God, I need Your wisdom and peace as I face the
storms of life. Your heavenly peace makes my life beautiful
because I can rest in it free from fear, sheltered in Your arms.
Thank You for the way You protect and preserve me! Amen.*

The Price

He personally carried our sins in his body on the cross so that we can be
dead to sin and live for what is right. By his wounds you are healed.
1 PETER 2:24 NLT

The Message paraphrases this verse like this: "He used his servant body to carry our sins to the Cross so we could be rid of sin, free to live the right way. His wounds became your healing."

The price of taking away our sin, giving us freedom, and making a way for us to live forever in heaven with God was the death of His Son. First Peter 2:24 reminds us of this truth. Jesus died on the cross so that we can be free from sin—not a slave to it anymore. Completely dead to it. And now we are free to live the right way: trusting in Christ, listening for His voice in our everyday life, following His lead.

The next part of the verse is a stark reminder: "By his wounds you are healed."

As you take time to pray today, remember: your freedom from sin came at the highest price. Allow this to bring you to your knees in worship and thanksgiving. God loves you so much that He sent His Son.

. . . .

Jesus, You sacrificed everything for me.
Help me live my life for You in return.

Eternal Choices

"Today I have given you the choice between life and death,
between blessings and curses. Now I call on heaven and
earth to witness the choice you make. Oh, that you would
choose life, so that you and your descendants might live!"

<small>DEUTERONOMY 30:19 NLT</small>

In the Old Testament, Moses was talking to the Hebrews and urging them to follow God and His ways. Their very lives and the lives of their children were at stake.

When someone makes a decision to follow Christ, it changes not only their lives but the lives of those around them and even their children's children. It has a trickle effect. That means that the goodness and blessing of living the Christian life gets passed on in families and relationships. Each individual person is still responsible to choose Christ or not, but the love and opportunity are there.

You get to make this same life-or-death decision. Choosing Christ means choosing life for eternity. Choosing sin now may mean death for eternity. The enemy is really good at making sin look good and easy now. But it has eternal consequences.

What will you choose?

. . . .

Lord God, I choose life. I choose Your ways. I want to follow
You and have life for all eternity. Let this blessing be passed
on to my family as I share Your love with them.

Day 227
Fix Your Thoughts

Now, dear brothers and sisters, one final thing.
Fix your thoughts on what is true, and honorable, and
right, and pure, and lovely, and admirable. Think about
things that are excellent and worthy of praise.
PHILIPPIANS 4:8 NLT

Have you ever used superglue? Maybe you tried and ended up getting your fingers stuck together. (It happens!)

Today's verse shares a fun concept: God wants you to superglue your thoughts to His Word. "Fix" your thoughts on what is true and honorable and right and pure and lovely and admirable. In other words, remain focused (fixated) on the good things, not the bad. When you spend your time thinking about things that are excellent (as opposed to, say, all the evil going on around you) you won't get so bogged down in the icky stuff.

It's not always easy. There's very real stuff happening. (Don't believe it? Turn on the news for five minutes, and you'll see!) People are angry. They argue. They fight over politics and all sorts of things.

But you? You're not engaging in those fights. Your thoughts are superglued to Jesus. You have His heart, His message, and His mindset. You're able to see beyond the mess to the bliss of loving Him.

. . . .

I'm supergluing my thoughts to Your Word, Jesus! Amen.

The Victorious Crown of Life

If your faith remains strong, even while surrounded by life's
difficulties, you will continue to experience the untold blessings
of God! True happiness comes as you pass the test with faith, and
receive the victorious crown of life promised to every lover of God!
JAMES 1:12 TPT

When you remain faithful to God's call on your life through all its difficulties and struggles, you receive true happiness and the victorious crown of life! Your faith will be tested as you live on this earth. Not everything comes easily to a person, but those of us who know the Lord have the promise that our faith can remain strong.

Keep the faith, stay in prayer, and focus on Him through each of the hard seasons. He will continue to shower you with blessings and bring you through those hard seasons even stronger than you were before! Trust in Him, for He sees the future and knows how to equip you.

. . . .

Father God, I need Your help to stay strong in my faith
when I begin to face difficulties. I often feel alone, like no one
understands what I'm going through, so help me to remember
that You do! You know my feelings and You know how to
strengthen me. Thank You for never leaving my side.

Restoration and Victory

But he was pierced for our rebellion, crushed for our sins. He was beaten so we could be whole. He was whipped so we could be healed.
Isaiah 53:5 NLT

Why is it important to take our sin seriously? Because God did. He sent His Son to die for our sins. That's why saying, "I'm sorry, okay?" and stomping off just doesn't cut it. God wants our hearts. He wants full repentance, where we are truly sorry for the sin that caused Jesus to die. It's a big deal.

Once we've come to Jesus and confessed our sins in repentance, He doesn't want us to live in shame and defeat anymore. Psalm 34:5 (NIV) says, "Those who look to him are radiant; their faces are never covered with shame."

When you come to God wholeheartedly, He cleanses you from your sin and sets you on the right path again. Your relationship with God is restored and you can move forward in victory.

. . . .

Jesus, I don't ever want to take Your death for granted. You died to save me from my sin. I'm sorry for turning away from You and choosing my own way. Please restore our relationship and set me on the right path again.

The Old You Is Dead and Gone

*Therefore, if anyone is in Christ, he is a new creation.
The old has passed away; behold, the new has come.*
2 CORINTHIANS 5:17 ESV

Did you realize you died and rose again, just like Jesus? It's true.

How, you ask? If you're a believer in Jesus, if you've truly given your heart to Him, then He took the old you (the one with the shame, the guilt, and the pain) and buried her under the covering of His blood. He tossed your sins as far as the east is from the west. When He came to live inside of you, you were reborn, girl. No, really. The old you is gone. The new you is here for good!

It's an interesting concept, but it's true. There's no more old you. There's only the new and improved version, the one He wants to present to the world. Now you see why it's so important to live a holy life! You can't go on living like you used to. That girl is gone. The girl who lives now is a reflection of the Creator of the world! She's got to shine bright for all the world to see.

All things are made new in Him, even you!

* *

*I get it, Jesus! You made me brand-new! I won't live
like the old me. I'm now the new me. Amen.*

Day 231
Faithful and True

*Then I saw heaven opened, and behold, a white
horse! The one sitting on it is called Faithful and True,
and in righteousness he judges and makes war.*
REVELATION 19:11 ESV

John, a close friend of Jesus, wrote these words about Jesus in heaven.
Jesus rides on a white horse and is called Faithful and True. He judges
in righteousness. On earth we saw Jesus as a peaceful man, living a
sinless and relatively quiet life. In heaven, it's another story. He is a
Warrior-King who fights for justice and righteousness. He is known
by His faithfulness and truth.

Rest today in knowing that the Jesus who is your Lord and Savior
is the same Jesus who judges righteously and makes war against the
enemy. You can rest easy knowing He is fighting your battles. He
won't let any weapon formed against you prosper. He will always
be faithful and true to you, His beautiful daughter.

. . . .

*Jesus, You are so powerful. I trust You to fight my battles.
I don't need to worry about the things the enemy tries to
throw my way, because I am safe with You. Amen.*

Day 232
Wise Words

Don't be impressed with your own wisdom. Instead, fear the Lord and turn away from evil. Then you will have healing for your body and strength for your bones.
PROVERBS 3:7–8 NLT

Proverbs is a book about wisdom, so if you're in need of wisdom, it's the place to go. Many interesting proverbs, like the one above, suggest that what's going on in your heart and mind can affect your physical body. Basically, instead of being a know-it-all, honor God and keep away from evil. Doing this can help keep your body healthy.

Remember what the verses right before verses 7–8 say? Here's a reminder: "Trust in the Lord with all your heart; do not depend on your own understanding. Seek his will in all you do, and he will show you which path to take" (Proverbs 3:5–6 NLT).

Chew on these wise words today. If you want to stay healthy in heart and mind, and stay on the right path in life, follow Jesus!

. . . .

I need wisdom, Lord. I'm growing up, and things feel overwhelming at times. Help me to stay on the right path with You.

Day 233
I'm All Yours

Dear friends, we are already God's children, but he has not yet shown us what we will be like when Christ appears. But we do know that we will be like him, for we will see him as he really is. And all who have this eager expectation will keep themselves pure, just as he is pure.

1 JOHN 3:2–3 NLT

Can you imagine actually seeing Jesus face-to-face for the first time? This might actually happen in your lifetime! The Bible tells us amazing things that will happen to us in the end times. While we wait for Jesus to return, God wants us to be pure like He is. But remember, we can't do this on our own.

The Bible says that if you are a follower of Jesus, you are being transformed into His likeness day by day (2 Corinthians 3:17–18). His Spirit invades your life and changes you, keeping you pure for what is to come.

Jesus, thank You for Your Spirit who is always at work in my heart. Thank You that I don't have to be afraid or worried that I have to become pure all on my own. I'm Yours, Jesus!

Glisten with Glory

Gaze upon him, join your life with his, and joy will come. Your faces will glisten with glory. You'll never wear that shame-face again.
PSALM 34:5 TPT

I love the way this verse is worded. Never wear that shame-face again! Joining your life with God and gazing on Him will bring you joy and cause you to glisten with glory! How beautiful to glisten with the glory of God!

Is there something in your life that is causing you guilt and shame? Have you been wearing the shame-face lately? It's time to trade it in, friend! Go exchange that shame for God's love, joy, peace, and glory! You will never want to go back to your old guilt again! Living with Christ as your Lord and Savior is so much more than saying a prayer; it is trading in your old life and leaving behind any desire to return to your sin. It's time to glisten with His glory, beautiful one!

Lord, I've held on to some of my shame and guilt because I don't feel worthy of trading it in for joy. But I know You call me worthy, and I'm ready to exchange that shame for glory now! I want to shine Your light to all I meet! Amen.

Day 235

Guardrails

Where there is no [wise, intelligent] guidance, the people
fall [and go off course like a ship without a helm], but in the
abundance of [wise and godly] counselors there is victory.
PROVERBS 11:14 AMP

Have you ever taken a road trip up a mountain? It can be a little frightening. Most places have guardrails to prevent serious accidents like going over the side of the mountain. But some more remote places don't have guardrails. You have to keep your eyes on the road at all times or you might be in big trouble. The guardrails help keep you safe.

God gives you guardrails in life too. He puts wise people in your path to help you when you look like you might be a little too close to the edge. He has given you the Holy Spirit to give you warning signals when you're straying off the path He has for you.

If you are in need of wise counsel, talk to God about this. Ask Him to send you some godly mentors who can help when you need wisdom and answers for life's great adventures.

. . . .

Lord, thanks for putting guardrails in my life.
Help me listen to wise counsel when You send it.

My Comfort and Safe Place

Whoever dwells in the shelter of the Most High will rest in the shadow of the Almighty. I will say of the LORD, "He is my refuge and my fortress, my God, in whom I trust."
PSALM 91:1–2 NIV

What comes to your mind when you think of a safe place? Your house? Your bedroom? The Bible tells us that God is our safe place—our refuge.

As you become an adult, your safe places will change as you move and change. But your safe place in God will never change. You can always count on Him to be the same. He wants to protect you, comfort you, and tell you how loved you are.

Psalm 46:1–2 (NIV) says, "God is our refuge and strength, an ever-present help in trouble. Therefore we will not fear."

Sit in the quiet with God and thank Him for His comfort. Ask Him to fill you with His love as you sit in His presence. Picture yourself leaning on God's welcoming shoulders and letting Him love you.

Lord, You are my comfort and safe place. I'm thankful I can come to You, and You take away all my fears.

Day 237

Being Pruned

"I am a true sprouting vine, and the farmer who tends the vine is my Father. He cares for the branches connected to me by lifting and propping up the fruitless branches and pruning every fruitful branch to yield a greater harvest."

JOHN 15:1–2 TPT

Pruning sounds like such a nice concept. Yet it sure doesn't feel nice to the plant being pruned! Being cut back to the node seems counterintuitive. Why would you cut back in order to get *more* fruit? Thankfully, God's ways are higher than ours and He knows that trimming back the branches will yield a greater harvest. Trimming back the things in our lives that don't serve Him will yield a greater harvest of spiritual fruit.

God loves us enough to show us what in our lives needs to be cut back for us to bring greater glory and honor to Him. Next time you feel convicted of something in your life that needs to be cut back, thank God for revealing it to you and ask for His help in trimming it away from your life.

. . . .

Father God, I don't usually like the process of being pruned. There are things in my life I want to hold on to, even after I realize they aren't serving You. Help me to be submissive to the pruning process so that I can be a better servant of You!

Day 238

When You Trip Up

The godly may trip seven times, but they will get up again.
But one disaster is enough to overthrow the wicked.

PROVERBS 24:16 NLT

Have you ever played a video game not knowing what you were doing? The game ended quickly, and you got to start all over. You tripped or fell or died again and again until you got the hang of it. Or remember when you were learning to ride a bike? You probably crashed a time or two, but someone was there to help. And especially when you were just learning to walk as a toddler, you tripped a bunch! But your parents were there to help you get up again.

This verse in Proverbs sounds a bit like that. God's children may trip, but He is with them and will help them get up again. But people who have no hope get completely overwhelmed when disaster strikes. They've not chosen to follow Jesus, and there is no one to help.

You can always count on Jesus to be with you when you trip up.

. . . .

Jesus, I'm so thankful that You help me up even if I trip again
and again. I know Your hand is there to grab ahold of.

Loving God

And so we know and rely on the love God has for us.
God is love. Whoever lives in love lives in God, and God in them.
1 John 4:16 niv

Do you ever wonder if you're loving God well? Do you find it sometimes difficult to say, "I love You, God," and wonder if you really mean it?

Sometimes it's hard to know how to love God back after He sacrificed everything for you. His great love can be overwhelming! But when we obey God's Word, listen for His voice, and love others, that is how we show love to God.

And when those times come when you aren't sure that you are loving God very well? Today's verse answers that question: "We know and rely on the love God has for us." The only way we can love at all is because He loved us first. He is the author of love, and He'll continue to show us how to love better and better as we follow Him.

. . . .

Lord God, please help me to listen for Your voice in my life and
to follow after You, relying on the love You have for me.

Kindness Leads to Repentance

Or do you show contempt for the riches of his kindness,
forbearance and patience, not realizing that God's
kindness is intended to lead you to repentance?
ROMANS 2:4 NIV

We can become so accustomed to God's kindness that we take it for granted. When we begin to take it for granted and expect it without gratitude, we begin to lose sight of the reason for His kindness. His kindness is to draw us to repentance. He is kind and patient with us so that we will reject our sin and shame and walk in His marvelous light.

Take a moment right now to reflect on the riches of His kindness and patience to you this week. What blessings did you skim past but now can thank Him for? Did you get somewhere early? Did you get to take a nice long shower? Did you get a good grade? Did you make a new friend? These may seem like regular, day-to-day things, but when you shift your perspective, you'll see that these are blessings from God that show His kindness!

. . . .

Lord God, You've shown me so many blessings this week that I simply
took for granted and failed to appreciate. I don't want to become
so blind to Your blessings that I become self-absorbed and sinful.
I want to recognize Your kindness and patience at all times! Amen.

Day 241
The Future Starts Now

All praise to God, the Father of our Lord Jesus Christ. It is by his great mercy that we have been born again, because God raised Jesus Christ from the dead. Now we live with great expectation, and we have a priceless inheritance—an inheritance that is kept in heaven for you, pure and undefiled, beyond the reach of change and decay.
1 PETER 1:3–4 NLT

The Message paraphrase of these verses says, "Because Jesus was raised from the dead, we've been given a brand-new life and have everything to live for, including a future in heaven—and the future starts now!"

Heaven is real and waiting and glorious! Your inheritance is waiting there for you. God's Word promises that His chosen ones (you!) will live eternally with Him in heaven where " 'He will wipe every tear from their eyes. There will be no more death' or mourning or crying or pain, for the old order of things has passed away" (Revelation 21:4 NIV).

But you don't have to wait for heaven to start living a victorious and joyful life. The future starts now! As you walk closely with Jesus, He shows you the path of life and fills you with joy in His presence (Psalm 16:11).

. . . .

God, I'm so thankful that You're with me,
filling me with joy now and forever.

Day 242

Thank God for His Compassion!

You, O Lord, are a compassionate and merciful God.
You are patient, always faithful and ready to forgive.
PSALM 86:15 GW

How many times has God given you second chances? Too many to count, right? Have you ever wondered why He's so compassionate and merciful? Why He's always patient and ready to forgive? It's in His nature, girl! And because you're created in His image, it's in your nature too. He wants you to treat others that way.

Think of it this way: If you had a toddler who kept bumping into things and breaking them, would you continue to scold? No doubt you would remove the items and then train the child—with love and compassion leading the way. Your ultimate goal wouldn't be the things but the child. That's how love works!

God is that loving parent. He's compassionate. He wants the best for you. And even when you bump into things and make a mess, He's not mad. He just moves them over, hugs you, and says, "Try again, girl!"

. . . .

Thank You, Jesus, for your compassion and mercy! I don't know why you keep forgiving me for the mess-ups, but I'm so glad You do. Amen.

Promises and Thanks

*You are being kept by the power of God because you
put your trust in Him and you will be saved from
the punishment of sin at the end of the world.*

1 Peter 1:5 nlv

Wow! What a promise! When you decided to follow Jesus, you became
God's child. And the Bible says, "He cares about you [with deepest
affection, and watches over you very carefully]" (1 Peter 5:7 amp).

Think about that for a minute. How does it make you feel that
God cares about you deeply and watches over you very carefully?
That you are being kept and held by the power of God? Consider
writing these thoughts down in your journal.

Spend some time in prayer now, thanking God for being with
you and watching over you. Praise Him for His deep love for you.
Honor Him in your heart and mind. Thank Him for saving you from
the punishment of sin and preparing a place for you in heaven. Tell
Him how you feel about all of that.

God calls you His! Lift your heart to Him in worship.

* *

*Lord God, I'm grateful to be called Yours!
I worship and honor You today.*

Living in Fellowship with God

*And we know that the Son of God has come, and he has given us
understanding so that we can know the true God. And now we live
in fellowship with the true God because we live in fellowship with
his Son, Jesus Christ. He is the only true God, and he is eternal life.*

1 JOHN 5:20 NLT

The Bible makes it clear that God has made Himself known to us
through His creation. Signs of God are everywhere. Miracles are
everywhere. We are without excuse when it comes to believing that
intelligent design is behind every natural wonder.

Jesus Christ is the one true God. He proved it by coming alive
after He was put to death. Everything He ever said was and is true.
Isaiah 42:5–6 (NLT) says, "God, the LORD, created the heavens and
stretched them out. He created the earth and everything in it. He
gives breath to everyone, life to everyone who walks the earth. And
it is he who says, 'I, the LORD, have called you to demonstrate my
righteousness. I will take you by the hand and guard you.'"

. . . .

*Jesus, my one true God, I'm amazed that You want to take me by the
hand and guide me forever. Thank You for giving me eternal life!*

You're a Conqueror

*Little children, you can be certain that you belong to God
and have conquered them, for the One who is living in
you is far greater than the one who is in the world.*

1 JOHN 4:4 TPT

There have been times in my life when I've felt like David when he was a young man facing Goliath. My Goliaths have never been a giant on a battlefield, and yours haven't either. Our Goliaths are the things we face that are much bigger than we could conquer on our own. My Goliaths have been things like depression, anxiety, broken relationships, and financial difficulty. Perhaps you've had the same Goliaths as I have.

This verse has always been a source of hope for me and can bring hope to you as well. We are told that we belong to God and have conquered the things of this world that are not of Him. He is greater than the enemy, and He is greater than the things of the world. God is greater than depression, anxiety, friendship troubles, financial strain, school headaches, and any other hard thing you might experience. Ask Him to deliver you today from the Goliaths you are facing. He is stronger than any giant you encounter!

* *

*Lord, You are the conqueror who has overcome anything
I could face. The enemy wants to steal, kill, and destroy.
He wants to bring me down and make me afraid. I won't be
afraid of the things I face because I know that I have a God
who is bigger than anything that comes against me!*

New Every Morning

This I remember, and so I have hope. It is because of the Lord's
loving-kindness that we are not destroyed for His loving-pity
never ends. It is new every morning. He is so very faithful.
LAMENTATIONS 3:21–23 NLV

Have you ever noticed that a brand-new day puts new hope in your heart? Say you spent all day Tuesday fretting over a situation with a friend. But then randomly, you woke up on Wednesday morning and it was the farthest thing from your mind. Somehow, in the night, you let it go.

God wants to remind you today that His mercies are new every single morning. Every day is a fresh start, a chance to begin again. (That's 365 second chances a year, for those who are keeping track!)

It should give you hope to know that the Creator of the universe knows how to recreate your heart every single day. And He does so out of loving-kindness toward you. Each new morning, He glances down at you with love in His eyes and says, *"I'm crazy about this one!"* Then with great joy, He offers a fresh, new start.

. . . .

I'm so grateful for new chances and new days, Lord.
Bye-bye yesterday. Glad you're gone! Amen.

Day 247

Be Like the Holy One

Get your minds ready for good use. Keep awake. Set your hope now and forever on the loving-favor to be given you when Jesus Christ comes again. Be like children who obey. Do not desire to sin like you used to when you did not know any better. Be holy in every part of your life. Be like the Holy One Who chose you.

1 PETER 1:13–15 NLV

These are some really important scriptures as a child of God. Jesus is coming soon! Are you ready? It's easy to get distracted with growing up and friends and school and endless activity. But remember that God has a special plan for your life. Set your mind and your hope on Jesus as you go through life. God calls you to obey. He wants you to be holy in all you do.

Whoa! That sounds hard. How is it possible to be holy in every part of your life? Remember that the Holy Spirit lives inside you, guiding you, teaching you, counseling you, and prompting you to follow Jesus in everything. He'll help you make decisions that honor God. He'll give you wisdom when you ask.

• •

Lord, I want to be like You. Fill me with Your Spirit and help me to listen and obey.

God Cares for You

*I will instruct you and teach you in the way you should
go; I will counsel you with my eye upon you.*
PSALM 32:8 ESV

Here's your daily reminder that God loves you! He is near. He cares
about the things that are on your heart and mind. Check out these
awesome scriptures that show how much God cares about you:

- "The LORD is close to the brokenhearted and saves those
  who are crushed in spirit" (Psalm 34:18 NIV).

- "Even though I am afflicted and needy, still the Lord
  takes thought and is mindful of me. You are my help and
  my rescuer. O my God, do not delay" (Psalm 40:17 AMP).

- "You keep track of all my sorrows. You have collected all
  my tears in your bottle. You have recorded each one in
  your book" (Psalm 56:8 NLT).

- "Cast all your anxiety on him because he cares for you"
  (1 Peter 5:7 NIV).

God cares deeply about you, friend! He will lead you, watch
over you, and give you the very best advice. You can trust Him with
your whole heart.

. . . .

*God, thank You for Your love and care for me!
Please plant these scriptures in my heart so that I never forget.*

Until You're Old and Gray

"I will be your God throughout your lifetime—
until your hair is white with age. I made you, and I will
care for you. I will carry you along and save you."
Isaiah 46:4 nlt

It may be hard to imagine, but one day you will be old and have gray hair. You will be weaker than you are now, and slower too. God promises that no matter how old, weak, or slow you get, He will *always* be by your side. He will care for you and guide you in His path for your life. Not even age can separate you from Him.

As a young lady who is just beginning her life, you have so much promise ahead of you! God will be with you throughout your entire lifetime. No other friend or family member can be with you for as long as He can and will be! How beautiful that God is not only your Father but your friend and that He will always be right with you!

· ·

Father God, thank You for never leaving my side.
Right now, I can't even imagine being an old woman, but
I can trust that even when I am elderly, You will be the same
God You are to me today. I look forward to the deep relationship
I will have with You then—formed over decades together.

Day 250

Forget about It!

Forget what happened in the past,
and do not dwell on events from long ago.
ISAIAH 43:18 GW

"Just forget about it!"

Maybe you've heard those words. Maybe you've spoken them. Imagine you've borrowed a pen from the girl who sits next to you in your Spanish class. She asks about it the following day, but you realize you must have lost it somewhere. When you tell her, she says, "Oh, don't worry about it! Just forget about it!"

It's not a big deal to her. In fact, she really doesn't care at all.

That's how you should view your past, girl. It's behind you now. It's in the rearview mirror. Sure, you messed up. You were a different person back then. But now? Now you're focused on today and aiming toward tomorrow. You don't have time to get bogged down in all of the junk from yesterday.

Forget about it.

Sure, it matters. And yes, there might be some consequences. But don't let guilt and condemnation rob you of the joy of today. Jesus wants His girls to walk with a forward posture, not a backward one!

· ·

I won't keep looking back over my shoulder, Jesus. I'm so grateful for Your forgiveness. Thanks for helping me let go of my yesterdays. Amen.

Day 251

A Good Father

You call out to God for help and he helps—he's a good Father that way. But don't forget, he's also a responsible Father, and won't let you get by with sloppy living. Your life is a journey you must travel with a deep consciousness of God. It cost God plenty to get you out of that dead-end, empty-headed life you grew up in. He paid with Christ's sacred blood, you know.

1 Peter 1:17–19 MSG

God is a good dad. He's not only good; He's perfect. He will never sin against you. He always gets it right. He sees the beginning of your life, all the way to the end. He sees what you can't. That's why trusting Him is so important. You can obey Him wholeheartedly. He wants the very best for your life.

Would a good dad let you go on hurting yourself through sin and bad choices? No, parents have a responsibility to correct and discipline their children. God, the perfect parent, disciplines those He loves too (Hebrews 12:6).

The good news is that God doesn't guilt and shame you. He wants you to repent by coming to Him and allowing Him to change your heart.

· ·

Lord, show me anything in my life that doesn't honor You. I want You to have my whole heart. Thanks for being the very best dad!

The Perfect Inheritance

*We are reborn into a perfect inheritance that can never
perish, never be defiled, and never diminish. It is promised
and preserved forever in the heavenly realm for you!*

1 PETER 1:4 TPT

Imagine finding an envelope in the mail one day with a letter saying
you had a distant aunt who left you her entire fortune in her will. If
you're anything like me, you'd have an easy time spending all that
cash on the things you've wanted and needed. You might tithe some,
give some to family and friends, and save some, but in any case, you'd
find a use for all of it!

Now take a moment to realize that you are the heir to the greatest fortune in history. You are receiving the perfect inheritance of
God's kingdom! This inheritance is one that can never diminish or
dwindle, even if you share it with everyone you know! God promises
it to you, and He even gives you access to His kingdom while you're
here on earth!

. . . .

*Father God, I'm so amazed that You chose me to be part of
Your family. I thank You that I am an heir to Your kingdom.
Give me the boldness to share my inheritance with others so that
they too can have access to You and Your gift of eternal life.*

He Came to Save, Not Condemn

Whenever our heart condemns us, God is greater than our heart, and he knows everything.
1 JOHN 3:20 ESV

You've tried to let it go, but it's driving you crazy. That thing you did. . .you can't stop thinking about it. Yes, you've already confessed it. Yes, Jesus has forgiven you. The people you've hurt are working hard to forgive you too. But you're having a hard time forgiving yourself. How did you mess up like that? You knew better.

Guilt is a tricky thing. It wraps its tentacles around you and tries to keep you from moving forward. But here's the truth: if you've truly asked God to forgive you for what you did and if you're making an effort to make things right with the people you hurt, you have to forgive yourself.

That's easier said than done, for sure. But you have to try. Don't let the enemy consume your thoughts with negative self-chatter. It's so pointless, and it weighs you down. Instead, proclaim, "I'm set free from that!" as you move forward. God has a lot for you to do. So no self-condemnation, girl.

. . . .

It's hard, Jesus, but I'll do my best to forgive myself. I'm truly sorry for what I did. Help me do better next time. Amen.

Day 254

Growing Up

*So get rid of all evil behavior. Be done with all deceit,
hypocrisy, jealousy, and all unkind speech. Like newborn babies,
you must crave pure spiritual milk so that you will grow into
a full experience of salvation. Cry out for this nourishment,
now that you have had a taste of the Lord's kindness.*

1 PETER 2:1–3 NLT

Peter has some direct commands to share: Stop every form of evil. Don't lie or be jealous. Say nice things! Pretty clear, right? These apply to Christians today too. You may think this should be easy for Christians, right? But many people struggle with jealousy, and it can be hard to say nice things to a crabby teenage brother sometimes!

Like newborn babies who need their mamas, you need the Holy Spirit to help you grow as a child of God. You're never alone as you try to do the right thing. God is good and kind, and He helps you carry out His will through His Spirit who is alive and at work in you!

. . . .

*God, thank You for Your kindness to me. Thanks for giving me Your
Spirit to help me know right from wrong and to grow up in You!*

Instruct and Guide Me

I hear the Lord saying, "I will stay close to you, instructing and guiding you along the pathway for your life. I will advise you along the way and lead you forth with my eyes as your guide. So don't make it difficult; don't be stubborn when I take you where you've not been before. Don't make me tug you and pull you along. Just come with me!"
PSALM 32:8–9 TPT

What a promise we find in these two verses! The Lord promises that He will be by your side to lead and instruct you on the path for your life! His eyes will be your guide! Wow! This is the type of faith and dependence on God that we all need. We need to walk in such a way that each step we take is guided by His voice.

As He leads you today, don't be like a stubborn donkey that has to be pulled and tugged along. Be a willing follower. His plan for you is a million times better than what you could conjure up for your own life. Trust Him as He guides you. The journey might be scary sometimes, but it always leads to a better and more peaceful way of living!

· ·

*Father God, give me strength to be a willing follower.
I want to trust You with all that I am and all that I have. Amen.*

Beauty Within

*Don't be concerned about the outward beauty of fancy hairstyles,
expensive jewelry, or beautiful clothes. You should clothe yourselves
instead with the beauty that comes from within, the unfading
beauty of a gentle and quiet spirit, which is so precious to God.*

1 PETER 3:3–4 NLT

Peter talked about beauty at the beginning of 1 Peter 3. In that time period, wealthy women would spend hours having their hair braided intricately and being dressed by their servants. Peter said that beauty comes from the inside, and that is a message we all need to be reminded of.

God gave you your body purposefully. You devalue God's creation when you turn from your mirror in disgust. Get in the habit of thanking God for every part of your amazing body. Even the parts you don't like. As you look in the mirror, begin thanking God for every part of you. That your eyes can see. That your ears can hear. That your teeth can chew to keep you healthy. Instead of feeling defeated by the flaws you see, ask God to help you take good care of the body He gave you, and trust in faith that He will.

. . . .

*Creator God, help me to see myself as You see
me: beautiful from the inside out.*

Well-Known

You know what I am going to say even before I say it, Lord. You go
before me and follow me. You place your hand of blessing on my head.
PSALM 139:4–5 NLT

Psalm 139 begins: "O Lord, you have searched me [thoroughly]
and have known me! You know when I sit down and when I rise
up.... You understand my thought from afar. You scrutinize my path
and my lying down, and You are intimately acquainted with all my
ways" (verses 1–3 AMP).

Girl, you are well-known and valued by your Father in heaven.
He cherishes you and delights in you. Whenever you are feeling far
from God, open your Bible to Psalm 139. Read it slowly and allow
God's Word to fill you with His love and truth.

. . . .

Heavenly Father, I'm so glad I can come to You with all
my thoughts and feelings because You know them already.
Thanks for loving me and helping me sort everything out.

God Has Your Back

What then shall we say to these things?
If God is for us, who can be against us?
Romans 8:31 esv

There is a story of a boy who was being bullied at school. He finally told his family about it at dinner one night. As he shared, his older brother sat quietly and took in the story. The next day at school, the bully approached the little boy and began to taunt him again. The little boy stood up to him, and suddenly the bully backed down and ran away. The little boy felt awfully proud of himself until he turned around and saw his older brother quietly standing behind him. It was the presence of the big brother that scared the bully away.

We are like that little boy. We are faced with the bullying tactics and taunting of the enemy and people in the world who don't know Christ. Yet we have a Defender standing right behind us. With God on our side, who can bring us harm? We have hope that no matter what happens in this life, we are backed by the Creator of the world! What an undeniably beautiful truth!

· ·

Jesus, because You are for me, I have nothing to fear!
Nothing the enemy throws my way can separate me
from You. I am held in Your arms in this life and for
eternity. Thank You for having my back. Amen.

Better Than Vitamins

For the Scriptures say, "If you want to enjoy life and see many happy days, keep your tongue from speaking evil and your lips from telling lies. Turn away from evil and do good. Search for peace, and work to maintain it. The eyes of the LORD watch over those who do right, and his ears are open to their prayers. But the LORD turns his face against those who do evil."

1 PETER 3:10–12 NLT

This little nugget of truth for life is tucked away in the book of 1 Peter, and it's better than your daily vitamin. Want to see happy days? Follow God's plan for your life! Verse 11 in the Amplified Bible explains it this way: "He must turn away from wickedness and do what is right. He must search for peace [with God, with self, with others] and pursue it eagerly [actively—not merely desiring it]."

God is watching over you, and His ears hear your prayers. He is with you, helping you to follow Him throughout your life. His Spirit prompts you to turn away from evil and to pursue God. This doesn't mean that life won't be hard sometimes. But it does mean that God will help you enjoy the life He gave you!

· ·

My happiness is found in You, Lord. Help me follow Your ways.

It Isn't Clear Yet

Dear friends, now we are God's children. What we will be isn't completely clear yet. We do know that when Christ appears we will be like him because we will see him as he is. So all people who have this confidence in Christ keep themselves pure, as Christ is pure.

1 JOHN 3:2–3 GW

Sometimes, like today's verse says, things just aren't clear yet. You wish you could see the road ahead, but there's a thick fog hanging overhead, and you're just not sure.

Imagine you're getting ready for school and you need to fix your hair and put on some makeup. You go to the bathroom mirror, but steam from the shower you took earlier has clouded it over. What do you do? You take your hand and swipe it across the mirror to clear the image.

Don't you wish you could do that with God? Don't you wish He would reveal everything all at once? (Have you ever wondered why He doesn't?)

He loves you, girl. And He wants you to know that, little by little, you're becoming more like Him. It's not going to happen overnight. But with every right choice you make, the image in the mirror is becoming clearer. The fog on the road is lifting. You're on the path to holiness, and it's looking good on you, girl!

. . . .

Lord, I don't even know how or why You keep forgiving me and giving me second chances. But I do know You're working in me. And one day I'll see it all clearly. Until then, I will trust You! Amen.

Day 261

The Bible Is God's Word, for Real

All of Scripture is God-breathed; in its inspired voice, we hear useful teaching, rebuke, correction, instruction, and training for a life that is right.

2 TIMOTHY 3:16 VOICE

It has become a popular lie to say that the Bible is just a book written by men about God. The enemy is trying to convince the world that the Word of God is not truly God's words written down by men. This lie has convinced many that Scripture can be flawed, untrue, and not a real authority over our lives. Paul knew, even during his time, that this lie would be spread about Scripture, and he headed it off with this verse.

All of Scripture is God-breathed and is for our instruction and training for living a holy life, set apart for God. We can trust the Bible as God's true Word about life, about love, and about ourselves. The Bible is not a list of dos and don'ts meant to keep us from having fun. That's the beauty of it—the Bible is a gift from God to teach us how to live in a way that honors Him and ourselves! As you read your Bible, remember that it is God's Word written just for you to be in a right relationship with Him!

. . . .

Father God, give me a hunger to know Your Word and to find the deeper meaning in every verse. Reveal Your heart to me through Scripture. I want to know You more! Amen.

Day 262
Get Ready!

*But in your hearts revere Christ as Lord. Always be prepared
to give an answer to everyone who asks you to give the reason for
the hope that you have. But do this with gentleness and respect,
keeping a clear conscience, so that those who speak maliciously against
your good behavior in Christ may be ashamed of their slander.*

1 PETER 3:15–16 NIV

If you love God and treat other people with kindness, people are
going to wonder what makes you different. They may even ask you
questions about why you act the way you do. Get ready to share!

Some people will disagree with your faith in unkind ways. But
before you get angry, ask for God's help. He is right there with you,
and He sees everything that's happening. He wants you to answer
with gentleness and respect, not anger and embarrassment.

The reason people ask is because they are looking for hope too!
And they want to know if yours is real or not!

. . . .

*God, help me remember that everyone else is looking for
hope in You too. You created them that way. Help me be
gentle and respect others when I share my faith in You.*

His Searchlight
Is on Your Heart

*Search me, O God, and know my heart! Try me and
know my thoughts! And see if there be any grievous
way in me, and lead me in the way everlasting!*

PSALM 139:23–24 ESV

Have you ever heard the expression, "You can run, but you can't hide!"? It's true. God will always find you out. And just because you haven't shared something openly with a friend or loved one doesn't mean no one knows it. God searches your heart and sees all.

Maybe that idea creeps you out. You kind of wish He couldn't see inside your heart. After all, you've had some not-so-nice thoughts go through there. Some ugliness has taken up residence in some of your heart's chambers over the years.

God is searching, like a janitor with a broom in hand. He wants to sweep out the cobwebs, the dust bunnies. If He finds anything that might cause trouble, He sweeps it up, bit by bit. He won't leave anything behind.

Why? Because He adores you. He wants His girls to have clean hands and pure hearts! He wants to set you free from the pain of hanging on to the icky stuff. He's a master cleaner. No doubt about it.

· ·

Come on in and clean up, Jesus! I'm ready. Amen.

Becoming His Poetry

*We have become his poetry, a re-created people that will fulfill
the destiny he has given each of us, for we are joined to Jesus,
the Anointed One. Even before we were born, God planned in
advance our destiny and the good works we would do to fulfill it!*

EPHESIANS 2:10 TPT

Can you believe that God has given you a destiny through Jesus?
That, even before you were born, God knew the course of your life
and the way you would live it out? He knew the good works you
would do in His name! You are His *poetry*, the beautiful words He
has written. How incredible is it that God sees you this way?

Honor Him with your words and the things you do. Not only
were you created in the image of God from your mother's womb,
but you've been *re-created* in the image of Christ—a holy daughter
of the King! When you received Christ as your Lord and Savior,
you inherited a new identity. Ask God for the direction He has for
you; His way is so much higher than ours!

. . . .

*Lord God, I find it so amazing that you wrote my life story as Your
poetry. You have designed a perfect plan for my life, and I want to live
it out to honor You. Give me the direction I need today and every day.*

Love Lasts

The end of all things is near. Therefore be alert and of sober mind so that you may pray. Above all, love each other deeply, because love covers over a multitude of sins.
1 PETER 4:7–8 NIV

"The end of all things is near." This sounds like a quote from *The Lord of the Rings* movies! But Jesus really is coming back. The Bible promises this is so. Epic movie series like *The Lord of the Rings* and *The Chronicles of Narnia* point to the restoration of our world and the return of our King.

So keep on praying and following Jesus along the way. Keep your focus on Jesus, and He will lead you in love. School, hobbies, careers, and possessions are given to you for the time being and can be used to share God's love—but love is the most important thing. We need to share the love of God with others while we await Jesus' return.

When you love others deeply and put their needs above your own, you are representing Christ to a world that desperately needs to be loved.

Lord, help me to keep my focus on You and not get too distracted by earthly things that pass away. Help me love others deeply. That's what lasts.

Day 266
Continually Renewed

You've become a new person. This new person is continually renewed in knowledge to be like its Creator.
COLOSSIANS 3:10 GW

Have you ever had a subscription to a magazine? They can be fun, but if you're not careful, the magazine company might set you up for an automatic renewal. That means they can charge your bank account every year, without your knowledge, so that you go on receiving new editions—whether you want them or not!

God has an automatic renewal policy too! He's making everything inside of you new. And tomorrow, it'll be new again. And the day after that too. Every day, He renews your life. He zaps you with fresh starts, new energy, new excitement to face the tasks ahead.

Today's verse from Colossians explains that you've become a new person. You're continually being renewed to be more like Jesus. Every minute of every hour of every day of every year. You're becoming more like Him. . .in increments!

Sure, you wish it could happen all at once, but here's the cool part: you're on a journey! And every day is an adventure as you become more like your heavenly Father.

. . . .

Thanks for taking me on the journey, Jesus!
I want to be more like You. Amen.

Favored and Blessed

And Mary sang this song: "My soul is ecstatic, overflowing with praises to God! My spirit bursts with joy over my life-giving God! For he set his tender gaze upon me, his lowly servant girl. And from here on, everyone will know that I have been favored and blessed."

LUKE 1:46–48 TPT

Can you imagine the joy that Mary felt knowing she was chosen by God for a holy purpose? You should be able to, because you too have been chosen by God for such a time as this! God has set His tender, loving gaze upon you and shown you His favor and blessings.

The Holy One of Israel, the God of all creation, has set His tender gaze on you. He calls you beautiful and worthy, friend! We can never know the extent of His love for us, and yet we could not exist without it! Take a page out of Mary's book and sing a song of thankfulness to God right now for the ways that He has shown you His favor!

. . . .

Father God, I have a song of gratitude in my heart and on my lips for the way that You have looked on me, a teen girl like Mary, with Your tender gaze and love. You have blessed me beyond what I ever could have imagined! Thank You, Lord! Amen.

God's Temple

*Don't you know that you yourselves are God's temple
and that God's Spirit dwells in your midst?*
1 Corinthians 3:16 niv

When you commit your life to Christ, His Spirit miraculously comes to live inside you, and you become a temple of the Holy Spirit. The secular (non-Christian) dictionary defines *temple* like this: "a building for religious practice."

First Corinthians 6:19–20 (niv) says: "Do you not know that your bodies are temples of the Holy Spirit, who is in you, whom you have received from God? You are not your own; you were bought at a price. Therefore honor God with your bodies."

Isn't that amazing? Your very own body is a place where God Himself dwells! And as a dearly loved daughter of the King, God wants you to honor Him in your body. You are loved and set apart for a purpose. God wants to help you keep His temple pure and healthy. You don't have to manage all that in your own strength, though! Being a temple of the Holy Spirit is a big responsibility, and God Himself will give you the strength and power you need to do what He asks.

. . . .

*God, help me to honor You in my body. Give me the
strength and power to keep Your temple pure.*

He's Doing a New Thing

"Forget the former things; do not dwell on the past. See, I am doing a new thing! Now it springs up; do you not perceive it? I am making a way in the wilderness and streams in the wasteland."

ISAIAH 43:18–19 NIV

Have you ever felt that the things in your past define who you are? You can probably recall times when you have made a mistake and it impacted a friendship, ruined your reputation, or caused your parents to lose their trust in you. It feels terrible to walk out the consequences of a mistake. However, God says that the old things have passed away. Those mistakes you've made? They don't define you!

God says He is making a way in the wilderness and streams in the desert! He can create something new and beautiful from those mistakes. Learn from the mistakes you've made; ask God to help you correct them and grow from them. But don't let your past determine how you view yourself. Only God can define your worth, and He calls you worthy!

. . . .

Jesus, thank You for not seeing me through the lens of my sin, guilt, or mistakes. I rest in the promise that I am worthy of Your love. I want to define myself by Your truth and find my identity in You alone. Help me remember that You make me worthy today and every day! Amen.

Abilities and Pride

So humble yourselves under the mighty power of God,
and at the right time he will lift you up in honor.
1 PETER 5:6 NLT

Are you awesome at basketball and other sports? Do you have a beautiful singing voice? Or maybe gymnastics is your thing. Whatever gifts and talents you have, it's okay to be confident in your skills and giftedness. God has given you those gifts for a purpose.

But God doesn't want you to be prideful about those gifts and abilities. Romans 12:3 (NLT) says, "Don't think you are better than you really are. Be honest in your evaluation of yourselves, measuring yourselves by the faith God has given us."

Your gifts can be used for God, to bring Him attention and glory, or they can be used to bring attention and glory to yourself. Which one will you choose? Here's the thing: people who brag about their talents usually don't have a lot of real friends. People who bring attention to Jesus have an inner joy that comes from loving Him. The choice is yours to make.

. . . .

Lord, I'm thankful for the talents You've given me.
I commit them to You. Let them bring You attention and glory.

Day 271
Blotted Out

Change the way you think and act,
and turn to God to have your sins removed.
ACTS 3:19 GW

Picture an artist working on a painting. He's almost done when he accidentally spills a can of paint across his canvas. His whole painting is now buried under the big blob. Awful!

When something is covered by something else, you can't see what was there originally. That's how it is when your sins are covered by the blood of Jesus. You can't see them, and He can't see them either! They've been blotted out.

You have to trust His work on the cross, girl. When you feel like your sins are still there, trust Him that they're gone. And while you're at it, go ahead and change the way you think and act. This is an important part of the equation. It wouldn't make sense to keep coming back to Him for a repeat performance of the same sin. (How awkward would that be?)

Let Him blot out your sin once and for all. When it's gone, you'll have a fresh start, an amazing do-over. That's how much He loves you, girl!

. . . .

Thank You for blotting out my sin, Jesus!
It's washed away, never to be seen again.
Help me live a life that's pleasing to You. Amen.

Always Be Praying

Pray always. Pray in the Spirit. Pray about everything in
every way you know how! And keeping all this in mind,
pray on behalf of God's people. Keep on praying feverishly,
and be on the lookout until evil has been stayed.

EPHESIANS 6:18 VOICE

I don't know about you, but when I begin to pray, all the anxieties and worries of the day begin to lift off my shoulders. I feel light as air and can smile and find God's peace even in the midst of the hardest times I've ever experienced.

The apostle Paul was encouraging the Ephesians, and us today, to pray all the time, about everything, in every way we know how. When we pray about all things, big or small, we build a stronger and deeper relationship with God. A relationship that can weather storms. Through knowing Christ, we come to know who we are as coheirs with Him. And that, friend, is beautiful.

. . . .

Father God, remind me to come to You with everything
I face. You don't mind if it's big or small, You care
about everything I bring to You in prayer. Let me be
diligent to pray for others, myself, my future, the global
church—remind me to pray for it all! Amen.

Tricks of the Enemy

*Stay alert! Watch out for your great enemy, the devil.
He prowls around like a roaring lion, looking for someone to
devour. Stand firm against him, and be strong in your faith.
Remember that your family of believers all over the world
is going through the same kind of suffering you are.*

1 PETER 5:8–9 NLT

Even though the enemy knows he has already ultimately been defeated by Jesus, he's still trying his best to get into your head and discourage you so that you won't be able to live well for God. That's why Jesus wants you to stay alert. Don't fall for Satan's tricks; he's the father of lies (John 8:44).

Remember that James 4:7 (AMP) says, "So submit to [the authority of] God. Resist the devil [stand firm against him] and he will flee from you." You have power in the name of Jesus to get rid of any evil you come up against.

You don't have to be afraid, just alert. Don't focus on fear of the enemy. Focus on Jesus and His power to fight your battles!

. . . .

*Lord, You have given me everything I need to live my life for You.
Help me to stay alert and not fall for any of the enemy's tricks.*

Day 274

The Greatest Is Love

Now these three remain: faith, hope and love.
But the greatest of these is love.

1 CORINTHIANS 13:13 NIV

Because God sees you as His worthy child, He's poured out awesome gifts on you. (Hey, if He didn't think you deserved them, He wouldn't lavish them on you!)

You've been blessed with amazing relationships and many other blessings besides! He's taken care of your needs from the time you arrived on the planet until now, and He doesn't plan to stop anytime soon. But if you took every single thing He's ever given you—every single one—there would be *one* that would sit at the top of the list.

Love.

Love trumps everything. Literally, everything. It trumps joy. It trumps hope. It trumps financial blessings, healings, and anything else you could imagine. Why is love the most valuable of all the gifts? Because it was love that sent Jesus to the cross. It was love that convinced Him to come as a babe in a manger. It was love that caused Him to lay down His life for you. If not for love, none of the other gifts would bring fulfillment or peace. Everything else hangs on this one word: love.

· ·

I get it, Jesus. You gave the greatest gift when You gave Yourself.
Nothing else even comes close. I'm so grateful! Amen.

Delight in Him

Trust in the LORD and do good; dwell in the land
and enjoy safe pasture. Take delight in the LORD,
and he will give you the desires of your heart.
PSALM 37:3–4 NIV

What are the desires of your heart? Take a moment right now to reflect on your deepest desires. You may have certain hopes and dreams mapped out that will take years to see happen. These desires and passions are things that God has put in your heart. They are hopes and dreams that align with His plan for your life.

Trust in His plan and His faithfulness. When you take delight in serving God and following His will as He has laid it out in His Word, you will begin to see those desires take shape and become a reality. His plans and ways are so much better than ours. You can trust Him to have your best in mind all the time. Don't worry when things seem to fall out of place; God knows exactly what He is doing. Trust Him completely!

. . . .

Father God, I trust Your plan for my life. I know You have made
a "safe pasture" for me to rest in—it's the safety of Your will
for me. Show me how to delight in Your Word, and direct the
desires of my heart to align with Your desires for me. Amen.

Anytime Now

*The Lord isn't really being slow about his promise, as some
people think. No, he is being patient for your sake. He does not
want anyone to be destroyed, but wants everyone to repent.*

2 PETER 3:9 NLT

The Bible tells us that Jesus is coming back for all of us who love
Him so that we can be with Him forever. James 5:7 (MSG) says,
"Meanwhile, friends, wait patiently for the Master's Arrival. . . . Stay
steady and strong. The Master could arrive at any time."

Many people wonder why Jesus hasn't come back already and
removed all the bad things from this world. The Bible has an answer
for that: God loves us, and He wants everyone to trust Him. So He is
patient, giving people more time than they deserve to make a choice
for Christ. His timing is perfect, and He knows exactly what He's
doing. He wants people to repent and turn back to Him.

While we wait for Jesus' return, God wants us to be steady and
strong in our faith.

*God, please help me to be steady and strong as I wait
for Jesus' return. Help me to share Your love with
friends and family who need to know about You.*

The God Who Sees You

Then she called the name of the LORD who spoke to her,
"You are God Who Sees"; for she said, "Have I not even
here [in the wilderness] remained alive after seeing Him
[who sees me with understanding and compassion]?"

GENESIS 16:13 AMP

There was a young Egyptian girl in the Bible named Hagar who was a servant of Abram's wife, Sarai. Sadly, Sarai thought God needed help delivering on some of His promises, and she used and abused Hagar in the process.

Hagar was so upset that she ran away from Abram and Sarai. In Genesis 16, we see that an angel of the Lord was sent to Hagar to comfort her and give her hope and direction. He found her alone in the desert. Hagar was amazed that God cared about her—an Egyptian servant-girl! She named God the "God Who Sees Me."

God sees you too, dear one. He cares about your struggles and your concerns. He cares about your hopes and dreams. He planted many of them inside you, after all. Go to Him about everything. You will never be rejected.

. . . .

God, I believe You see me. Thanks for caring about what's on my heart.

Day 278

Rescued!

*For he has rescued us from the dominion of darkness
and brought us into the kingdom of the Son he loves,
in whom we have redemption, the forgiveness of sins.*

COLOSSIANS 1:13–14 NIV

Beautiful friend, you are the daughter of the King! You share an inheritance with Christ Jesus—the kingdom of God here on earth and in heaven. You received this special status without doing anything to deserve it. You were not born into it. You were not elected or specially trained for it. You were rescued into this inheritance by Christ's sacrifice on the cross.

No one wants to imagine a life without Christ once they've been born again into His family. It is a dark life, full of shame and regret. We once were in the dominion of darkness, but now we've been brought into a marvelous light! We are redeemed, our sins forgiven! The beauty of forgiveness is that it is limitless. You will still come up short, you will still sin, you will still do things that hurt the heart of the Father. Yet the forgiveness He offers you never runs out. So much freedom can be found in knowing that we can be forgiven whenever we need it!

. . . .

*Thank You, Lord, for Your never-ending forgiveness!
Thank You for rescuing me from my sin and offering me new life
in Christ. I am proud to be a daughter of the King of kings!*

No Rock like Our God!

*No one is holy like the LORD! There is no one
besides you; there is no Rock like our God.*

1 SAMUEL 2:2 NLT

No one compares to God. No king. No president. No pastor. No actor. No politician. No billionaire. Absolutely no one on planet earth who ever lived or who will ever live in the future can even come close.

Can any of them bring about world peace? Can any of them claim to save others? Can any say that they are truly holy? Absolutely not!

Can any of them provide comfort and shelter like God can? Can any of them remain steady as a rock when the world is shaking? Can any of those people rise from the dead? Definitely not!

There is no one like our God. He's worthy of your praise, no matter what you're facing. He alone is the Savior who gave His life for you. He'd do it again too if He had to. Who else would do that for you, girl?

No one but your rock, Jesus. He is above all, in all, and through all. . .and yet He would drop everything in an instant just to be with you.

. . . .

Thank You, Jesus! You stand alone. No one is holy like You. Amen.

Because of Jesus

*So then, dear friends, since you are looking
forward to this, make every effort to be found
spotless, blameless and at peace with him.*

2 PETER 3:14 NIV

Being spotless and blameless sounds like an impossible task, doesn't it? That's because it is. There is absolutely no way you can keep yourself spotless and blameless in your own strength. If you could, you wouldn't need Jesus, right? It's in Christ's strength alone that we are made holy.

When God looks at you, He sees you as spotless and blameless because Jesus took all of your sin and made you perfectly clean. That's how you have peace with God. The only way you can live a spotless and blameless life in this confusing world is in the power of Jesus Christ Himself. He's the one at work in you. When you get close to Him, He'll help you sort out the good from the sneaky and evil. Aligning yourself with Him and His Word daily is how you keep from being deceived by the enemy and the things of this world.

. . . .

*God, I know there is no way I can be spotless and
blameless on my own. I'm so thankful that You
see me as clean and pure because of Jesus.*

Confession

If we confess our sins, he is faithful and just and will forgive us our sins and purify us from all unrighteousness.

1 JOHN 1:9 NIV

We all mess up. It's part of being human. Sometimes you might be tempted to hide from God when you sin. I mean, that's what Adam and Eve did, right? But God wants you to come to Him instead. Talk to Him about it. Turn back to Him and trust Him to be faithful to you.

The Amplified Bible explains that God "will forgive our sins and cleanse us continually from all unrighteousness [our wrongdoing, everything not in conformity with His will and purpose]."

There is something very powerful about coming to God and confessing your sins to Him. He wants to cleanse you "continually." He wants to help you through your situation and give you peace. He wants to remind you of who you really are to Him.

Jesus already paid the price for your sin—once and for all on the cross. Your salvation is secure. And when you come to Him again when you've messed up, you get to clear the air. Your relationship with God gets deeper and stronger.

. . . .

Lord, thanks for being so faithful to me! I come to You with all my sin and ask that You would change me and restore our relationship.

Day 282

Unconditional Love

But God demonstrates his own love for us in this:
While we were still sinners, Christ died for us.
ROMANS 5:8 NIV

The most beautiful love is love that is unconditional. God demonstrated this pure, unconditional love for us when He sent His only Son, Jesus Christ, to die for our sins. Even though we were sinners and were unable to please God, He made a way for us to come into relationship with Him.

Can you imagine sacrificing your life or the life of someone you love for people who, at best, don't honor or respect you or who, at worst, completely hate you? This is what God did. Jesus sacrificed Himself for those who hated Him, for those who disobeyed His commands, and for those who did not even know who He was. What an awesome God, full of unconditional love! Truly, nothing is more beautiful than this.

. . . .

Father God, long before I ever knew the truth of Your love,
You sent Your only Son to die on the cross for my sin and shame.
You made the sacrifice of love so that I could be saved and be
in relationship with You. Thank You for this gift that is mine
simply by receiving it and becoming part of Your family!

Day 283

God's Correction

See what great love the Father has lavished on us, that we should be called children of God! And that is what we are!

1 JOHN 3:1 NIV

Our great God is a good Father. The very best. You may struggle with the way you are parented, but God parents perfectly. He always welcomes you with love and grace, even when you've made a mistake. He lavishes you with His love because You're His child. His correction is clear and kind; His discipline is loving and hope filled. He won't shame you.

The Bible tells us in Romans 2:4 that it is God's lovingkindness that brings us to repentance. Hebrews 12:8–11 (MSG) helps us understand this better: "Only irresponsible parents leave children to fend for themselves. Would you prefer an irresponsible God? We respect our own parents for training and not spoiling us, so why not embrace God's training so we can truly live? While we were children, our parents did what seemed best to them. But God is doing what is best for us, training us to live God's holy best."

. . . .

Thank You for parenting me perfectly, Father God.
I'm thankful that You care about the choices I make in life.
Thank You for seeing me and setting me on the right path.

Who Ya Gonna Call?

I call upon the LORD, who is worthy to be praised,
and I am saved from my enemies.
PSALM 18:3 ESV

Who do you call when you're in trouble? What's the first number you punch into your phone when you're in crisis mode? Your dad? Your mom? Your best friend? A leader from your church? No doubt a name came to mind right away as you read that question. You've got a short list of people you could count on to rescue you.

Here's a fun fact: God wants to be your first call. He wants you to remember that He, alone, is worthy. So call on Him. Cry out His name. He will sweep in and rescue you. He'll save you from your enemies. (Could anyone else do that? No way!)

His capabilities are so far beyond that of mere humans. Some people will come to your rescue in a pinch or offer great advice. But when it comes to the big stuff? Only God is able. Only God is willing. Only God is worthy.

Run to Him, girl. He's waiting with open arms.

· ·

I'm coming straight to You, Lord! You're my first call, and not just when I'm in trouble! I'm so honored to be Your kid! Amen.

Led Astray

Dear children, do not let anyone lead you astray.
1 JOHN 3:7 NIV

The Message paraphrases 1 John 3:7–8 like this: "So, my dear children, don't let anyone divert you from the truth. It's the person who acts right who is right, just as we see it lived out in our righteous Messiah. Those who make a practice of sin are straight from the Devil, the pioneer in the practice of sin. The Son of God entered the scene to abolish the Devil's ways."

Sometimes sin isn't easy to spot, right? The enemy can be very sneaky. That's called *insidious evil*, evil that's right in your face but you can't even see it. A good example is Rapunzel's mom. She kept her hidden away for her own selfish reasons, all the while pretending to love Rapunzel and be her mother.

That's a fairy tale, but it happens all the time in the real world. People say they are Christians, but they are selfish and dark on the inside. So how do you keep from being led astray? You stay close to Jesus. His Spirit who is at work in you will tell you right from wrong. If you are listening for Him in your life every day, you'll hear Him speaking.

. . . .

Jesus, please continue to speak to me. I want to stay close to You.

Let Them Hear It!

"But when I speak with you, I will open your mouth,
and you shall say to them, 'Thus says the Lord GOD.'
He who will hear, let him hear; and he who will refuse
to hear, let him refuse, for they are a rebellious house."

EZEKIEL 3:27 ESV

A beautiful part of being in God's family is sharing His truth with others in love. God will give you the words to speak to others to draw them to Him.

Is there someone in your life who is hungry to know more about God? God is giving you the wisdom to know how to speak to them and invite them into relationship with Him. Invite your friend to church or to a Bible study, or even give them a copy of this book and ask them to go through it with you. You know what a treasure it is to be in relationship with God, so share that treasure with others! Even if they're not quite ready to hear it, eventually they may be receptive to what you have to say about God's love!

. . . .

Lord God, open my eyes to see those in my life who are
hungry to know more about You. Give me the wisdom
to share Your truth with them in love and in a way they
will receive. Help me walk in Your truth. Amen.

Day 287

He Alone Is Worthy

They sang a new song, saying, "Worthy are you to take the scroll and to open its seals, for you were slain, and by your blood you ransomed people for God from every tribe and language and people and nation."

REVELATION 5:9 ESV

There's coming a day when death and sadness will end, when we'll all be safely in heaven with the one who created us. And when we're there, we'll see—once and for all—that the price Jesus paid on the cross was worth it, for all of mankind.

Today's verse gives us a glimpse into a story that will one day come to pass. Jesus, the spotless Lamb, will be given a scroll to open. And, as He opens it, all in attendance will be absolutely sure of one thing: only *He* is worthy to open it. None of them are able, but Jesus is! Only He is sinless, spotless, holy. And because of who He is, He's given sole permission to do what no one else can do.

Think of a jailer with a key to the cell. He's the only one trusted to keep it. Jesus is like that jailer, holding the keys in His hand. And He uses them to unlock the doors to our hearts.

. . . .

Jesus, You alone are worthy! No one even comes close. I worship You for who You are! Amen.

Day 288
A Thousand Words

Dear children, let's not merely say that we love each other; let us show the truth by our actions.
1 JOHN 3:18 NLT

Have you heard the saying "A picture is worth a thousand words"? Think about that for a minute. You could go on an amazing trip to another country and try to tell your friends about it over the phone, but no amount of words could help you explain the beauty. But a picture might! The picture still might not capture all the details, but it works a lot better than words sometimes.

That's a bit like this verse. You can say you love someone for years and years. But until you show them with your actions, the words don't mean much. Take chores, for example. Does anyone actually like them? Not really, but you do them because you are part of a family and you love your parents. Doing chores with a happy heart is one way to show your love.

What are some other ways you can show your love for someone with your actions? Talk to Jesus about this.

. . . .

Lord, help me love with my whole heart.
And help me show it with my actions.

Held

The Son is the image of the invisible God, the firstborn over all creation. For in him all things were created: things in heaven and on earth, visible and invisible, whether thrones or powers or rulers or authorities; all things have been created through him and for him. He is before all things, and in him all things hold together.

COLOSSIANS 1:15–17 NIV

These scriptures tell us some very amazing things about Jesus. Jesus is how we can see God. He made everything, and He holds the whole world together. He is more powerful than anything you can imagine; and yet He loves and cares for you.

Sometimes that can be hard to believe, but the Bible tells us it is true. And Jesus will show up and be very real in your life if you let Him. Have you invited Him in?

Jesus wants you to talk to Him about everything. Is there a problem you are facing that feels too big or too small for God? Talk to Him about it. Tell Him how you really feel. Let Him hold you in the palm of His hand.

. . . .

Lord, thank You for holding me together. I need You every day.

Chill Out

*If our hearts condemn us, we know that God is greater
than our hearts, and he knows everything.*
1 John 3:20 niv

Let's take a look at this verse in a few different translations and
paraphrases and see what we learn:

> Amplified Bible: "For God is greater than our heart and
> He knows all things [nothing is hidden from Him because
> we are in His hands]."

> *The Message*: "For God is greater than our worried hearts
> and knows more about us than we do ourselves."

> New Life Version: "Our heart may say that we have done
> wrong. But remember, God is greater than our heart. He
> knows everything."

> New Living Translation: "Even if we feel guilty, God is
> greater than our feelings, and he knows everything."

One Bible commentary suggests that John was talking to people
who were worried that they weren't doing enough for Jesus. And this
verse is a reminder that God knows our hearts better than we know
ourselves. So chill out. God will lead you to do what He wants you
to as long as you're listening for His voice and obeying Him.

- -

*Lord, You know my heart. I want to listen and obey. Lead me
to do what's right, and help me to leave my worries behind!*

God Is Your Strength

"There's no need to fear for I'm your God. I'll give you strength.
I'll help you. I'll hold you steady, keep a firm grip on you."
ISAIAH 41:10 MSG

When you read the verse above, did you think of something that you need God's strength to face? When you're facing a challenge, whether a troubled relationship or an issue with school, work, or your parents, you have God's reassurance that there is no need to fear.

God promises to give you strength. He promises to help you and hold you steady. Don't read this verse and assume its message was only for the people of the Old Testament. This promise is for you. Right here and now, God is promising to hold you up with His firm grip. Think back on that difficulty you are facing and imagine that you are facing it with God's help and strength. Knowing it is in His hands sure removes a lot of the fear and anxiety from the equation!

. . . .

Father God, You know all the difficulties I face. Nothing is hidden
from You. You know all the things that cause me anxiety, all the
things that make my heart feel heavy. I claim this promise today
that there is no need to fear, because You will give me strength.
Thank You for helping me and holding me steady. Amen.

Day 292

God's Favorite

And this is his commandment: We must believe in the name
of his Son, Jesus Christ, and love one another, just as he
commanded us. Those who obey God's commandments remain
in fellowship with him, and he with them. And we know
he lives in us because the Spirit he gave us lives in us.

1 JOHN 3:23–24 NLT

John was known as the disciple "Jesus loved." This never made sense to me (because didn't Jesus love all the disciples?) until I met Grammy B. She loved God deeply. And she was fond of often saying, "God loves you, but I'm His favorite." She had such a deep relationship with God that she felt like God's favorite daughter.

John wrote the books of 1 John and the Gospel of John. In John 13:23 (NIV), John wrote, "One of them, the disciple whom Jesus loved, was reclining next to him." If Grammy B had been writing a book, that's what she'd write too. God's love can make you feel like you're the only one in the world.

And that unmatched love pours out of us to everyone around us because of God's Spirit who lives in us.

. . . .

Lord, Your love is one of a kind. Thanks for pouring Your love into me.

Day 293

A Voice from Heaven

He was still speaking when a bright cloud overshadowed them.
Then a voice came out of the cloud and said, "This is my Son,
whom I love and with whom I am pleased. Listen to him!"
MATTHEW 17:5 GW

One of the first indicators that Jesus really was who He said He was came on the day He was baptized by John the Baptist. When He came up out of the water, a voice from heaven came out of a cloud and spoke over the group that had gathered there: *"This is my Son, whom I love and with whom I am pleased. Listen to him!"*

Whoa. Imagine if you had been in the crowd that day. How startling that must have been! And yet how convincing! You would never doubt that Jesus was the Savior of the world if His own Dad spoke up and told you so, after all.

Jesus got a great endorsement that day. And guess what? God's given you an endorsement too! He says that you are worthy because the Savior (His Son) died on the cross for you. So in a way, that proclamation from heaven included you too!

Cool, right?!

* *

I get it, Lord! When You said You were well pleased
with Your Son, You knew that He would one day die
on the cross for me. I'm so grateful He did! Amen.

Day 294

God Lives in You

If anyone acknowledges that Jesus is the Son of
God, God lives in them and they in God.
1 JOHN 4:15 NIV

God Himself chooses to live within you—what a wild thought! The Creator of the universe looked at you and thought you would make the perfect home for His Spirit to dwell within. It is through your obedience to God and your acknowledgment of Jesus as the Son of God and Savior of your life that you become part of His family.

God's goodness and beautiful character shine through you when He lives in you. You radiate His glory and shine His light to others. Nothing can separate you from His love, even when you fail. He pursues you every moment of the day. He delights in you! Remember who lives in your heart today and walk around with the knowledge that you are chosen, wanted, and loved. God's glory shining through you makes you even more beautiful than you already are!

. . . .

Holy Spirit, I'm always amazed when I remember that You choose me!
I don't always feel like the best vessel for You, but You say I am worthy
of Your love! I just want to spend time today praising You for being
holy, full of kindness, mercy, and grace. Bring to my mind worship
songs that I can sing to You to thank You for who You are. Amen.

Day 295
Look It Up!

Dear friends, do not believe everyone who claims to speak by the Spirit. You must test them to see if the spirit they have comes from God. For there are many false prophets in the world.
1 JOHN 4:1 NLT

The Message paraphrases this verse, "Don't believe everything you hear. Carefully weigh and examine what people tell you. Not everyone who talks about God comes from God. There are a lot of lying preachers loose in the world."

Remember that the enemy likes to trick people. And he's really good at it. He likes to deceive, and the Bible says that he even disguises himself as an angel of light (2 Corinthians 11:14).

Often, people who have been deceived like to take certain verses out of the Bible and use them to say what they want them to say. So always test what people say about God with His Word. Look it up. Find a study Bible or an online study Bible and find out what God's Word really says.

You have the Spirit of God right there in your heart, so if someone says something about God and it doesn't feel right, check it out.

. . . .

God, please give me wisdom about You.
Thank You that I have Your Spirit to guide me.

He Does No Wrong

He is a rock. What he does is perfect. All his ways are fair. He is a faithful God, who does no wrong. He is honorable and reliable.
DEUTERONOMY 32:4 GW

Today's verse is so powerful, and it can only be used to describe one person: your heavenly Father. Who else could be called a rock? Who else is perfect? Who else is always fair? Who else is always faithful? Who else does no wrong? Who else displays honor and reliability at all times? Only God. He's in a class of His own! No one even comes close.

When you need a rock (a defender), call on Him.

When others let you down, He never will.

When others treat you unfairly, He's 100 percent fair.

When others are unfaithful, He's sticking with you till the end.

This is your trustworthy, holy Father. And best of all, He created you—His worthy daughter—to be like Him. So do your best to live up to these high standards. Be fair. Be faithful. Be honorable. Be reliable. In other words, be just like Him.

. . . .

I want to be more like You, Jesus! Help me, I pray. Amen.

Corrected for Holiness

Our parents corrected us for a time as seemed good to them, but God only corrects us to our good so that we may share in His holiness.
HEBREWS 12:10 VOICE

Being corrected or disciplined is never a *fun* experience. None of us likes to find out that we did something wrong, even inadvertently. Yet we know that when our parents, teachers, or other leaders correct us, they are usually doing it for our good. Still, our parents and other authority figures are human, and sometimes they miss the mark in their correction.

The author of Hebrews reminds us that anytime God corrects us, however, it is always for our good. It is so that we can be made holy and drawn into closer communion with Him. If you are convicted about something you've been doing, listen to the Holy Spirit's correction. Turn away from that sin and reconnect with the Lord in repentance. He corrects in love, and when you respond in love and humility, you are brought closer to Him!

. . . .

Father God, I don't like to be convicted. I get that sick feeling in the pit of my stomach, and I feel ashamed. I know You can't dwell in the same place as sin. I want to clean my heart and mind from any sin that I've let take up space there. Please forgive me and draw me closer to You every day. Amen.

Jesus Is Greater

Little children, you are from God and have overcome them,
for he who is in you is greater than he who is in the world.
1 JOHN 4:4 ESV

Do you have a certain fear that you struggle with on a regular basis? Maybe it's getting up in front of people or being alone. Maybe you struggle with nightmares or being alone in the dark.

Philippians 2:10 (NIV) says, "At the name of Jesus every knee should bow, in heaven and on earth and under the earth." Jesus is always bigger than anything you fear.

If you are in the middle of a situation that is causing you to be afraid, sometimes simply saying the name of Jesus in faith is the best prayer you can pray. When you call on Jesus' name, you're asking Him to take your fears and fill you with His love and peace instead. Darkness has to leave when Jesus enters. Memorizing 1 John 4:4 (ESV) is a great way for the Holy Spirit to bring this to mind too: "He who is in you is greater than he who is in the world."

. . . .

Jesus, I trust that there is power in Your name.
Thank You for rescuing me from fear.

Supersonic Vision

The eyes of the LORD are in every place,
keeping watch on the evil and the good.
PROVERBS 15:3 ESV

God has supersonic x-ray vision. He sees what's going on across the globe and can keep track of it all at the same time! He can see inside of a prison cell in America while viewing a child's broken heart in India. He sees the senior citizen struggling to live alone in South America and the hungry homeless woman who lives in Africa.

He sees it all, and He cares about it all. (How could He not care? It must break His heart to witness the brokenness of humanity.)

Who else do you know with supersonic vision like this? Who else sees across the globe and inside of the human heart? No one. Only God! And He's watching over you, girl. He loves you so much, cares about you so deeply, that His eyes are on you, making sure you're well provided for and safe. What a tender, loving, worthy Father!

. . . .

I want eyes to see like You do, Lord! Make me more like
You, I pray. I don't want to overlook anyone. Amen.

Day 300
Choosing Love

Dear friends, let us continue to love one another, for love comes from God. Anyone who loves is a child of God and knows God.
1 JOHN 4:7 NLT

John really wanted brothers and sisters in Christ to love one another. He told them over and over again to love one another. If love came easy, why would we need so many reminders? Because love isn't a feeling.

Movies and television shows and social media may present love as a feeling you get when you're around "the one." That's not real love. That's being "in" love. But that feeling comes and goes depending on the circumstances and the other person's response to you. People fall out of love all the time. That's why the divorce rate is so high in the world.

Agape love is different. It's love from God that lasts forever. It's making a choice to love another person even when you don't feel like it. You can show agape love to everyone around you. You can choose love and let your actions tell the truth about your words. This shows a watching world the true love of God.

* *

God, please fill me with Your love and strength to love even when my feelings tell me otherwise.

The Eternal Gift

*"I give to them the gift of eternal life and they will never be lost and
no one has the power to snatch them out of my hands. My Father,
who has given them to me as his gift, is the mightiest of all, and
no one has the power to snatch them from my Father's care."*
JOHN 10:28–29 TPT

What a comforting promise—no one has the power to snatch you
from the family of God! No one but you can make the choice to accept
Jesus as your Lord and Savior, and by the same measure, no one can
ever make you walk away from God. You never have to worry if you
have "lost" your salvation. Jesus reassures us that when we choose to
walk with Him, we have the gift of eternal life.

Jesus calls you a gift, a gift the Father gave to Him. He won't let
the enemy take you from His care because He loves you so much He
laid down His life for you. Spend your prayer time thanking Jesus
for the gift of salvation that can never be taken from you!

*Jesus, thank You for giving me the gift of eternal life. I will never
take for granted Your tremendous sacrifice to ensure my salvation.
I can rest in the reassurance that my salvation and righteousness
can never be taken from me. I am safe in Your hands!*

Day 302
Come Alive

*This is how God showed his love among us: He sent his one
and only Son into the world that we might live through him.
This is love: not that we loved God, but that he loved us and
sent his Son as an atoning sacrifice for our sins. Dear friends,
since God so loved us, we also ought to love one another.*

1 JOHN 4:9–11 NIV

Jesus came for you so that you might come alive through Him. In
Luke 4:18–19 (NIV), Jesus said, "The Spirit of the Lord is on me,
because he has anointed me to proclaim good news to the poor. He
has sent me to proclaim freedom for the prisoners and recovery of
sight for the blind, to set the oppressed free, to proclaim the year of
the Lord's favor."

He was not just talking about poor people and prisoners. These
words from Jesus are for you! Jesus came to bring you healing and
freedom from sin and death. He also came to bring you abundant
life through Him that starts right now (John 10:10).

Life can be hard, but you are never alone. Jesus is with you, carrying your burdens and breathing new life into you in each moment.

. . . .

Jesus, breathe new life into me this day as I follow You.

Full of Promise

*And we know that in all things God works for the good of those
who love him, who have been called according to his purpose.*
ROMANS 8:28 NIV

The Bible is full of promises for your future. You never have to be
worried or afraid because God always keeps His promises. Here are
just a few to encourage you today:

- "Praise be to the God and Father of our Lord Jesus Christ!
  In his great mercy he has given us new birth into a living
  hope through the resurrection of Jesus Christ from the
  dead, and into an inheritance that can never perish, spoil
  or fade" (1 Peter 1:3–4 NIV).

- "We look forward with hope to that wonderful day when
  the glory of our great God and Savior, Jesus Christ, will
  be revealed" (Titus 2:13 NLT).

- "I consider that our present sufferings are not worth
  comparing with the glory that will be revealed in us"
  (Romans 8:18 NIV).

- "'He will wipe every tear from their eyes. There will be
  no more death' or mourning or crying or pain, for the old
  order of things has passed away" (Revelation 21:4 NIV).

*Lord, I trust You to keep Your promises.
Thank You for the hope I have in You.*

Day 304

Let Your Beauty Rest on Me

O Lord our God, let your sweet beauty rest upon
us. Come work with us, and then our works will
endure; you will give us success in all we do.
PSALM 90:17 TPT

You know that God finds you beautiful! You are His creation, His highest achievement. Have you ever thought on *His* beauty, though? Have you considered that everything you've ever seen, ever found beautiful, was created by Him and for His glory?

When we let His sweet beauty rest on us, we reflect His beauty back to Him. When we do all things for His glory, we find success. Find time today to simply reflect on the beauty around you and thank God for His hands that made it. Ask Him to lead you in everything you do today so that you may find the success He desires for you!

. . . .

Father God, I want to do what You lead me to do. I want to have
the same measures for success that You have. Success to You is
doing anything that brings You glory, aligns with Your Word,
and spreads Your love. Show me how to walk in Your ways today
and every day. Teach me to reflect Your beauty, Lord! Amen.

Nothing Is Too Hard for Him

*"Ah, Lord GOD! It is you who have made the heavens
and the earth by your great power and by your
outstretched arm! Nothing is too hard for you."*
JEREMIAH 32:17 ESV

Think of the hardest math problem you've ever tried to solve. Did it drive you crazy until you figured it out? Now think of the biggest family problem you've ever faced. Did you finally get past it?

Life is filled with problems and complications and many of them will seem impossible to you. When you reach the point where things are beyond your capabilities, never forget that God is capable. What you cannot do, He can. Nothing is too hard for Him. There's no problem too big for Him. He can solve every one.

He created the heavens and the earth. That should convince you that He knows how things work. And because He knows how they work, He knows how to fix them when they're broken. You can trust Him when you're going through stuff, girl. He won't let you down. That's a promise.

. . . .

*You're the great Fixer, Lord! I'm glad You're
able, even when I am not. Amen.*

Wisdom Comes from Above

*"But I see I was wrong—it's God's Spirit in a person, the breath
of the Almighty One, that makes wise human insight possible."*

JOB 32:8 MSG

These words were spoken by Elihu, a young man. He was describing
his misconception that age makes a person wise. He admitted that he
was wrong and that he finally understood that only the Holy Spirit
in someone allows them to be wise and insightful.

When you are filled with God's Spirit, you receive a great gift.
Not only does God's joy make you beautiful inside and out, you also
become wiser. Your mind begins to align more with the Lord's, and
your heart is moved by the things that move His heart. Your age
doesn't matter, but your relationship with the Lord does! Godly
wisdom doesn't always make sense in earthly contexts, but it is *always*
the best path to follow!

*Father God, sometimes I question my wisdom and insight when
it's time to make choices. Help me to follow Your Spirit and to
trust that You will lead me in Your wisdom. Thank You for not
seeing me as the world sees me, as young and inexperienced, but
for seeing me as wise and insightful through Your Spirit. Amen.*

God at Work

No one has ever seen God. But if we love each other, God lives in us, and his love is brought to full expression in us. And God has given us his Spirit as proof that we live in him and he in us.

1 JOHN 4:12–13 NLT

One day we'll be able to see Jesus face-to-face. That's the promise we have as God's children. But for now, the Bible tells us that we see God by seeing His Spirit alive and at work in us and in believers around us. God is love. And when you see love in action, you are seeing God at work.

We also see evidence of God in all of His creation. God can speak to us in many ways. He is the master artist. He paints us a new picture with every sunrise and sunset. Do you see God at work around you? Journal some of the ways You've seen Him work as part of your prayer today.

. . . .

Thank You for Your amazing creation that speaks to me every day, God! Help me love others well so that they can see You at work in me.

His Understanding
Is Beyond Measure

Great is our Lord, and abundant in power;
his understanding is beyond measure.

PSALM 147:5 ESV

He gets it. That thing you're worrying about—God gets it. He understands. He sees all and knows all.

Now ponder this for a moment. On the other side of the planet, there's a woman who's struggling to feed her family. She doesn't speak your language. You have nothing in common. But God gets her too. He understands her situation, and He cares.

He gets that man who is agonizing over losing his job. He understands that elderly woman in the hospital bed who wonders if she'll die alone. He gets the yard worker, slaving away in the heat to care for someone else's lawn. He understands all of them. He knows where they're coming from, what they're going through, even what they're thinking. (Wow!)

Your heavenly Father is all-knowing, all-powerful, and filled with love and compassion for all of creation. His love knows no limits. His knowledge knows no bounds. Now that's a God who's worthy to be praised!

. . . .

I can't even fathom how You know all of that, Lord!
But I'm in awe of You, for sure. Amen.

Make Me Holy

"Your Word is truth! So make them holy by the truth."
JOHN 17:17 TPT

True means "in accordance with reality." God's Word is in accordance with reality. It is not fictional. It is not a fairy tale. God gave every word in the Bible to those who would write it down and send it out. You can trust God's Word to be accurate, factual, and true.

Jesus prayed these words for you. He prayed that you would be made holy by His truth—the truth that is found in His Word alone. Jesus made you, He loves you, and He wants you to pursue holiness. To be holy means to chase after Him continually and resist the temptation to sin. Pray today that Jesus would make you holy as you study and follow His true Word!

. . . .

Father God, I want to be holy because You are holy.
Your Word is holy and true, and I want to know it
inside and out. Reveal to me the deeper things of Your
Word. Give me a hunger for Your truth. I want to
resist sin and follow You with my whole heart.
Help me to desire You more than anything else. Amen.

Day 310

No Fear in Love

There is no fear in love. But perfect love drives out fear,
because fear has to do with punishment. The one who fears is
not made perfect in love. We love because he first loved us.
1 JOHN 4:18–19 NIV

The biggest blessing in your life is that you have access to God. You can always approach Him without fear because He sees you through the love and sacrifice of Jesus. Jesus made a way once and for all. So God is not angry with you. A person who is afraid of God's punishment doesn't understand who they are in Christ. He is a good Father, longing to hold you and love you well all the days of your life.

You don't have to work harder or be a better Christian to earn God's love. When you begin to believe who you are in Christ, it changes everything. You start living differently. You realize how deeply loved you are, and that sets you free. Remember this: as Jesus pours His love and His Spirit into your life, it spills over into the lives of those around you.

. . . .

Thank You, God, that I'm able to come to
You without fear because of Jesus!

Born of God

Everyone who believes that Jesus is the Christ has been born of God,
and everyone who loves the Father loves whoever has been born of him.

1 JOHN 5:1 ESV

The Bible says in several places that you are "born of God." First
John 5:18 (NIV) says, "We know that anyone born of God does not
continue to sin; the One who was born of God keeps them safe, and
the evil one cannot harm them."

So what does "born of God" mean? The Amplified Bible explains
that being born of God means "a divine and supernatural birth—
they are born of God—spiritually transformed, renewed, sanctified"
(John 1:13).

This supernatural truth is more binding than your physical
reality. It's eternal! In Christ, you are God's child with rights to His
full inheritance. You are born into His family. He keeps you safe,
He frees you from slavery to sin so that you don't have to go back to
it again and again, and the evil one is not permitted to destroy you.
Are you walking in this truth? Keep your chin up! You are chosen
by God and kept safe in His love for eternity.

. . . .

Lord, I choose to believe Your Word. I'm Your child.
I will live with gratitude in my heart for all You've done.

Day 312

Come into His Presence
with Thanksgiving

Oh come, let us sing to the LORD; let us make a joyful noise to
the rock of our salvation! Let us come into his presence with
thanksgiving; let us make a joyful noise to him with songs of praise!
PSALM 95:1–2 ESV

How sweet it is to hear a genuine "Thank you" for something you did or a gift you gave! My love language is acts of service, so I love to see the joy on someone's face when they see that I did something special for them, and they appreciate it. That is how the Lord feels when we come to Him with thanksgiving!

When we sing to Him joyfully, entering His presence with our thanks and praise, He is blessed! He considers your thanksgiving to be a beautiful sound, a song of praise from His beautiful daughter! Take some time today to thank God for the things He has done for you and sing to Him your praise!

. . . .

Lord, I enter Your presence with my gratitude today.
I thank You for sending Your Son, Jesus, to take on my sin
and give me His righteousness. I praise You for always
being good and never making me feel inadequate to come
before You with my heart's burdens and desires. Amen!

A Banner of Love

He brought me to the banqueting house,
and his banner over me was love.
SONG OF SOLOMON 2:4 ESV

In ancient times, soldiers would lift their banners to identify their country, their allegiance, their pride and glory. Think of the Olympics today. . .athletes lift up their banners showing the country they are proud to represent.

These verses in Song of Solomon help us know more of God's amazing love for us. He invites us into His palace and raises a banner of love over us. The Amplified Bible says it this way: "his banner over me is love [waving overhead to protect and comfort me]."

God's banner of love indicates the country we belong to as well. His banner over us tells the world that our home is in heaven with our Father who loves and protects us.

This mixed-up world can feel like a warzone sometimes, so remember to stand firm under the banner of God's love. You are deeply loved and protected by God who is preparing a place for you with Him in heaven for all eternity!

. . . .

Lord, I'm so thankful for the banner of love that You are
waving over me! I need that protection and comfort as
I face the attacks of the enemy. Give me strength and
courage to share Your love with those who need it.

Day 314

Your Thoughts Are a Big Deal

You will keep in perfect peace all who trust in
you, all whose thoughts are fixed on you!
Isaiah 26:3 nlt

The Bible talks about taking every thought captive and making it obedient to Christ (2 Corinthians 10:5). This is a big deal if you want to have a close and personal relationship with God. It means that whenever anything happens to you—good, bad, boring, you name it—take it immediately to God. Talk to Him about it.

Perfect peace happens only in the presence of God. It doesn't mean that nothing bad will ever happen to you, but it does mean that God will give you peace for each moment that you share with Him.

Wouldn't it be great to live out your life in perfect peace? Well. . .you can! If you're waiting at the dentist's office, bored or nervous, talk to God. If you are happy or sad or mad or excited, talk to God. Share each moment with Him. He offers perfect peace in every moment for anyone who fixes their thoughts on Him!

. . . .

Lord, please help me to get in the habit of bringing my thoughts to
You. Please help me to remember You in all things and all situations.

Day 315

Confidence in
What We Can't See

*Now faith is confidence in what we hope for
and assurance about what we do not see.*

HEBREWS 11:1 NIV

There is no faith or hope in heaven. Wait, what? There is no faith or hope in heaven. Why? Because all things are fulfilled in His presence. There is no need for faith because we see Him face-to-face. There is no need for hope because all things have come to pass in Him. We only get to experience the beauty of faith and hope here on this earth.

When we are confident in the Lord and in His promises, we are doing something so unique. We are bringing heaven to earth, just as we pray in the Lord's Prayer. Our faith and hope on this earth bring to light the things that God has promised. We have faith in our salvation; we have hope for a beautiful eternity. Walk out your confidence in God's promises today—that is the expression of your faith in Him!

. . . .

*Father God, thank You for trusting me with Your gifts of faith
and hope. I believe Your promises are truth. I know You are
who You say You are, even when I can't physically see You.
Increase my faith day by day, Lord. I want my hope and faith
to increase as I learn more about You and Your Word.*

Day 316

Fearless

Perfect love expels all fear. If we are afraid, it is for fear of punishment, and this shows that we have not fully experienced his perfect love.

1 JOHN 4:18 NLT

The love we all deserve as Christ's daughters has no reason to cause fear. God proclaims that His love casts out fear. In God's house, "fear" and "love" cannot be in the same room.

I am so afraid that others' love for me has expectations I can never meet. I sometimes think I will be punished by them taking away that love and leaving me alone. In those moments, I have so much fear. How can God call me "fearless"?

Only God is perfect in loving us the way we need. In heartache and pain, He calls us to Him and asks us to leave our fears behind—fears of abandonment and loneliness and of being left out. This world may hurt us and scare us, but God has promised to one day take away that pain and let us live in wholeness with Him.

When I fully accept the loneliness this world offers me, I am fully embraced by the love of a perfect God. Not because of anything I've done. It's all because of who God is and who He makes us when we do our best to follow Christ.

. . . .

Father God, help me to love myself as You love me. It won't be easy, but it will be a start to accepting the love You created me to receive.

Day 317
Stronger Than Ever

I can do all things through him who strengthens me.
PHILIPPIANS 4:13 ESV

Think back over some of the tough times you have been through in your life. I bet looking back you can see all the ways the Lord helped you through His power and strength. When you look back and remember the ways He has strengthened you in the past, you are building up your faith and your trust that He will do it again.

Nothing you will go through is too tough for Him. He can strengthen and uphold you through anything you encounter in this life. Even when the trials seem too tough to handle, you don't have to go it alone. He is there with you, and He alone can take the burden from you. Trust in Him to strengthen you.

. . . .

Lord, You are strong enough to help me in the situations that just seem too hard to handle on my own. I know I can walk out these trials with confidence because You give me the strength. Help me to remember the ways You have strengthened me in the past and to trust Your promise that You will continue to do so!

Lovely

But for right now. . .we have three things to do. . . .
Trust steadily in God, hope unswervingly,
love extravagantly. And the best of the three is love.
1 CORINTHIANS 13:13 MSG

Paul tells us in 1 Corinthians 13 that we can be the smartest person in the room, the most talented, the prettiest. . .but if we don't possess love for others—real love that only God provides—we have nothing. These amazing parts of life that we view as lovely and life-giving are only that way because God has touched them with unimaginable grace and beauty.

I want to be lovely. I want to extend agape, accepting love to those around me. But I have to tell myself every day that being lovely doesn't mean being the girl everyone wants. Paul writes, "All that I know now is partial and incomplete, but then I will know everything completely, just as God now knows me completely" (1 Corinthians 13:12 NLT). Paul also writes a list to live by in 1 Corinthians 13:4–7. And I want my actions to align with this list. Am I being patient and kind? Am I being jealous, boastful, proud, or rude? Am I demanding my own way, holding grudges, rejoicing in others' hardships? Am I giving up, losing faith? Am I being hopeful and enduring by trusting in my God?

If you try your best every day to love others as Jesus did when He walked this earth, God calls you lovely.

· ·

God, help me to be the lovely daughter You
know and created me to be. Amen.

Day 319

Just Right

But you are not like that, for you are a chosen people.
You are royal priests, a holy nation, God's very own possession.
1 PETER 2:9 NLT

I've been told I'm just too much. I've also been told I would never be enough. Both hurt because both reactions told me that I needed to change who I was to fit the perfect mold of whom others wanted in their life. And so, I prayed for God to change me.

Spoiler alert: God didn't answer my prayer.

The truth?. . . God doesn't want any of His daughters to change who we are because He made us with a purpose in Him and not for a partnership on this earth. He made us to have a relationship with Him before anyone else. That's why we are never too much for the Lord. And He loves us in a way no one else in this life can.

Moses was stuck between two very different worlds. He felt both burns from both the Egyptians and the Israelites—for not being good enough for one group and not fitting in the other.

But Moses didn't fit in because *God didn't want him to*. Moses was created by the Lord to deliver the Israelites out of bondage. He wasn't meant to find peace in this world. Only with His Father.

And the story is the same with us. Our reward for trusting God, for doing Christ's good work, will be worth it. You're just right for your heavenly Father.

. . . .

God, when I'm feeling like I'm "too much" or "not enough,"
remind me that I'm just right because You created me.

It Was Always about His Love

He is the radiance of the glory of God and the exact
imprint of his nature, and he upholds the universe by the
word of his power. After making purification for sins,
he sat down at the right hand of the Majesty on high.
HEBREWS 1:3 ESV

Jesus is worthy, sweet girl. And because He's worthy, His gift of salvation has made you worthy. What a gift!

You'll make mistakes, sure. You'll mess up every day. You're still human. But because of His worthiness and His compassionate nature, you'll get a second chance. And a third. And a fourth. Tomorrow will be better. And you'll keep growing and getting closer to Him over the years ahead.

But here's the truth: your worthiness was never based on your actions. You're His kid, and He made you worthy the day He adopted you into the family. So enjoy your relationship with the one who thinks you hung the moon! (You are pretty special, you know!)

. . . .

Jesus, thank You! I love being Your daughter. I feel like
such a mess-up sometimes, but You're so forgiving and
gracious to me. Even on days when I don't feel worthy at
all, You remind me that all You ever wanted from me was
my heart. It's Yours, totally and completely. Amen.

Day 321

Forgiving

Bear with each other and forgive one another if any of you has a grievance against someone. Forgive as the Lord forgave you.

COLOSSIANS 3:13 NIV

Life is full of disappointments, injustices, and hurt. And you have a right to be angry. Feeling angry doesn't make you a bad Christ follower.

However, along with this anger we feel, we have a choice. We can either give anger the power to control our actions, interactions, and relationships—or we can give our anger to God, trusting that He will heal the hurt and make His presence known.

We want a perfect ending, but that "perfect story" is rarely God's will for you and me. All the wrongs of our lives were made right on the cross.

God understands our pain through Jesus, who lived through every human heartache—including the betrayal of friends. Jesus never let His emotions control Him. He never let any part of being human take precedence over the will of God in His life. God wants the same for us. If we are too focused on our anger, we lose focus of our connection to our Savior.

God calls you to forgive because He loves you too much to let you live in distrust and hate. One day, you will live a life of no tears and no pain. Until then, we must trust that God is working all things for the good of those who trust and believe in Him.

. . . .

Father God, help me to forgive those who have hurt me. I trust You and ask for Your eyes as I try to move forward in mercy and grace.

New Creation in Christ

Therefore, if anyone is in Christ, he is a new creation.
The old has passed away; behold, the new has come.
2 CORINTHIANS 5:17 ESV

Sometimes I look back on the things I've done and see where I missed the mark of what God had for me. This kind of reflection could make me sad and disappointed that I allowed my sin to separate me from God. Yet thanks be to God that anything wrong I have done in the past is dead and buried. The old me no longer exists. I now exist as a new creation in Christ. I have been made holy because He is holy.

Spend today's quiet time thanking God for the ways that you have been made new. You no longer need to feel guilt or shame over mistakes you made in the past. Let those be buried and thank Him for the new life you've been given now that you are one with Christ!

. . . .

Jesus, thank You for making me a new creation. Thank You
for no longer seeing my past sin but rather covering it by
Your blood on the cross. Remind me of my new life in You
anytime I'm tempted to fall back into old patterns. Amen.

Day 323
Beloved

*"Those who were not my people I will call 'my people,'
and her who was not beloved I will call 'beloved.'"*

ROMANS 9:25 ESV

How much does God loves you? How much does He adore every part of your mind, even the deepest, darkest bits you don't let anyone else see?

I can describe the simple grace of your beating heart, the marvelous body you were given to live in and live out God's calling, praise for the people who care for you, the talents you have and the hobbies you love. I can describe the creation of the world in Eden, the promises of a Savior and the tale of repeated forgiveness throughout the Bible until the miracle of Jesus and His death and resurrection from the cross.

But since the Fall, there is *that* voice. You know the one. It whispers when you're alone and when you're hurting. It says you don't deserve love. It says God could never forgive someone like you. This voice comes from false ideas from the enemy. He is "a liar and the father of lies" (John 8:44 NIV). The enemy does not have the power to be in your head, but he will set things in your life to change your way of thinking. That's why God asks us to be so cautious of what we focus on.

And when we receive the truth that we belong to God, we take back power. The enemy's words can't change God's way. Every time the enemy battles holy truth, he loses.

. . . .

God, thank You for loving me. Amen.

Day 324
Ambitious

For we are God's handiwork, created in Christ Jesus to do good works, which God prepared in advance for us to do.
EPHESIANS 2:10 NIV

"What do you want to be when you grow up?" That's the question adults love to ask kids.

As you get closer to graduation, the answer to that question could change. Or it could stay the same. Maybe you don't have any answer at all. That question that used to fill you with awe and excitement might now fill you with dread.

The good news is there is no deadline for knowing the answer. You might stay on one path all the way through your life, steady and true. Or you might take detours, rest stops, and U-turns. The most important part of any decision is that you are listening to and following God.

Just trust that you are well equipped to do what the Lord has called you to. God calls you "ambitious." He knows exactly what you need to do to get exactly where you need to be. He knows you have the ability to learn, work hard, fail, and try again. God knows what you'll go through, and He promises to be beside you, hold you, and encourage you every step of the way.

Father, I choose to go to You when I start worrying about my future. I know I'm in Your hands. You have a beautiful plan for Your creation, and I am so thankful that I am an important part of it. Amen.

She Shall Not Be Moved

God is in the midst of her; she shall not be moved;
God will help her when morning dawns.
PSALM 46:5 ESV

Have you ever had a really terrible night? You might've been up sick, awake from nightmares, cramming for a test, or crying because of a broken friendship or relationship. These nights seem so long and hopeless, but somehow you know you just have to make it until morning. The morning light brings clarity and comfort after a difficult night.

This verse is a good reminder that even when we're going through those long nights, God is still in our midst. His presence steadies us and keeps us from falling. The terrible nights can't take us out because He is holding us upright. We see His help and strength clearly when the morning light dawns, but He was right beside us even through the night.

. . . .

Father God, I want to thank You for being right beside me
even when I go through difficult nights of stress, loneliness,
or heartbreak. Thank You for always bringing Your
morning light to shine clarity on any situation. Amen.

Day 326
Accepting

He stood up again and said, "All right, but let the one
who has never sinned throw the first stone!"
JOHN 8:7 NLT

In the book of John, a woman was caught in the act of adultery. With the whole town watching, she was dragged into judgment in front of Jesus. The crowd was in full view of her sin and her shame. The Pharisees called Jesus to condemn this woman to a stoning. And Jesus said they could stone her, but only if one who had never sinned threw the first stone. No one in the crowd was able to say they'd never sinned. The only one who could say that didn't even touch one rock. Slowly, they all dropped their stones. And their judgments.

The story ends with verses 10–11 like this:

"Then Jesus stood up again and said to the woman, 'Where are your accusers? Didn't even one of them condemn you?' 'No, Lord,' she said. And Jesus said, 'Neither do I. Go and sin no more.'"

Jesus shows that accepting someone doesn't mean accepting what they've done as right. It also doesn't mean we pretend it never happened. It means we take a good long look at how God has forgiven our sins and share that truth with a fellow sinner. This means open communication—so it will get awkward.

God wants you as one of His "accepted" to show others they are "accepted" too.

. . . .

Lord, instead of judgment, fill me to the brim with Your love.

Day 327
A Leader

Fight the good fight of the faith. Take hold of the eternal life to which you were called when you made your good confession in the presence of many witnesses.

1 TIMOTHY 6:12 NIV

Leaders must make sure the job gets done. They have to stand up for what they believe in. They have to do what's right, not what's popular.

You might not consider yourself a leader, but if you share your faith with others, people are watching you. They look at where you go and what you do and listen to what you say. They're waiting to see if living a life with faith is different than living a life without it. God is using you as a leader, as an example of what a young Christian woman is.

That's why God must be our source for strength, peace, and wisdom. He knows we can't point people toward Him without His help.

Paul tells Timothy in 2 Timothy 1:7, "For the Spirit God gave us does not make us timid, but gives us power, love and self-discipline."

God calls you a leader that has authority, one that speaks and acts in kindness, and one with the determination and wisdom to solve problems and work hard. You can rise above conflict and difficulty by fighting for faith and joy and trusting in the Lord for all things. In this way, you are grabbing hold of the eternal life Jesus promises you.

* * *

Father, when I am offered a leadership role or find myself in one, I will step into it gladly, knowing I'm exactly where You want me to be. Amen.

Who I Really Am

For the word of God is alive and powerful.
It is sharper than the sharpest two-edged sword.
HEBREWS 4:12 NLT

Knowing who you are in Christ will change your whole life forever. Because of what Jesus has done for you, all these things are true:

- I am free and clean in the blood of Christ (Galatians 5:1; 1 John 1:7).

- He has rescued me from darkness and has brought me into His kingdom (Colossians 1:13).

- I have direct access to God (Ephesians 2:18).

- I am a precious child of the Father (Isaiah 43:6–7; John 1:12; Galatians 3:26).

- I am a friend of Christ (John 15:15).

- Nothing can separate me from God's love (Romans 8:38–39).

- God is for me, not against me (Romans 8:31).

- I am chosen by God (Colossians 3:12).

- God will meet all my needs (Philippians 4:19).

- I am dearly loved (John 3:16; Jeremiah 31:3).

God, thank You for telling me the truth about who I am.

The Lord Is for Me

So we can say with great confidence: "I know the Lord is for me
and I will never be afraid of what people may do to me!"
HEBREWS 13:6 TPT

We know that God promised He would never leave us or forsake us. This promise is what allows us to say that we will never be afraid of what others may do to us. Yes, the world can be uncertain, and there are evil people in the world, but Jesus has overcome the world. Even when people do hurt us and we do go through trials, we can lean on the Lord and He will give us strength.

When you face uncertainty or begin to fear, speak His promises over yourself, even aloud. He will never leave you or forsake you. He is for you. His presence is with you always, even to the very end. Remind yourself whose daughter you are and how He cares for you!

* *

Lord, thank You for being in my corner. I need Your presence
with me always. I am so grateful that You have promised
never to leave me or forsake me. I will not fear what the world
could throw at me, because I know You are by my side.

Day 330
Your Everything

You are my strength, I sing praise to you; you, God, are my fortress.
Psalm 59:17 niv

God calls His daughters many names in His Word, but characters in the Bible also called God certain names too. These names can still be used today. David wrote Psalm 59:17 to ask the Lord for safety and deliverance from men trying to kill him. He was afraid and alone.

David was on the verge of giving up. So he declared the truth that God was his strength. David's strength didn't come from himself or anywhere else. His safety didn't rely on his circumstances. David decided that he would wait and rely on the Lord for his rescue.

Can you do that in the circumstance you're in? Can you rely on His strength and His timing?

God is on His way to save you. This doesn't mean all your hardships will disappear, but it does mean that God is going to rescue you from hopelessness and fear. He will give you strength to find joy, peace, and acceptance wherever you are.

The hard things and the loneliness we experience in this life never define the Lord's love for us. We may not know yet the good that God is working in our lives, but we can have faith that He is near, that He is intentional, and that He is strong when we aren't.

We never have to be alone. Call God your strength, your fortress, your everything. "He will never leave you nor forsake you" (Deuteronomy 31:6 niv).

. . . .

God, thank You so much for Your strength. Let it wash over me today.

Day 331
Prayerful

*"Then you will call upon me and come and pray to
me, and I will hear you. You will seek me and find
me, when you seek me with all your heart."*
JEREMIAH 29:12–13 ESV

Jeremiah 29:11 reads, "For I know the plans I have for you, declares
the LORD, plans for welfare and not for evil, to give you a future
and a hope." It's a verse to lean on as you approach graduation. But
when it's taken out of context, we can lose sight of what the Lord
wants us to do.

God has plans for us, but He doesn't want us to just sit and wait
for those plans to happen. He asks us to call upon Him—and *pray*.
He cares about our plans, and He wants us to actively care about
our plans too.

God gives His children another promise in Jeremiah 29. Right
after He speaks of His plans for us, He says that our prayers will
always be heard. He promises that if we search for Him with good
intentions and our whole heart, we'll find Him. He promises to help
us find His plans if we do our part.

You are called *prayerful* by your heavenly Father. You were created
with a need to connect with Him. When we pray to Him about our
future, we show that we value His plans over our own.

. . . .

*God, lead me to a quiet place away from life's
daily distractions. I want to share everything on
my heart: my day, my plans, my worries.*

Day 332

God Only Speaks the Truth

*This is he who came by water and blood—Jesus Christ;
not by the water only but by the water and the blood. And the
Spirit is the one who testifies, because the Spirit is the truth.*

1 JOHN 5:6 ESV

You look in the mirror and groan. You hate the pimples. You can't stand your eyebrows. You wish your lips were prettier. And that hair! You'd change everything about it. Why can't you have great hair like the other girls?

When you stare at your reflection, you may not feel beautiful. In fact, you may not feel remotely pretty. But God's Word says you are! Consider these words from Song of Solomon 4:7: "You are altogether beautiful, my love; there is no flaw in you" (ESV). When God looks at you, He sees His beautiful daughter, cleansed and set free, thanks to the work that Jesus did on the cross.

You're beautiful. Even on the days when you're not feeling it. You're beautiful because He says so, and your amazing heavenly Father doesn't lie. In fact, He only *ever* speaks the truth. So if He said it, it must be 100 percent true.

. . . .

*You find me beautiful, Lord? Wow! I don't understand how,
especially on the days when I'm looking rough. But Your
Word says that You only tell the truth, so I'll have to believe
You on this one, even when I'm not feeling it. Amen.*

Handmade with Love

Yet you, LORD, are our Father. We are the clay,
you are the potter; we are all the work of your hand.
ISAIAH 64:8 NIV

Creating with clay is a precise art. If just one small thing goes wrong, the whole design will come out wonky. Even professionals have to scrap a piece they're working on every now and then because it just doesn't come out the way they thought it would.

Thankfully, God has never once made a mistake. When He crafted you in your mother's womb, He did so with deft and expert hands. He already knows the end from the beginning and accordingly equipped you for each situation you would face in your life. Praise Him today for crafting you with care and excellence. Nothing about you is a mistake or an accident—the Lord created you with purpose and for a purpose!

· ·

Father God, You made me with excellence. I am the work of Your hand. It is because of Your love and care that I know I am beautiful and that nothing about me is a mistake. Remind me of this truth when I start to criticize something about myself. Amen.

Loveworthy

You are altogether beautiful, my darling, beautiful in every way.
SONG OF SOLOMON 4:7 NLT

Loveworthy is an old word. It sounds like it belongs in a Jane Austen novel or a Shakespeare play. It means exactly what you think—it's an adjective for someone who is worthy of love.

God calls every one of His daughters loveworthy.

Eros is a Greek word for love that describes a physical, intimate love. This is the blooming love of a new relationship and a major part of a fully grown and mature marriage.

Eros love is defined in the Bible book Song of Songs, also known as Song of Solomon. Two people are declaring their love for one another, but there are plenty of meanings we can find in the verses to apply to our relationships today.

Twice the book says, "Do not arouse or awaken love until it so desires" (2:7; 3:5 NIV). It's saying that even though we crave someone to love and for someone to love us, God still has the perfect plan in mind for our love story. When we rush things, we can hurt ourselves and others.

If you don't have a desire for marriage, that's okay! We aren't all supposed to have the same story. The most important thing is that we are putting God first and trusting Him in everything we do.

. . . .

Lord, You are the only constant reminder in my life that I am loveworthy because Your love is best of all. Thank You!

Friend

Jesus said to him, "Friend, do what you came to do."
Then they came up and laid hands on Jesus and seized him.
MATTHEW 26:50 ESV

God is omnipotent—all-powerful and all-knowing. And Jesus was all man and all God. He had knowledge that surpassed every human's understanding. Jesus knew what was going to happen on the cross. And He also knew that one of His disciples would betray Him (Matthew 26:21).

Judas was one of Jesus' followers and His friend. He had been through everything with Jesus—the healings, miracles, and expressions of the Word made flesh. In the end, however, he chose to betray Jesus. Yet Jesus still called him "friend."

Remember that Jesus came for the sole purpose of saving Judas. He came to save all humanity. Our sin today is the same act of Judas' betrayal.

I don't like comparing myself to Judas. But every time I choose anger over love; every time I choose an idol over God; every time I tell myself, *Jesus doesn't care* or *Jesus isn't looking*, Jesus—all man and all God—still calls me "friend."

I know how the story ends, and the sin of this world still separates me from my Savior. The cross brings us back together again.

No matter what you've done, Jesus looks at you and says, "Friend."

God, thank You for Jesus and what He's done for me. Thank You for Your forgiveness. Thank You for calling me Your friend. Amen.

Day 336

The First of All His Creatures

He gave us our new lives through the truth of His Word only because He wanted to. We are the first children in His family.
JAMES 1:18 NLV

If God lined up all of His creation in order of importance, guess who would be at the front of the line? You, girl! Well, you and all the other human beings. People get the first spot in the line because God created them in His image.

He didn't create frogs in His image. Or sharks. Trees, bushes, clouds. . .they do not reflect the image of a holy God. Neither do the fish in the sea or the birds flying overhead. And none of those things have souls either. But you? You're His masterpiece, made to look and act like Him. And you've got a soul inside of you. It's the perfect dwelling place for God's Spirit, which sets you apart from the rest of creation.

So don't start cutting yourself down! Whenever you feel like you're less than, remember that you're really more than ten billion other amazing things God made.

. . . .

*Thanks for putting me at the front of the line,
Jesus! I don't always feel like I deserve the top spot,
but You do! I'm grateful for Your love. Amen.*

Learning to Walk

Make me hear of Your faithful love in the morning, for I trust in You. Teach me how I should walk, for I offer my soul up to You.
PSALM 143:8 VOICE

Are you a morning person or does it take you longer to ease into the beginning of your day? I think there is something special about spending the first moments of the day with the Lord. You set a good tone for the rest of the day when you remember God's faithfulness first thing.

In this psalm David is asking the Lord for guidance in his life. What better way to set up your day than to begin it by acknowledging God's faithfulness and then asking Him to direct your actions for the rest of the day? He is faithful to show you the way that is best for you. Trust Him and offer up your needs and desires to Him. He will lead you with His faithfulness.

. . . .

Lord God, remind me to begin each day by spending time with You. Don't let me forget that it is the best time of my day and sets the rest of my day on the right path. Teach me to trust You and follow Your guidance in all that I do. Thank You.

Day 338

More Than One Thing

We also pray that you will be strengthened with all his glorious power. . . . May you be filled with joy.
COLOSSIANS 1:11 NLT

Strength from the Lord is more than just our ability to survive day to day. Strength from the Lord lets us actually enjoy living for God every day.

We gain this goodness because we've been qualified for an inheritance by Jesus Christ. When we receive that inheritance, we have access to all the benefits of living with the Spirit in us. This includes the fruit of the Spirit which is "love, joy, peace, forbearance, kindness, goodness, faithfulness, gentleness, and self-control" (Galatians 5:22–23 NIV). We know that what happens in this life isn't the end of the story. We have an eternity in heaven with our Savior.

When Jesus died on the cross and rose from the dead three days later as He promised, we were rescued from our darkness and our sins were forgiven. He left the Spirit with us so that we are never away from His presence. That is where our strength comes from. The strength, the "glorious power" that lifted Jesus from the grave is in us through the Holy Spirit.

God calls you "strong" because He created you that way. He made it possible for you to withstand this life so that you can live in eternity with Him, the way you were always meant to.

. . . .

God, thank You for the strength You give me every day.

Day 339
The Best Dad

Many sorrows come to the wicked, but unfailing
love surrounds those who trust the LORD.

PSALM 32:10 NLT

Isaiah continued to call God's people to turn back to Him. He said: "Come, descendants of Jacob, let us walk in the light of the LORD" (Isaiah 2:5 NIV).

Put yourself in your parents' shoes for a minute. If your kid continued making unhealthy choices that were harming you, how would you handle that situation? Parents who follow Jesus do the very best they can, but even good parents mess up sometimes. God never does. He's the perfect parent. He sees everything from beginning to end and knows all sides to every situation.

Not only did God send Isaiah to warn the people, He also sent him to give God's people a message of hope: Jesus was coming! The Savior of the whole world! "The people walking in darkness have seen a great light; on those living in the land of deep darkness a light has dawned" (Isaiah 9:2 NIV).

The answer to the problem of sin was going to come and make everything right. God promised He would bless His children and give them another chance. God is a good dad—the best! He knows exactly what His children need.

Thank You for Your love, Lord. You are a good Father.

Day 340

He Knows Your Name!

But now, this is what the L<small>ORD</small> says—he who created you,
Jacob, he who formed you, Israel: "Do not fear, for I have
redeemed you; I have summoned you by name; you are mine."
Isaiah 43:1 niv

I remember when I was working wardrobe at a concert one time and a famous musician asked me to come help them, and they called me by name. Wow! I felt so honored that this talented and well-known artist knew me *by name*! How much more honored should we feel realizing that the Creator, the King of kings, knows us by our names!

God Himself says that we don't have to fear because He redeemed us. What a comfort! He calls us by our names, and we are His. He doesn't see our sin, guilt, or shame, but He sees us as His daughters, pure and holy. Remember today that the Most High King is calling you by name to spend some time with Him!

. . . .

Lord, forgive me for the times that I have forgotten how special it is that You know me and call me by name. I love to spend time with You. Thank You for redeeming me and calling me Your own. Amen.

Day 341

You

*Your hands made me and formed me; give me
understanding to learn your commands.*
PSALM 119:73–74 NIV

Is there anyone you can think of who has qualities you wish you had? If it's their talents, you're probably noticing them because this person is out there using them. We can be happy when we see others taking the gifts God has given them and multiplying them here on earth.

But it can be hard not to feel jealous sometimes. I once heard a member in a Christian band say, "If I'm too busy wanting to do what someone else is doing over there, I'll miss out on what God wants me to do here."

If you're too busy trying to be someone else, you won't be trying your best to perform the work God asks of you.

Trust that God has prepared you to be exactly where you are right now. We were created to *create*! He made us all with special talents and abilities to do what He wants us to. God created you to be the imperfectly perfect you.

When you start believing that God made you "you" for a reason, you'll start searching out ways that only you can glorify His name. When people see you, they'll know something is different. They'll know that your talent, grace, and power are coming from something bigger than this world.

. . . .

*God, show me how I might use the talents You gave
me to help others and, ultimately, glorify You!*

He's Looking at Your Heart

The Lord said to Samuel, "Don't judge by a man's face
or height, for this is not the one. I don't make decisions
the way you do! Men judge by outward appearance,
but I look at a man's thoughts and intentions."

1 SAMUEL 16:7 TLB

Today's Bible story is about King David. Well, let's back up. He wasn't a king yet. He was just a boy. The prophet Samuel was instructed by God to choose the future king for the nation of Israel. He took a close look at David's older brothers, who were bigger and better suited for the job. But in the end, God told Samuel to choose the little shepherd boy. (No doubt David's father was confused! "Hello? What about my older boys?")

Let's face it: the world judges by appearance. The pretty girls? Yeah, they get the attention. The handsome boys? They're the ones all the girls drool over. But the "average" ones? Many times, they get overlooked. It stinks, especially because you've already discovered that looks aren't the important thing.

But back to David. He was just a kid, but God saw extraordinary potential in him. And He chose David for the highest office in the land!

God sees potential in you too! He sees your value, even when others do not. (He's pretty cool like that!)

. . . .

Thanks for seeing more than just the physical, Lord! Amen.

Day 343
Fully Known

For now we see only a reflection as in a mirror;
then we shall see face to face. Now I know in part;
then I shall know fully, even as I am fully known.
1 Corinthians 13:12 niv

Go to your bathroom and turn the hot water on in your shower. Let it run for a few minutes. It won't take long before the mirror is covered in fog by steam. What was once a clear reflection is now distorted.

Now turn off your hot water. Take a clean cloth and wipe down the mirror. It may be streaked, but now you can see everything again, including your face.

The world is a lot like that. Before the Fall, Adam and Eve lived in clarity. Then sin entered the picture and made everything blurry.

When humans blurred this way of life, God took His clean cloth and wiped away the sin with His Son, Jesus. But sin still leaves streaks on the world. It won't be perfect until He returns to make everything right.

We see our life as only a reflection. But God promises us that if we believe in Him, we will see things for real in time. You only know part of the story, but soon you will know the whole thing. This is where your faith and trust come in.

The best part is that God already calls you "fully known." I hope this encourages you to love yourself and God even more, knowing that He understands and loves every part of you.

. . . .

Lord, I trust that I'm fully known by You.
I believe that You are doing good things for me. Amen.

Day 344

Reservoirs of Wisdom

Since we first heard about you, we've kept you always in our prayers that you would receive the perfect knowledge of God's pleasure over your lives, making you reservoirs of every kind of wisdom and spiritual understanding.

COLOSSIANS 1:9 TPT

Friend, ever since I began writing this devotion, I have prayed for you. I prayed this exact prayer, that you would receive perfect knowledge of how much God loves and delights in you. That you would know how beautiful He finds you. That you would begin to see yourself through the same eyes that Jesus sees you through!

Today, spend some time in prayer asking Him to share with your heart the things He loves about you. Keep your focus on the identity you have in Him. When you realize the delight He takes in you, you will start to become a deep well of wisdom and spiritual understanding. You will realize that neither Satan, the father of lies, nor other people can determine your worth. You are the daughter of the King, and you never have to question your worth and identity in Him!

. . . .

Father God, let me see myself the way You see me. I want to be a reservoir of wisdom and understanding. I want to know the goodness of Your love and truth, because I believe in it with everything inside of me. Let me receive the perfect knowledge of Your pleasure over me without doubt or skepticism. Thank You for loving me! Amen.

Abiding

As the Father has loved me, so have I loved you. Abide in my love.
JOHN 15:9 ESV

God wants you to know that you are so, so loved. We weren't made to live in brokenness, in hurt. No matter what you have done or what has been done to you, God is calling you back to Him. He wants you to come as you are to abide forever in His perfect and full love and forgiveness.

We have to live on this side of heaven. We have to live in suffering, hurt, and pain we were never meant to. But Jesus promises that if we abide in Him, He'll abide in us. We're never alone in our suffering. Jesus suffered to rid the world of suffering and promises when He returns, He'll heal all of our hurt and tears for good.

Sometimes we need a little more help while here on earth. Sometimes we need to go to a doctor to help with these feelings and thoughts inside us. Allow God to give you the strength to reach out for help. If you're scared, let Him fill you with courage. If you feel weak telling others about this hurt, remember that God is calling you "abiding." He sees you trying to live out His love for you by trying to love and take care of yourself. He is right there with you.

Lord, please give me the courage to reach out to those I trust. You don't want me to live in pain. You created me to live in everlasting love. Amen.

Seen

And she conceived again and bore a son, and said,
"This time I will praise the LORD." Therefore she called
his name Judah. Then she ceased bearing.

GENESIS 29:35 ESV

Leah wasn't Jacob's first choice. Her father tricked Jacob into working for him for seven years to marry his youngest daughter, Rachel, but didn't tell Jacob he had to marry the eldest daughter first. So he was given Leah instead of Rachel. Because of this deceit and his feelings toward the younger sister, Jacob didn't like his first wife.

Is there someone in your life who makes you feel like a second choice? It doesn't feel good when our deep feelings for someone go unnoticed or unreturned.

God saw that Leah was unloved, so He blessed her with children (Genesis 29:31). Leah thought the first son would make her husband love her, but no. She thought the birth of their second or third son might win her husband's affections. . . . After her fourth son, scripture says that Leah didn't mention her husband in her prayer. All she said was that she would praise the Lord. While the hurt of rejection still stung, Leah decided to shift her attention to the one who had always seen her, loved her, and provided for her.

God sees you too. When you feel like you're being ignored and unnoticed, the Lord is listening and cheering you on. Lean into His love today.

. . . .

God, thank You for letting me be first place to You.

Day 347
New

*And to put on the new self, created to be like God
in true righteousness and holiness.*
EPHESIANS 4:24 NIV

Sometimes the biggest decision we need to make on certain days is what we're going to wear. Maybe it's easy because your school has a uniform or a dress code. Maybe what you wear isn't very important to you. Or maybe you want to use your clothing to express yourself but are afraid of doing so because of what people will say.

It's hard making decisions in high school. It's hard feeling like every decision will be mocked by somebody—especially if that decision is about expressing yourself and being who you want to be.

Galatians 3:26–27 (NIV) reads, "So in Christ Jesus you are all children of God through faith, for all of you who were baptized into Christ have clothed yourselves with Christ." We may not know what to wear every day on our bodies, but Jesus is pretty clear about what we should wear on our souls.

When we put on the truth that we are children of God, the Lord calls us "new." We are made new in Christ.

We don't have to think about what the world calls us when we know what His truth says.

This decision to be like Jesus might bring you struggles, but you can believe that Jesus is beside you in them all. You are not alone.

*Father God, remind me that the only opinion
that really matters is Yours. Amen.*

His Plans > Our Plans

"I know what I'm doing. I have it all planned out—plans to take care of you, not abandon you, plans to give you the future you hope for."
JEREMIAH 29:11 MSG

Have you ever sat around thinking about how your life will look five or ten years down the road? You probably imagine college, a career, marriage and kids, world travel, or even fame. How great is it to know that God knows what He is doing so much better than we do? He has plans for us that are better than we could hope or dream. He cares for us, protects us, and stays by our side through every difficulty.

God delights in providing a future for us that is so much greater than our imagination could conjure. His timeline isn't always the same as ours. Yet when you look back on the times you thought He wasn't coming through, you'll see that you were walking a path that was infinitely better than the one you wanted for yourself!

. . . .

Father, I am so thankful that You have my best interests in mind. You never want me to fall or fail. You will never hurt me or abandon me. Thank You for Your promise to give me the kind of future I can only hope for right now! In Your name. Amen.

Called

*Therefore, brothers, be all the more diligent to confirm your calling
and election, for if you practice these qualities you will never fall.*
2 Peter 1:10 esv

How do we "confirm" our individual callings? Peter creates a list to help us get there. Second Peter 1:5–7 reads, "For this very reason, make every effort to supplement your faith with virtue, and virtue with knowledge, and knowledge with self-control, and self-control with steadfastness, and steadfastness with godliness, and godliness with brotherly affection, and brotherly affection with love." All these qualities get us closer in relationship to Christ and also closer to who He was as an example of how to live on earth.

We have these qualities because we know that we have been forgiven and our sins have been washed away. Because we have been loved, we have the chance to share that love with others. Not only are you promised a home in the kingdom of heaven, you can also help others receive that promise for themselves.

It may seem like a lot of rules to live by, but God doesn't expect perfection. He expects constant communication with us as we live *in* this world but not *of* it. He expects us to choose Him above all idols. He expects us to sometimes fail at those things. And He always expects us to come to Him in humility when we mess up so that we can be shown forgiveness and grace.

. . . .

*Lord, help me to remember that all I do on earth to follow Your
ways may not be easy, but it is the best way to love myself and
others with the love You give Your creation every day.*

Upside-Down Kingdom

*If you cling to your life, you will lose it; but if you
give up your life for me, you will find it.*
MATTHEW 10:39 NLT

The Bible has a bunch of sayings like this: Wait and get new strength.
Walk and don't get tired. Trade your ashes for beauty. Lose your
life to gain it. These sound a little mixed up, right? But it's what
the Christian life is all about: *faith*. Some call it the "upside-down
Kingdom."

God asked Cory to do some difficult things. Many people didn't
understand. She lost some of her best friends because she was willing
to follow God no matter what. Cory didn't have all the answers, and
she didn't completely understand why God was leading her in that
direction, but she trusted Him anyway.

When you trust God even when something doesn't seem to
make any sense, He will always come through for you. He loves to
show Himself to His people. He wants you to know how close He
is. He wants you to know that He sees you and that He's working
on your behalf.

. . . .

*Lord, I choose to trust You even when things don't make sense to
me. I'm thankful to be a part of Your upside-down kingdom!*

Precious in His Eyes

To me, you are very dear, and I love you.
That's why I gave up nations and people to rescue you.
ISAIAH 43:4 CEV

Who's your favorite person—right now, at this very moment? Of all the people on the planet, who came to mind right away as you read those words? Your BFF? Your mom? A kid sister? That guy you have a crush on?

The love that you have for that person doesn't even come close to the intense feelings your heavenly Father has for you. He's nuts about you. He believes you're far more valuable than gold or silver and even more precious than rubies or diamonds. If you lined up all of the jewelry in the world, it wouldn't come close to your value. Wow!

God would split heaven and earth wide open to care for you, girl. His love for you is that deep. He sacrificed everything, even His Son, so that He could prove that love. Rest easy in knowing your heavenly Father is flipping out over you, His child.

. . . .

I have to admit, I don't always feel very "precious,"
Jesus. Some days I'm just not feeling worthy at all. I don't know
why You love me like You do, but I'm so grateful. Amen.

Trusty as a Tree

"Blessed is the man who trusts in the LORD, whose trust is the LORD. He is like a tree planted by water, that sends out its roots by the stream, and does not fear when heat comes, for its leaves remain green, and is not anxious in the year of drought, for it does not cease to bear fruit."

JEREMIAH 17:7–8 ESV

Putting your trust in God is like having a strong root system. You don't have to worry when the storms come or the fierce winds blow, because your trust and faith in God go deep. How do you build a strong root system of trust and faith, though? You choose day by day to turn to Him in the trivial things, and that builds your faith for the bigger things.

I hope you never have to encounter a trial so big that you feel like you're caught in the middle of a storm, but these kinds of trials are a reality in our fallen world. Hardships press in on us like a drought or a sudden storm, but our faith in the goodness of God can remain steadfast.

. . . .

Father, thank You for Your goodness and faithfulness that never change or waver. Help me to build a strong root system of trust in You so that I don't bend or break when the hardships come. Thank You, Father.

Day 353

Consecrated

*Then Joshua said to the people, "Consecrate yourselves,
for tomorrow the LORD will do wonders among you."*
JOSHUA 3:5 ESV

What does the word *consecrate* mean? In English it means "to set apart." If we look at the ancient Hebrew, it actually means "a filled hand." How do those two connect?

God wants us to set ourselves apart from others. He already set His beloved apart before the Fall. Now that we are separated from God by sin, we must receive that truth through Jesus to fully live in it on this side of heaven.

While the English version tells us *what* we need to do to consecrate ourselves, the Hebrew version tells us *how* we consecrate ourselves. God wants to set us apart by filling us with His Spirit.

When we live that way, full of the Holy Spirit and God's love, we're bound to set ourselves apart as different. If we are following God correctly, we're hopefully showing others a different type of joy, peace, and love that they've never seen before and want to know more about.

After we fully put our lives in God's hands is when the wonders start to happen. Our circumstances may not change, but our view of them sure does.

In every outcome we must continue to consecrate ourselves with prayer.

. . . .

God, thank You so much for setting me apart for a high purpose. Amen.

Day 354

Why Worry about
Your Clothes?

*"And why would you worry about your clothing? Look at all the
beautiful flowers of the field. They don't work or toil, and yet not even
Solomon in all his splendor was robed in beauty like one of these!"*
MATTHEW 6:28–29 TPT

Jesus Himself said these words! He said not to worry about anything
because God will take care of you! That seems like a big task—trying
not to worry! Sometimes worrying seems like what we do best! We
worry about what to wear, what to eat, where we will go to college,
what to do for a career, and the list goes on. . . . Yet when we investi-
gate the trees and discover the birds within their branches, or when
we go for a walk and pass through a meadow filled with beautiful
wildflowers, we see that God takes care of even the smallest animals
and plants. How much more does our Creator take care of us!

What is one worry that you can give back to God today? Maybe
it's your concerns about your appearance or your questions about
school. Give them up to the one who cares for even the tiniest
creatures. He has your back!

· ·

*Jesus, my cares and concerns are Yours. You know my
needs and my wants, and You take care of me. Help me
to remember that worrying doesn't change anything, but
coming to You in prayer does! In Your holy name. Amen.*

The Good Things of Heaven

*If then you have been raised with Christ, keep looking for
the good things of heaven. This is where Christ is seated on
the right side of God. Keep your minds thinking about things
in heaven. . . . Christ is our life. When He comes again, you
will also be with Him to share His shining-greatness.*
COLOSSIANS 3:1–2, 4 NLV

Being raised with Christ means you are a Christian who believes in Jesus as your one and only Savior. It means you believe Jesus is God in human form, the Son whom Father God sent to live on earth and then die on the cross to take away your sin. Jesus did not stay dead but rose again. And when you believe in Him, you have been raised spiritually from the death that sin causes and you have the gift of forever life in heaven with Jesus. You are blessed by God, girl, and you get to keep looking ahead for the good things of heaven that are coming your way!

. . . .

*Dear Jesus, I believe You are God and that You came to
earth to teach us. Then You died to take away our sins and
show us how much You love us. You rose again to life, and
You make me rise to forever life because I trust in You as my
one and only Savior. Thank You! Please help me to keep my
mind always thinking about You and Your love. Amen.*

Day 356

Everything Really
Will Be Okay

*We know that God makes all things work together for the good
of those who love Him and are chosen to be a part of His plan.
God knew from the beginning who would put their trust in
Him. So He chose them and made them to be like His Son.*

ROMANS 8:28–29 NLV

"Everything will be okay." We hear that a lot, and often we say it
too. We need a lot of reassurance in this crazy, uncertain world. But
sometimes things don't seem okay at all in the middle of hard situations and terrible circumstances. When major plans fall through,
when we fail big-time, when a loved one dies, when our hearts are
broken, and on and on—we don't feel like anything will be okay ever
again! So we must trust in God's promise that says He is working all
things together for the good of those who love Him and are part of
His plans and purposes. Notice that the promise is not just for some
things but for *all* things—even what seems like the absolute worst.

. . . .

*Heavenly Father, please help me never to grow discouraged or
hopeless, no matter how hard things get or how disappointed or
heartbroken I may be. Keep me trusting in Your promise that You
work all things together for good for those who love You. Amen.*

Clay Jars Containing Priceless Treasure

We now have this light shining in our hearts, but we ourselves are like fragile clay jars containing this great treasure. This makes it clear that our great power is from God, not from ourselves.

2 CORINTHIANS 4:7 NLT

When you know Jesus, you contain a priceless treasure. It is a light shining in your heart that is difficult to contain—you just want to let it out and share it with others! You may fail sometimes; you will slip up and even sin. But when you confess your sin and repent of it, you continue to grow stronger in your walk with the Lord.

You are like a clay jar, fragile and not extraordinarily strong on its own. You know that you can't boast in your own strength and power but only in God's. He alone empowers you to share His great treasure of shining light. When the world tries to crush you, you will not be broken, because you are strengthened by His power!

. . . .

God, I love that You choose a fragile jar like me to pour out Your Good News to others. I love to shine Your light and to represent You to a hurting world. Remind me that I'm not able to do anything of real significance in my own strength, but rather I'm empowered by You. I love You, Jesus!

Day 358

Jesus Will Return

*The Spirit teaches you everything you need to know, and what
he teaches is true—it is not a lie. So just as he has taught you,
remain in fellowship with Christ. And now, dear children,
remain in fellowship with Christ so that when he returns,
you will be full of courage and not shrink back from him in shame.*

1 JOHN 2:27–28 NLT

As Christians, we're supposed to be ready for Jesus to return to earth
at any time (Matthew 24:44; Luke 12:40). To some people, that
might sound ridiculous or scary, but for those of us who stay close
to Jesus, it should be exciting and remind us how blessed we are! It
should fill us with hope and joy! This scripture says that if we remain
in fellowship with Jesus, meaning in close connection, then we will
be full of courage and not shrink back with fear or be ashamed in
any way when Jesus returns to earth.

* *

*Dear Jesus, I believe You will return right on Your perfect schedule.
Please keep me close to You. Help me to form good habits of spending
time with You and to crave ever closer fellowship with You! Amen.*

Day 359

My Armor

*Therefore put on the full armor of God, so that when the
day of evil comes, you may be able to stand your ground,
and after you have done everything, to stand.*

Ephesians 6:13 niv

As God's Warrior Princess, you are deeply loved and valued. You
have authority to wield these weapons because of your position in
Christ. Here's what's included in your armor:

- The belt of truth
- The breastplate of righteousness
- Shoes of the gospel of peace
- Shield of faith
- Helmet of salvation
- Sword of the Spirit

Can you picture Jesus putting this armor on you? The belt of
truth keeps everything in the right place. When you know the truth
about who God is and who He says you are, you can make it through
any battle. Add your breastplate of righteousness (covered by Jesus),
the shoes of the gospel of peace, the shield of faith to extinguish the
enemy's flaming arrows, the helmet of salvation, and the sword of
the Spirit which is God's Word.

You are covered and ready to keep the faith in a messy world!

Thank You, Lord, for giving me Your armor of protection.

Day 360

Flawless Beauty
Because of His Sacrifice

Every part of you is so beautiful, my darling.
Perfect is your beauty, without flaw within.
SONG OF SOLOMON 4:7 TPT

Song of Songs (or Song of Solomon) is a beautiful book of love between Solomon and his bride. Though it's a love note between spouses, it's included in the Bible because of the way it represents God's love for us and the way we respond to Him. When we read this verse, written by the king to his bride, we see the connection of our bridegroom-King, Jesus, speaking to His bride, the church, like this. He knows us to our very core and calls us beautiful. He says we are perfect and flawless because He sees us through the lens of His own righteousness.

When we repent of our sin and become one with Jesus, we are clothed in righteousness and made pure by His blood. Through His death on the cross, He made us perfectly beautiful and without flaw. Don't ever doubt how much He loves you. He sees you with eyes so full of love that He can't take His eyes off you!

. . . .

Jesus, thank You for seeing me through the lens of Your sacrifice on the cross. You have put my sin as far away from me as the east is from the west. You see me as holy and clean, without spot or blemish. Let my life be a living sacrifice to You! In Your holy name. Amen.

Every Spiritual Blessing

All praise to God, the Father of our Lord Jesus Christ, who has blessed us with every spiritual blessing in the heavenly realms because we are united with Christ. . . . So we praise God for the glorious grace he has poured out on us who belong to his dear Son. He is so rich in kindness and grace that he purchased our freedom with the blood of his Son and forgave our sins. He has showered his kindness on us, along with all wisdom and understanding. God has now revealed to us his mysterious will regarding Christ—which is to fulfill his own good plan. And this is the plan: At the right time he will bring everything together under the authority of Christ—everything in heaven and on earth. Furthermore, because we are united with Christ, we have received an inheritance from God, for he chose us in advance, and he makes everything work out according to his plan.

EPHESIANS 1:3, 6–11 NLT

Wow! If ever you're in need of a huge dose of encouragement to remember just how blessed you are, girl, come again and again to Ephesians 1 and be filled with gratitude, joy, and praise that God gives you *every* spiritual blessing because you are united with Jesus Christ!

. . . .

Father God, You're beyond amazing, and I love You! I can never thank You enough for every spiritual blessing You so generously give! Amen.

Day 362
The Original

God created humans in his image. In the image of God
he created them. He created them male and female.
GENESIS 1:27 GW

Have you ever taken a photo of a friend and tried to turn it into a sketch? Making a replica isn't easy! Rarely does the copy end up looking like the original.

Girl, you look like the original. You were created in the image of God, and you look like Him. You've got His DNA. Your personality, your quirkiness, the way you talk, these are all things you got from Him.

You have a "true likeness" to the original. And because you were created in His image (an amazing replica) you're part of Him. He's your Father. And your heavenly Father thinks you're all that and a bag of chips! You're His kid, after all.

Parents love their kids, and this is especially true with God. He stays up nights trying to think of ways to bless you. And nothing you do—not even the wickedest thing—will change His opinion of you, though He is especially proud when you set a great example.

You're worthy, girl. Your Daddy says so.

. . . .

Thank You for creating me in Your image, Lord! Amen.

Better Is One Day

Better is one day in your courts than a thousand elsewhere; I would rather be a doorkeeper in the house of my God than dwell in the tents of the wicked. For the LORD God is a sun and shield; the LORD bestows favor and honor; no good thing does he withhold from those whose walk is blameless. LORD Almighty, blessed is the one who trusts in you.

PSALM 84:10–12 NIV

Nothing you can do is better than loving and worshiping and obeying the one true God. Nowhere you can go is better than being in His courts, within His kingdom. No one is worthy of your worship like Him. No one is able to protect and provide for you like Him. No one loves you like Him. Girl, you are so indescribably blessed to be His child!

. . . .

Almighty God, I praise You that I get to call You my Father and Provider, my friend and Savior through Jesus Christ, My Comforter and Helper through the Holy Spirit. One day with You is truly better than being anywhere else. I'm so grateful that all of my days are with You! Amen.

You Don't Know It All—
and That's a Good Thing!

*Trust G<small>OD</small> from the bottom of your heart; don't try to figure
out everything on your own. Listen for G<small>OD</small>'s voice in
everything you do, everywhere you go; he's the one who will
keep you on track. Don't assume that you know it all.*

P<small>ROVERBS</small> 3:5–6 <small>MSG</small>

We can get into trouble when we assume that we know it all. Not having all the facts can really make for some embarrassing moments. One way to avoid this trap of thinking we know it all is by trusting God to lead us down His path for us.

We can listen for His voice and know what He wants us to do. How? By reading His Word, praying, and worshiping. We know His voice and His will for us when we are in a relationship with Him. Trust is born from intimacy with God. If you don't have a personal relationship with Him, you'll struggle to trust Him. But when you've seen His faithfulness repeatedly in your life, you'll find it much easier to lean on Him when you don't know what to do! Always turn to Him in prayer with each decision you face. He will never steer you wrong.

* * *

*Lord, I want to lean on You and not on my own
knowledge of a situation. Direct me and keep me
on Your narrow path. I trust You. Amen.*

Day 365

God's Love Won't Run Out

Give thanks to the LORD, for he is good. His love endures forever. Give thanks to the God of gods. His love endures forever. Give thanks to the Lord of lords: His love endures forever.

PSALM 136:1–3 NIV

There are twenty-six verses in Psalm 136, and the phrase "His love endures forever" is stated twenty-six times! I think the author really wants us to get the point that God's love endures forever! This means that no matter what, God's love is so rich, so deep, so big. . .that it won't ever run out. It goes on forever and ever!

Just sit with that thought for a minute. Thank God for His deep well of love for you that never runs dry. How does this make you feel? Talk to God about it. Write a prayer of thanks to God in your journal.

Remember this, dear one: you are loved and cherished by God with a love that will not run out, not ever.

. . . .

God, here I am again, amazed at Your great love for me! I'm so thankful to know that Your well of love will never run dry.

Scripture Index

OLD TESTAMENT

NEW TESTAMENT

More Encouragement for Your Beautiful Spirit!

You Belong
Devotions and Prayers for a Teen Girl's Heart

You Were Created with Purpose by a Loving, Heavenly Creator. . .You Belong!

This delightful devotional is a lovely reminder that you were created with purpose by a heavenly Creator. . .and that you belong—right here and now—in this world. Its 180 encouraging readings and inspiring prayers, rooted in biblical truth, will reassure your uncertain heart, helping you to understand that you're *never* alone and *always* loved. In each devotional reading, you will encounter the bountiful blessings and grace of your Creator while coming to trust His purposeful plan for you in this world.

Flexible Casebound / 978-1-63609-169-3